The Scandal of Divine Love

The Scandal of Divine Love

A Study on Biblical Christology
for Skeptics, Seekers, and Survivors

Robert P. Vande Kappelle

WIPF & STOCK · Eugene, Oregon

THE SCANDAL OF DIVINE LOVE
A Study on Biblical Christology for Skeptics, Seekers, and Survivors

Copyright © 2017 Robert P. Vande Kappelle. All rights reserved. Except for brief quotations in critical publications or reviews, no part of this book may be reproduced in any manner without prior written permission from the publisher. Write: Permissions, Wipf and Stock Publishers, 199 W. 8th Ave., Suite 3, Eugene, OR 97401.

Wipf & Stock
An Imprint of Wipf and Stock Publishers
199 W. 8th Ave., Suite 3
Eugene, OR 97401

www.wipfandstock.com

PAPERBACK ISBN: 978-1-5326-4060-5
HARDCOVER ISBN: 978-1-5326-4061-2
EBOOK ISBN: 978-1-5326-4062-9

Manufactured in the U.S.A.   10/12/17

Unless otherwise noted, Bible quotations are from the *New Revised Standard Version of the Bible*, copyright © 1989 by the Division of Christian Education of the National Council of the Churches of Christ in the United States of America. Used by permission.

To Evelyn Jane

"I know the plans for you; a future with hope."
—JEREMIAH 29:11

Contents

Preface | ix
Acknowledgments | xv

Introduction | 1

Part I: Human | 15

Session 1: Son of Man (Part I) | 17

Part II: Fully Human | 29

Session 2: Servant (Son of Man, Part II) | 35
Session 3: Teacher | 45
Session 4: Prophet | 58

Part III: God's Human | 69

Session 5: Son of God | 74
Session 6: Messiah | 83
Session 7: Savior/High Priest | 94

Part IV: God in Christ | 105

Session 8: Spirit/Angel of the Lord | 109
Session 9: Judge (Son of Man, Part III) | 121
Session 10: Wisdom of God | 129
Session 11: Word of God (Logos) | 143

Part V: Christ in God | 155
   Session 12: Lord | 160
   Epilogue: God in All | 174

Appendix A: Chronology of Biblical Events | 181
Appendix B: Guidelines for Leading a Group Bible Study | 184
Bibliography | 191
Subject/Name Index | 195

Preface

THREE CONCEPTS ARE TRUE of any ideology—political, social, economic, or religious: a problem (understood as a threat), a vision (a solution to the problem), and an exemplar (a role model who overcomes the problem by embodying the vision and fulfilling its hope). This book addresses one such paradigm: an apocalyptic hope embodied in a Jewish peasant that captured the ancient imagination en route to global domination. In my estimation, there is no more important topic for inquiry today than the meaning and message of Jesus, no more important concern than one's answer to Jesus' perennial question, "Who do you say that I am?" (Mark 8:29), for in this quest, I believe, lies the solution to individual malaise and humanity's woes.

Task and Guidelines

Who is Jesus Christ, and why is he so important for the Christian faith? The Christian doctrine of the person and significance of Christ, known as Christology, sets out to explore why the church believes that Jesus of Nazareth, a first-century Galilean peasant, holds the key to the nature of God and of human destiny.

Christology represents a narrowing of the wholeness of "the Christ-event," a reduction to mere words of the more than verbal impact of the historical figure and the risen Lord. Any insights in this study are complemented by viewing other aspects of the beginnings of Christianity from different perspectives. In addition, what follows is not intended as a comprehensive study of all aspects of New Testament Christology. The quest for Jesus' self-awareness, for example, is not a central concern, or an

Preface

investigation of the historical Jesus, or its relation to the "Christ of faith." No attempt is made to deal with the resurrection of Jesus as such, to analyze all christological titles, or to discuss the question of Christ's parousia (his return or "second" coming). The object is simply and solely to explore the meaning and significance of Jesus Christ by examining key christological titles found in the New Testament.

Two tasks appear necessary: (1) to begin with biblical texts and christological formulations, determining how to interpret them for our use and understanding today, and (2) starting with our own, twenty-first-century questions and concerns and applying them to the biblical texts. We will emphasize the first, but not at the expense of the second. We are, necessarily, citizens of our place and time, from which we cannot or should not escape, but because Christology is a subset of biblical study, because that is its initial and primary locus, its bedrock and quarry, it will serve as our focus. We will consult other literature of the times as necessary, both earlier and later, but primarily for context. To understand the language of the New Testament in its original intention naturally involves its background and wider usage at that time. Not, we might add, because the wider usage necessarily determines its meaning in the New Testament, but because without awareness of the historical context we will be unable to enter the thought world of the time and thus fail to grasp the nuances of New Testament usage.

Our concern, so far as is possible, is to allow the New Testament authors to speak for themselves, to understand their words as they would have intended, to hear them as their first readers would have heard them, and thus to allow their own understandings of Christ to emerge.

In our time there has been an explosion in the scholarly investigation of early Christology. Much of the work has been concerned with particular titles given to Jesus by early Christians. The range of material covered is clear and can be grouped under different headings. Son of God and Word/Logos language is significant, for these were the two most important categories for later confessional formulations. Son of Man language, used extensively in the Gospels, has also been the subject of extensive scholarly research. The discussion of Son of Man leads naturally to a discussion of the association between Adam and Christ within the New Testament. Other titles for Jesus, "Lord," "Christ," and "Savior," are significant, particularly when viewed in relation to the cultic veneration of Jesus by the earliest Jewish-Christian communities. Messianic language, filled with royal and priestly implications, is primary, as are Jewish apocalyptic and prophetic models. Recent

Preface

study reflects an interest in the concept of "divine agency," a reference to various figures from ancient Jewish tradition pictured as agents of God or intermediaries, including personifications of divine attributes (Wisdom, Spirit, Word), exalted patriarchs (Moses, Enoch, Elijah), and principal angels (including the Angel of the Lord, Michael, and Melchizedek).

From the outset, readers must become aware of four dangers in the study of Christology:

- The *danger of misrepresentation*: analyses of complex concepts or profound claims by individuals twenty centuries removed in time and culture are bound to be distorted. The vast differences between modern Western culture and that of first-century Palestine bring us to what the eighteenth-century philosopher G. E. Lessing called the "ugly great ditch" between faith and history. If we are serious in our desire to be not only hearers but doers of the Word, we must allow the New Testament evidence to speak for itself rather than superimpose later developments and clarifications upon the first-century material.

- The *danger of simplification*: definitions of terms that presuppose singularity or uniformity of meaning in christological usage across books of the New Testament or even within texts by the same author overlook nuance and subtlety and violates the importance of literary context. Those who define too quickly or too narrowly biblical elements restrict the study of their understanding, either by preventing the New Testament authors from speaking to us in their own ways or by limiting the material to presupposed meanings.

- The *danger of compartmentalization*: attempts to classify or divide christological terminology remain arbitrary and conjectural. Differing formulations may have been dependent on each other in the larger theologizing of the time, facets of complex and interlocking ways of assessing the significance of Jesus.

- The *danger of misinterpretation*: reading New Testament documents about Jesus Christ involves understanding the rich mixture of statements, assertions, and declarations offered by the biblical authors. Alert readers of scripture will notice that these data represent different kinds of information. Scholars have identified four independent rubrics, often combined in the biblical text, that convey christological information: (a) historical remarks (for example, that Jesus "was a Jew"); (b) mythic reports (for example, that Christ Jesus "was in the form of God"); (c) metaphorical statements (for example, that Jesus Christ "is God's Son"); and (d) theological assertions (for example, that Jesus Christ "is the end of the law," or that Jesus "died for sinners"). When readers encounter christological information in the New Testament, they must be able to distinguish the historical from the mythical (traditional), metaphorical (symbolic or figurative), and theological (confessional or doctrinal) meanings. Ultimately, however, christological information serves as a vehicle for communicating underlying theological convictions rooted in values, beliefs, and perspective.

It follows from the above that the author does not wish to promote specific titles of Jesus or disparage specific understandings of Christ. To know and grasp what the first generations of Christians believed concerning Jesus in their own terms and in the context of their own times is sufficient to shed light on why and how Christology has been so central in Christianity. Moreover, for those who, like the author, find the definition of Christianity more clearly provided by the New Testament than by the creeds of Christendom, the biblical answers to our questions could have a critical bearing on faith itself. However, all should bear in mind that to hear the New Testament writers speak in their own terms requires that listeners accept the possibility that some of their preconceived ideas may be challenged and possibly need to be rejected even as others are confirmed.

It is my hope that through this study readers will discover anew the magnificence of the life and person known to us as Jesus of Nazareth, both as guide, exemplar, and Lord.

Audience

While this study is designed for Christian believers (survivors), it embraces skeptics and seekers alike, mindful that within each of us are multiple voices, sometimes affirming, sometimes questioning, occasionally even denying, and at times all speaking simultaneously, whether in joyous cacophony or in bewildering confusion. The relative strength, dominance, and relationship of these voices may vary through the seasons of our lives, individually and communally, for our lives are always in flux, emotionally, psychologically, and spiritually, if we are growing in faith and understanding. Whether you consider yourself primarily as skeptic, seeker, or believer, and if the latter, whether as conservative, liberal, traditional, progressive,

Preface

or someone without label, this study is for you, for it encourages you to listen, appreciate, and cultivate each voice. In actuality, all three voices are latent—simultaneously present to some extent—in most of us. Though one may be dominant, each can contribute; all must be heard.

As there are numerous personality types, there are also numerous spirituality types. One approach, building on the insights of psychological type theory found in the Myers Briggs Type Indicator, connects typology to four paths in one's spiritual journey. Utilizing the principle that one's spirituality flows out of one's individuality, Peter Tufts Richardson[1] defines four spirituality types and relates them to four journeys:

- STs: Journey of Works; a task-oriented spirituality
- SFs: Journey of Devotion; an experience-based spirituality
- NTs: Journey of Unity; a highly-principled spirituality
- NFs: Journey of Harmony; a questing spirituality

Urban Holmes[2] presents a helpful typology for the spiritual life revolving around how people seek to understand the experience of God and its meaning for our times:

- Type I: sacramental (an intellectual, "thinking" spirituality)
- Type II: charismatic (a heartfelt, intuitive spirituality)
- Type III: mystical (a contemplative, introspective spirituality)
- Type IV: apostolic (an active, visionary spirituality)

Likewise, Jack Haberer[3] identifies five concerns (which he calls "Godviews") that drive and divide individual Christians:

- passion about conserving truth
- passion about unity in the church
- passion about promoting intimacy with God
- passion about caring for victims
- passion about welcoming the marginalized

---

1. Richardson, *Four Spiritualities*.
2. Holmes, *History of Christian Spirituality*.
3. Haberer, *Godviews*.

Preface

While specific factors motivate individual Christians, as priorities they can also be divisive. Vital communities of faith should provide opportunities for all such concerns to flourish. When congregations become one-dimensional or give preference to specific ways of being Christian, they stymy growth and heighten conflict.

What we noted about the spectrum and degrees of faith or doubt within each of us also applies to personality and spirituality. While we may identify primarily with one of the above options or types, we should not reduce our spiritual preferences to single attitudes, concerns, or approaches to God and others. Consistency is not always a virtue, for life is not static, and neither are personality and spirituality. How we view scripture, the church, Jesus, God, and truth can (and should) change over time. The biblical maxim, "I am fearfully and wonderfully made" (Ps. 139:14), allows a great deal of latitude. While we may be an enigma to others, the same holds true for ourselves. Our study of Christology will not only teach us about Jesus and God, but in the process, we will learn a great about others and ourselves. Expect to be surprised!

Acknowledgements

To paraphrase Charles Dickens, we live in the best of times, yet also in the worst of times. While it is easy to go low, that is, to focus on the negative, in our assessment of things, I wish to go high. Despite political and social climates bordering on frustration and despair, there are opportunities of great promise today, of collaboration between science and religion and philosophy and theology, disciplines occasionally hostile and suspicious of the other. In an age of globalism, multiculturalism, and ecumenism, courageous institutions and individuals are learning to think and live more holistically than ever before, embracing the new while exposing themselves to uncertainty and the unknown.

This book is written in the spirit of openness and inquiry, with the understanding that each generation of thinkers and believers is required to examine anew the relationship between theology and anthropology, how views of God impact what it means to be human. The bridge, it seems, is Jesus Christ.

We are witnessing today an explosion in the scholarly investigation of Christology, the study of the significance of Jesus Christ. *The Scandal of Divine Love* builds on that scholarship, beginning with the contributions of Donald Baillie and Emil Brunner in mid-century, incorporating the groundbreaking Christological contributions of Norman Pittenger, Oscar Cullmann, John Knox, John A. T. Robinson, Martin Hengel, and James Dunn in ensuing decades, and examining the promising current investigation of Dale Allison, Richard Bauckham, Larry Hurtado, and Bart Ehrman. Of these, the most influential on my thinking has been John A. T. Robinson, particularly his 1973 volume *The Human Face of God*.

This scholarly array represents a wide spectrum of views and interpretations, and it is precisely this multiplicity of perspective—this

Acknowledgements

divergence—that has pulled, prodded, and stretched my understanding of Jesus, leading me to believe that the fullest and best understanding of Jesus Christ lies dormant, yet to be discovered. It is my hope that this current volume may contribute in some small way to that discovery.

In writing this book, I am indebted to Georgia Metsger and Jess Costa, whose friendship has encouraged me to keep growing spiritually and intellectually. This book is a product of that alliance. Their workshops and study groups have provided an outlet for my research and a sounding board for my publications. I am indebted also to the Special Studies department at Chautauqua Institution, where I have taught adult classes for the past five years, and to the recruiting efforts of Lil Gervais, whose belief and trust in me is undeserved.

This book could not have been written without the ongoing encouragement and support of my wife Susan, whose advice challenges me literarily, aesthetically, and spiritually. I am also grateful to Washington & Jefferson College for granting me emeritus status and for providing the resources requisite for scholarly research. I dedicate this book to my granddaughter Evelyn Jane, whose conception, gestation, and birth coincide the creation and publication of this book.

Introduction

Important Biblical Verses and Passages: Philippians 2:6–11; Hebrews 13:8; 1 Corinthians 12:3; Acts 2:22–36; John 1:14; 1 John 1:1–3; 4:1–3; 2 Corinthians 5:19

Technical Terms and Concepts: Christology; Trinity; Nicene Creed; Council of Chalcedon; Council of Nicaea; Christology "from below"; Christology "from above"; mythological; ontological; functional; ancient Judaism; metaphysical/metaphysics; adoptionism (exaltationism); kenoticism; incarnationism; docetism

THIS STUDY GUIDE INTRODUCES readers to the topic of Christology, a theological endeavor that is meaningless to many today, because not only are they unfamiliar with the term ("Does it have to do with crystals"?), but also because they consider theological debate antiquated if not useless to modern issues and concerns. We live in a world dramatically different from that of the first century, indeed from the fifteenth and even the twentieth century. The question originally asked by Jesus, "What do you think of Christ?" (see Matt. 22:42), was a Jewish question, expecting a Jewish answer. The state of Christology is fluid today, more fluid perhaps than it has been since the earliest Christian debates with Judaism.

The word "Christology" consists of two Greek words: *logos*, meaning "talk about" or "the study of," and *Christos*, originally meaning "Messiah." For early Christians the term "Christ" quickly morphed from the narrow confines of Jewish messianism to become the Christian name for Jesus;

Introduction

Jesus the Christ became simply Jesus Christ. If theology is "God-talk," Christology is "Christ-talk," language about Jesus of Nazareth, his identity and significance (who he was and what he accomplished).

When I began researching the topic of Christology for this study, I asked family members and friends to identify a model or image that best represented their understanding of Jesus. The answers, as I expected, varied greatly:

- "He was a man, but one who changed history."
- "He was human, but not ordinary, because he was wholly human."
- "Jesus is the Son of God, the one who embodies God's hopes and aspirations for the world and its human inhabitants."
- "He is God, not simply second member of the Trinity, but God in human form."
- "Jesus is a compassionate healer, the one who grounds me and keeps me whole."
- "He is the Ever-present One, who represents and holds together the human family. I think of Jesus as 'Kin,' not 'King,' and his realm as 'kindom,' not kingdom.'"

Were the survey to continue, I suppose the variety of responses would be endless. The question posed above, asking folks to identify a single title, model, or image to summarize their understanding of Jesus, is of course misleading, for to our knowledge there never existed a Christian congregation that applied to Jesus only one title. Biblical writers, like the communities they represented, identified the enigmatic Jesus with the aid of numerous images. Nowhere in early Christianity was there an exclusive Son of God Christology, Messiah Christology, Servant Christology, Savior Christology, or the like. These titles and images flowed together, complementing one another. Such usage encouraged new titles, making the picture even richer. The Christology of the early church was inclusive, imaginative, and broadly conceived.

The first Christians had a stunning array of titles, names, and expressions for Jesus, ranging from Rabbi, Messiah, and High Priest to Lord, Son of God, Word of God, Wisdom of God, and Spirit of God. In the Pauline corpus alone we find a broad range of christological titles. In addition to common titles such as God, Lord, Messiah, and Spirit, we find also Angel

Introduction

(Gal. 4:14), Rock (1 Cor. 10:4), Destroyer (1 Cor. 10:10); Man of Heaven (1 Cor. 15:49); Power of God (1 Cor. 1:18); Wisdom of God (1 Cor. 1:21); the Glory (2 Cor. 4:4); Image of God (2 Cor. 4:4); Form of God (Phil. 2:6); the Name (Phil. 2:9); and the Head (1 Cor. 12:12–13); and that's only a start to the Pauline list. In addition to established titles, most books of the New Testament introduce unique titles of their own. For example, Colossians speaks of Christ as Firstborn (Col. 1:15); Beginning (Col. 1:18); and Fullness of God (Col. 1:19). Readers may wish to expand their understanding of Jesus by examining the New Testament book by book, exploring each author's Christology.

Over the next three centuries these titles would be fleshed out to incorporate a Nicene understanding: Jesus Christ was of the same substance as God the Father; he was equal with God in status, authority, and power; he was the one through whom God created all things in heaven and on earth; there never was a time when he did not exist. These were all quite exalted things to say about an apocalyptic itinerant preacher from rural Galilee crucified as a would-be messiah, a failed claimant to the vacant Jewish throne of Judea.

By AD 381, this understanding of Jesus, recited in the Nicene Creed—or, more accurately, the Niceno-Constantinopolitan Creed—served as a benchmark of orthodoxy for all succeeding mainstream Christian churches, whether Catholic, Orthodox, or Protestant. The classic Christian position, summarized in the "doctrine of the two natures," perfectly divine and perfectly human, was definitively stated by the Council of Chalcedon in 451. Generally stated, this position affirms the centrality of the two natures of Jesus Christ for the church, wisely noting that so long as we recognize that Jesus Christ is both truly divine and truly human, the precise manner in which this is articulated or explored is not of fundamental importance. Chalcedon defined the starting point for classical Christology to be the recognition that in the face of Christ we find the face of God.

As stunning as these claims remain, what is even more surprising is the rapidness of the development of the early church's Christology. According to biblical scholar Martin Hengel, more happened in the first decade or two after the death of Jesus than in the entire later centuries-long development of dogma. The historian of early Christianity, Bart Ehrman, concurs: "It must have been no more than twenty years after Jesus died, possibly even fewer, that the Christ poem in Philippians [Phil. 2:6–11] was composed, in which Jesus was said to have been a preexistent being 'in the form of God'

Introduction

who became human and then because of his obedient death was exalted to divine status and made equal with God, the Lord to whom all people on earth would bow in worship and confess loyalty."[1]

During subsequent centuries, Christian thinkers devoted a great deal of study to the topic of Christology, speculating about the two natures of Christ while closely connecting their study to doctrines of the incarnation, the atonement, and the Trinity. Over time, two main pictures developed: of a Christ who was God in disguise and of Jesus the perfect man. Sadly, both pictures, offered as objects of devotion and belief, distanced Jesus from ordinary people and led to his irrelevance for increasing numbers of people.

Dietrich Bonhoeffer spoke for many when he wrote from a Nazi prison in the 1940s: "What really bothers me incessantly is the question . . . who Christ really is for us today." For Jesus Christ to be "the same yesterday and today and forever" (Heb. 13:8), he has to be a contemporary of every generation and therefore different for every generation: he must be *their* Christ, *our* Christ.

The critical question is, "How does the 'Christ for us today' relate to the Christ for other ages—whether of the first century or the sixteenth or the twentieth?" One mistake of the liberal tradition is to wish too fervently that the biblical writers might say exactly what needs to be said today. It is the same error in reverse of the traditionalists who wish too fervently that the biblical message might be the exact word we ought to pronounce now. Our exploration of the meaning of Jesus Christ—then and now—presupposes a reality there to explore. According to a Quaker observation, "we do not 'seek' the Atlantic, we explore it." The same applies to Christ, or to what Teilhard de Chardin called the Christosphere. Christians begin with a given, gracious reality. They cannot assume this dogmatically or narrowly, nor can they presuppose it of others. When Paul and other early Christians state, often uncritically, "to me, living is Christ" (Phil. 1:21), or confess, "Jesus is Lord" (1 Cor. 12:3), what did these mean to first-century Christians, and what do they mean to us today? The center, thankfully, is given in scripture, but the periphery is teasingly and liberatingly open.

In the words of J. M. Creed: "Christian theology need not claim that the Christian religion contains within itself all truth, or even all truth that is of religious value, but if it loses the conviction that in Jesus Christ it has found the deepest truth of God, it has lost itself."[2]

---

1. Ehrman, *How Jesus Became God*, 370.
2. Creed, *Divinity of Jesus Christ*, 113.

Introduction

The Two Basic Types of Christology

In the words of the Chalcedonian formulation, Christ is God as well as man: "truly God and truly man." In other words, Jesus represents to us the reality of what God is, as well as the reality of what humankind is. The question that has dogged Christian theology is how to maintain equilibrium between the human and divine natures so that one aspect of this double reality does not overwhelm the other. The key, we shall argue, is to begin where the first Christians began, with the church's own experience of Jesus, and then to press forward with the development of that understanding in its experience of Christ.

It is important to recognize that the starting point of the classic debate on Christology at the Council of Chalcedon (451), which fixed its shape for the next fifteen hundred years, was determined neither by scripture nor by experience but by the earlier Arian controversy on the doctrine of the Trinity, which reached its resolution at the Council of Nicaea (325). With Christ established there as a distinct person (hypostasis) of the Trinity, fully God in every sense of the word, it was this aspect and not his existence as a historical person that could not be questioned.

Yet this is not where the first Christians began, nor where we should begin. As Martin Luther noted: The "humanity [of Jesus] is our holy ladder, by which we ascend to the knowledge of God.... Who wishes safely to ascend to the love and knowledge of God ... let him first exercise himself in the humanity of Christ."[3] For Luther, "The scriptures begin very gently, and lead us on to Christ as a man, and then to one who is Lord over all creatures, and after that to one who is God. So do I enter delightfully, and learn to know God. But the [church] philosophers and doctors have insisted on beginning from above, and so they have become fools. We must begin from below, and after that come upwards."[4]

There are, as Luther indicates, two types of Christology, "from below" and "from above." Both types can be expressed in orthodox or in heterodox ways, and both are present in the New Testament:

- Christology "from below" (upward ascending); the focus is historical, on the fully human Jesus. For believers, God is said to have acted

---

3. Luther, *Weimarer Ausgabe* 57.99.3; cited in Hamilton, *New Essence of Christianity*, 88.

4. Luther, *Weimarer Ausgabe* 10/I 2.297.5; English translation taken from Mackintosh, *Person of Jesus Christ*, 232.

decisively, unsurpassably, in Jesus; therefore, Jesus cannot be subsumed into the category of visionary or religious reformer. In his human form, Jesus is said to be not *an* address of God but *the* address of God to humanity.

- Christology "from above" (downward descending); the focus is metaphysical, on the preexistent divine Christ. For believers, Christ is the eternal "Son of God," as distinct from the Father. For believers, Christ became incarnate in Jesus.

While these two are compatible, they cannot be ultimately synthesized. Despite their mutual interrelationship, they cannot be reduced to one. They represent two basic types of Christology, and in their distinction they render pluralism of Christologies both inevitable and legitimate. However, the initiative "from above" does not cancel the solidarity "from below."

The Three-Story Universe: Ways to Read Reality

How humans view reality depends on how they find it convincing to represent reality. Although modern, post-Enlightenment people in the West no longer view themselves as living in a three-*storey* universe, cosmologically and scientifically speaking, we inhabit a three-*story* universe, literarily and theologically speaking. Over time, humans developed three ways (three languages or stories) to conceptualize their world, to express what is most real to them—the mythological, the ontological, and the functional. Each way of thinking represents a stage or era in the development of civilization, although the three ways overlap and interrelate in the minds of most individuals. Beginning with a *mythological way of thinking*, humans moved to an ontological, and now are shifting yet again to a functional way of thinking.

The mythological, epitomized by the literature of ancient (Second Temple) Judaism and early Christianity (historically these two periods are partly co-terminus), represents a way of thinking that is highly imaginative, where the line between the human and the divine is permeable and fluid. In this representation of reality, found in the language of the visions of Daniel or 1 Enoch, of the Epistle to the Philippians, the Gospel of John, or later gnosticism, the identity of God with the "Christ-figure" is expressed in terms of a personification of some aspect of God's being or will. The mediatorial figure is seen as a heavenly being who is constantly with God.

Introduction

As God's Angel, Wisdom, Spirit, Word, or Son, this figure belongs at God's side. As God's agent, he visits this earth in human form, subsequently to be reunited with God in glory and in judgment. Whatever the degree of hypostatization, the identity between the sender and the sent is rarely in doubt.

The second, *ontological representation of reality* translates the language from poetic to philosophical categories. Christian theologians safeguard the unity of Christ with God by positing identity of substance between Father and Son. This perspective views Christ as a co-equal person of the Godhead, sharing God's uncreated being, assuming personhood and developing biologically without for a moment ceasing to be God. The doctrine of the two natures preserves duality, but with metaphysical continuity: Jesus was God under the form of flesh.

In the fourth and fifth centuries, the attention of theologians centered almost entirely on ontological (metaphysical) matters, on questions of the nature of Christ and on whether Jesus was co-eternal with the Father and of the same substance. Such questions threatened to divide the church, although for many Christians, the councils of Nicaea and Chalcedon satisfactorily answered these questions.

The New Testament scholar John Knox blames much of the confusion and divisiveness among Christians about the person of Christ to the use of "static" and "metaphysical" categories rather than "event" categories.[5] Phrases such as the "deity of Christ" and "of the same substance with the Father" are examples of "static" expression, while "God acts in Jesus Christ," or "Christ reveals the Father," or "Christ event" are examples of "dynamic" expression. If Christ is the principle of Christian unity, as the New Testament writings affirm, then Christians should avoid abstractions about Christ and his nature and emphasize what was originally important. If Jesus was the person in whom God became incarnate, then the focus of Christology should be less on the *nature* of God and more on the nature of God's *activity* in Christ.

The first transition is reflected in Christology in the shift from Jewish categories to Greek. The former viewed finality in terms of the eschatological act of God in history, embodied in the sending of the Messiah as savior and judge. The latter saw ultimate reality not in terms of decisive act but of timeless being, in the categories of substance rather than will; from the Lord's Messiah to the second person of the Trinity, from the Son of God to

---

5. Knox, *Jesus: Lord and Christ*.

Introduction

God the Son. While it looks to us as if this is a heightening of Christology, this is more apparent than real, for under the mythological way of thinking Jesus is given "the name that is above every name" (Phil. 2:9) and given the title "Lord" (*kyrios*) that belongs to God. Whatever meaning these liturgical affirmations suggested to the first Christian Jews, there could be nothing more exalted for the Jews than to designate someone the agent of God's final act in history.

The third, *functional, way of representing reality* appear to say much less than the other two ways, having neither the perceptible tangibility of personification nor the solidity of substance. Yet it is another, equally effective way of asserting identity, but in terms of verbs or activity rather than agency or substance. Christ is the one who does what God does, who stands in the place of God, speaking and acting in God's stead. The focus is not his divine origin or divine substance but on his earthly task. He is a human figure raised up to be the instrument of God's decisive work and to stand in relationship to God to which no other human is called. The issue is whether in seeing him people see the Father, whether in mercy and judgment he functions as God, whether he is God to and for them. This way of thinking is both primitive and modern. It is much nearer the Hebrew prophetic tradition before it was influenced by streams of thought (primarily evident in wisdom and apocalyptic literature) that entered ancient Judaism (in the centuries immediately before and after the first Christian century).

With regard to Christ, the distinction between these ways of representing his identity with God can perhaps be brought out in terms of the human analogy of royalty. The mythological and ontological stories of the incarnation use the image of the divine visitant, of the king who becomes a commoner. This presupposes two orders of being: the king and the commoner. The king is a royal personage, not a commoner. He may enter the other estate, he may become in every respect a commoner, but, like the Japanese emperor, he remains a being of completely different blood.

The Swedish model of royalty, on the other hand, represents the opposite extreme to the Japanese. Here the king is a commoner, who holds royal office. He embodies royalty, he exercises it, but he is part of the ordinary human scene. He does not come into the scene or make a visitation; he has grown up within it. You may see him on the streets at any moment. There is nothing different to see, yet you have seen the king.

Similarly, we may view Christ as a divine being who takes on humanity, or as a human who embodies divinity yet is a commoner, a human being born and bred who discloses the will of God, who exercises fully the transforming love of God, so that those who have seen him have seen the King. One cannot say that any of these ways of representing the presence of God in his Son is the biblical one. All are traceable in the New Testament, though the ontological one less than the other two. It is perhaps possible to see the beginning of it in the Epistle to the Hebrews and in the prologue to John's Gospel. Though we often read the New Testament through the ontological spectacles of later church councils and creeds, we must not forget that its representation of Christ is partly "mythological" and its basic categories often remarkably "functional."

Four Ancient Christological Phases: The Evolution of Christology in the First Century

The story of Jesus Christ appears in the New Testament in several forms—or perhaps we might more accurately state that several stages in the development of the story are found there—so that the significance of Jesus is not always set forth in the same way. There are differences among the New Testament writers—differences even within an author or a text—regarding both the character of Jesus and his role in the story of God's act in Christ, differences, we might say, between the answers they would have given to the question, "How human—that is, how fully or normally human—was Jesus?" and the question, "Why did there have to be a human Jesus?"

As we examine the development of Christology in the early Christians' experience of Jesus as both human and as Lord, we need to consider two factors: the *memory* of the human Jesus and the *knowledge* of him as still alive and present after his death, as Christ and Lord. The distinctive character of the Christian church, both in its origin and in its historical development, is that "it thus *remembers* and thus *knows*. This is the concrete, experienced meaning of both the resurrection and the Spirit. The phrase 'Jesus Christ our Lord' designates, not primarily an historical individual in the past, nor yet a character in a symbolic story, but a present reality actually experienced within the common life. The story [of Jesus Christ] arose to account, as well as might be, for so marvelous a fact of experience and to set forth and convey, as adequately as possible, its realized inner meaning and effect."[6]

---

6. Knox, *Humanity and Divinity of Christ*, 2–3.

Introduction

As we examine the early (first-century) church's conceptualization of its Christology, we must recognize its "story" quality, its metaphorical and mythological nature. For how can humans express the inner meaning of Jesus, realized as divine meaning, without resorting to figurative speech? How can we speak of "the fullness of time," or of Christ's exaltation to God's right hand, or of Christ's return, without recognizing that we are telling a story, creating a picture, dramatizing, mythologizing? As we recalls the many titles of Jesus—Messiah, Prophet, Servant, Son of Man, Son of God, Logos, Lord, Savior, Christ, and the like—we note that each belonged originally to a specific literary and metaphysical context. However we understand these names and titles, appropriated for Jesus, each of them called attention to some important aspect of his significance. Whatever one concludes about the original meaning and subsequent influence of these early depictions, they became embedded in a story, which advanced through four phases, each having its own Christology. These four phases—adoptionism, kenoticism, incarnationism, and docetism, are present in the New Testament, though only the third was finally embraced by the church.[7]

The earliest phase in Christology, labeled *adoptionism* or "exaltationism," is indicated in the opening of Acts, especially in the speeches by Peter and others. The clearest example is Acts 2, Peter's speech on the Day of Pentecost, where the crucified "man" Jesus, by virtue of being "exalted at the right hand of God" (2:33), has been "*made* both Lord and Messiah" (2:36). This passage, like the confessional statement in Romans 1:3–4, leads us to believe that the earliest Christology affirmed that the man Jesus was at the resurrection exalted to his present messianic status.

This form of the story, however, could hardly have become final. Although it corresponded closely with the actual experience of the earliest community of Jesus' disciples, who remembered Jesus in the flesh and now, in the Spirit, knew him as Christ the Lord, it did not accord with the growing sense of the importance and the divine significance of his earthly career. That career, they realized, had meanings that at the time were hidden. That recognition required some changes to the original story of the human Jesus, some alteration at least to the first act of the two-act drama. Such rewriting eventually occurred, but not before an immediate solution emerged, which required not a revision of the initial story, but the addition

---

7. The material in this segment is adapted from John Knox's short study, *The Humanity and Divinity of Christ*, particularly his discussion in chapter 1: Three Ancient Christologies," 1–18.

INTRODUCTION

of a "prologue" to that story, an account of a divine preexistence to the human career of Jesus.

The reason for this affirmation of preexistence lay implicit in the story from the beginning. We find this reason in the early preaching in Acts, which views the death of Jesus to be in accordance to "the definite plan and foreknowledge of God" (2:23). It is but a short step from the idea that Jesus preexisted in the mind of God to the conception of Jesus as a preexisting hypostasis of God or as a personal and objective divine being in his own right. We can also assume that reflection on the resurrection and on the post-resurrection status of Christ led directly and immediately to his preexistence.

There are good reasons for believing that the attribution of divine preexistence to Jesus was not the final step in a gradual process of pressing back the moment of his exaltation to an earlier and earlier time—from resurrection, to transfiguration, to baptism, to birth—until finally it was pushed beyond the earthly life to the creation and beyond. Such a process required time and would not account for its presence in the writings of Paul, some twenty or twenty-five years after Jesus' crucifixion (see Phil. 2:6; Rom. 8:3; 9:5; 1 Cor. 8:6; 10:4; 2 Cor. 8:9; Gal. 4:14). Paul not only alludes to the preexistence of Christ, but also takes for granted that the conception was familiar enough to his readers that they did not need to be convinced of its truth.

If the words "adoption" or "exaltation" are useful labels for the earliest christological phase (a human declared Lord and Christ at the resurrection), *kenoticism*, from the term "kenosis" (emptying) summarizes the second phase in this development. Philippians 2:6-11, a poetic passage believed to have been borrowed by Paul from the church's liturgical tradition and inserted into his letter to exemplify the humility incumbent upon believers, aptly illustrates the second phase in the story's growth (see also 2 Cor. 5:21; 8:9). While the details of this poem or hymn are much debated, particularly how they conceive or view the preexistent Christ, a natural reading of the phrases "form of God" and "equality with God" suggests Paul has in mind a transcendent, heavenly nature or state that the preexistent Christ willingly exchanges when he takes on humanity at his birth.

As primitive adoptionism was short-lived, so also the second phase in the story's growth was brief. Though traces appear in Paul's writings, in the Epistle to the Hebrews, and in the Synoptic Gospels, this phase had ceased to exist by the time the earliest New Testament writings were composed.

Introduction

The third phase, *incarnationism*, is quite different from the preceding.[8] Not only do all New Testament writings exemplify this phase (as far as they exhibit any christological pattern), but for what proved to be orthodox Christianity, this stage has provided the prominent and continuing model. Its most prominent biblical example is the prologue in John's Gospel, particularly John 1:14: "And the [preexistent] Word became flesh, and lived among us." According to New Testament scholar John Knox, this phase emerged early on, when the original adoptionist two-act drama was being adjusted to conform to the insertion of the so-called "prologue." Ordinarily, the prologue of a literary or dramatic work lies outside the story proper, providing appropriate background for the action of the story. Adding a prologue does not normally require changes in the original story and thereby does not exert any pressure on the plot. Far from raising problems, its intention is to forestall problems that the story might otherwise create in the reader's mind.

The prologue to the church's story of Christ, however, while anticipating and dealing with difficulties in the story as it stood, nevertheless created new difficulties. By adding preexistence to Jesus, questions it raised for the first act of the original drama (the humanity of Jesus), such as "How could a heavenly being, especially one identified with God, actually become the authentic human being Jesus was remembered as being?" or "Could a divine person ever become an actual human being?" were as serious as those it answered for the second act in the drama (the exaltation of Jesus). The effect of inserting such a preface into the original story was that the prologue "insisted on becoming the first act in the drama, and the original first act, now become the second, had consequently to be rewritten."[9]

This "rewriting" took place in *docetism*, the fourth christological phase, with its forthright denial that Christ was ever a true human being. He *seemed* to be human—and it was important to human salvation that he should have appeared as such—but actually he was not. Christ was a divine being, something he could never cease to be. His humanity was a disguise he wore temporarily or, perhaps better, a role he played, to deceive the powers that ruled the planets, including the earth. This fourth story, while not consistently represented in the New Testament, was at one time

---

8. Knox views incarnationism as an interim between stories rather than as a new story, a phase "less clear-cut in its structure and more diversified in its actual forms," and therefore distinct from the others. He does not include incarnationism among his three ancient Christologies.

9. Knox, *Humanity and Divinity of Christ*, 16.

INTRODUCTION

widely prevalent in Christian circles (beginning in the late first century and flourishing in the second and third centuries), as evident by passages in late New Testament writings inserted as refutation (see Col. 1:22; 2:9; 1 John 1:1–3; 4:1–3; 2 John 7; cf. 1 Cor. 12:3).

If the early church's recollection of Jesus was that of a human being who lived, suffered, and died as a human, then, almost by necessity, adoptionism was the original Christology. Given the environment that developed with belief in the resurrection, it was inevitable that the divine preexistence of Jesus could have been avoided. Once that ascription was made, it is clear that only three possibilities remained—kenoticism, incarnationism, and docetism. Either a divine being (called by whatever name) became a human being, in all respects, or else he only appeared to be human. There is no other alternative.

If, under different conditions, the original adoptionist pattern had proven to be the final one, the church would not have found it inadequate. The Christian message, summarized in 2 Corinthians 5:19: "In Christ God was reconciling the world to himself," is really the whole of the gospel, and that message could have been fully proclaimed within the limits of the primitive story. But conditions changed. The story of what God accomplished in Christ became the story of Christ himself. And once that happened, the old pattern would no longer do. It was no longer enough to recognize that Jesus' human life and death belonged to God's saving deed. That deed became conceived, more and more, as Jesus' own deed, and his entire life, from conception and birth to death, as his intentional way of accomplishing our salvation. The preexistence of Christ, once affirmed, brought the kenotic story into being, and then the necessity of incarnation.

Docetism, however, was not a form of the story the church was willing finally to accept. It was rejected, not only for theological reasons, but also because it constituted an intolerable denial of essential elements in the church's life, particularly its remembrance of Jesus and its sense of being rooted in history, especially in the larger story of the history of Israel. By rejecting earlier forms (stages) of the story it found inadequate, the rejection of docetism meant that the church finally embraced a Christology that might be described as a "revised" story, or as falling between stories, or perhaps as being a mixture of stories.

Paul's letters, the Synoptic Gospels, Acts, Hebrews, and the Fourth Gospel, serve as primary sources, though the rest of the New Testament writings also exhibit evidence of the various stages in the development of the church's Christology.

Part I

Human

THE STATE OF THE christological question: "What do you think of Christ?" (Matt. 22:2) is fluid today, more so than perhaps it has been since the earliest Christian debates with Judaism. As originally put by Jesus to the Pharisees, it was a Jewish question, expecting a Jewish answer: "What is your opinion about the Messiah?" That question, if one asks it at all today, is practically irrelevant, for who except ardent ultraorthodox Zionists or fanatical apocalyptic Christians looks for a messiah who will be the simple solution to all the world's problems, spiritually and politically? On the other hand, if Christology is simply about Jesus and who he was, interest in it is increasingly confined to a narrowing circle of ardent believers. Not that this topic is unimportant, for I believe the need to think through intelligently who Jesus is for us today is as central as it ever has been to a dynamic faith.

I would like to suggest, however, that Christology is not simply about Jesus, though even as human he represents the ideal universal person, the embodiment of the highest and best in us all. Christology is also about Christ, in whom "all things hold together" (Col. 1:17). That Christ has very much to do with us today. If Christology is to be relevant today, it must relate to the central issues of our day, providing vision, focus, and coherence not only to religious concerns but also to political, economic, social, scientific, and aesthetic concerns as well. If we are interested in Christology, it should be because of the vital issues of our day, not despite them. If, as psychiatrist Carl Jung, puts it, the Christ-figure corresponds to the archetype of the self, the God-image in us all, then this universality of the Christ figure, representing the ultimate dimensions of human existence, alone

Part I: Human

makes Christology relevant today. In this sense, the discussion about Jesus addresses the relationship between the self and God, the mystery that lies at the center of reality. At this initial point in the discussion, the mystery of the Christ is not a matter of faith but rather one of recognition, not "Can you believe this individual to be the Son of God?" (that question comes later), but "Can you see the fullness of your humanity in him?"

The fundamental affirmation of Christianity is that Jesus is the clue to the mystery of *Christos*, just as Christ is the clue to the mystery of God and the meaning of human existence. For those who call themselves Christians, the human Jesus is decisive for interpreting Christ. So we begin with Jesus; he is the center, wherever the circumference; the master key, whatever other keys fit; the essential clue, however complex the final solution.

Session 1

Son of Man (Part I)

Questions for Individual or Group Reflection: At the outset of this study, how would you describe your present understanding of Jesus Christ? Is he God, God "in disguise," the perfect human, an extraordinary person, or something else? Would you characterize your Christology as "from below" or "from above"? (For clarification, see the introductory chapter.) When you read the Gospels, do you read them as mythological in nature, as theologically motivated, or as historically accurate accounts? Explain your answers.

Important Biblical Verses and Passages: Acts 7:56; Matthew 8:20; 11:18–19; Mark 8:31, 38; Psalm 8:1–9; Daniel 7:13–14; Hebrews 4:14—5:10; Romans 8:3; 2 Corinthians 5:21

Technical Words and Concepts: gnostic/gnosticism; docetic/docetism; dualistic/dualism; Son of Man; Synoptic Gospels; Fourth Gospel; midrash; evangelists; Aramaic; sabbath; Parousia; Christendom; patristic; *anhypostasia*; nativity story; *neos*; *kainos*; virgin birth; parthenogenesis

ONE OF THE FUNDAMENTAL claims of the Christian faith is that God became incarnate in human flesh. Such belief emphasizes two realities as the locus of God: humanity and history. The Christian story, then, places paramount importance on the physical dimension of life and its rootedness in historical fact. Christianity, for early Christians, was not only fixed in the unshakeable world of metaphysics but grounded in secular history, in an objectivity both tangible and accessible to the senses, to what has been

Part I: Human

seen and heard, to "what we have looked at and touched with our hands" (1 John 1:1–3). Whatever the element of myth in the gospel story, there was the surety of objectivity "under Pontius Pilate."

The earliest heretical movements in Christianity tended to overspiritualize Jesus, dissociating the spiritual Christ from the physical Jesus and thereby attempting to detach Christianity from history. Such views, gnostic in nature, found agreement in docetic views of Christ, denying he was ever a true human being. A basic conviction of the Greco-Roman world was that truth, eternal and supernatural, was changeless, and that it could not (or should not) be tied to ephemeral phenomena or transitory events. By inserting the name "Pontius Pilate," the Roman procurator who authorized the crucifixion of Jesus, into the second article of the Apostles' Creed, orthodox Christians were emphasizing the historicity of the Christian faith as grounded in a series of historical events while counteracting dualistic views of reality.

Traditional Christianity has had a large stake in historicity. From the start, much of classical Christology—particularly the doctrine of the two natures—has depended on being able to regard the words and deeds of Jesus in the Gospels as actual and reliable, and the resurrection, equated with the empty tomb as historical fact, has been seen as the hinge of the Christian faith. Yet modern Christians cannot escape the evaluation of critical biblical scholarship, which asserts that there is no certainty that Jesus did or said most of the things attributed to him in scripture.

The skepticism of the postmodern ethos, which questions traditional language about the mystery of Christ, has shattered the beliefs of the past, reducing universal religious, metaphysical, and moral truths to tentative, private, and subjective claims and opinions. The classic way of expressing ultimate reality had been to use the vocabulary of uniqueness, of finality, of timeless perfection. That Christian theology presented Jesus Christ as *the* Son of God and *the* Son of Man, *the* Alpha and *the* Omega, in whom all lines meet uniquely, perfectly, and finally. Our world, however, relativistic, pluralistic, and diverse, compels us to be more modest about our claims. For many today, to go on saying the same things in the old terms is to be in danger of rendering Christ meaningless, the answer to questions few are asking.

Thankfully, as we are discovering, the static model of reality is largely unbiblical, the imposition of a later and alien culture. The Bible is much more at home with God as active and dynamic, who confronts humans in and through the particularities and peculiarities of the here and now. The Bible does not portray God as one who is unmoved by human need, who lags behind social and biological change, but as one who is characteristically found on the shifting frontiers of such change and need, incarnated in mundane and timely events rather than in a timeless absolute beyond them all.

With regard to the historical Jesus, two closely connected questions arise: "What *can* we know of him?" and "What do we *need* to know?" The latter question, of course, is significantly more important. Our intent is not to reduce God or Christ to our level, but to relocate "the beyond" and "the ancient," the absolute and the metaphysical, to our midst. This does not mean denying the dimension of transcendence or the supernatural, but it does mean starting where modern skeptics and postmodern seekers might have the best chance of encounter. It means beginning with the familiar and the contingent. In this process, the claims of honesty and integrity, of justice and freedom, of solidarity with universal suffering may be taken seriously and without reserve. One may not see how it all adds up or discern any final truths or laws that cannot be broken, but in the particular, concrete situation, one knows that persons matter more than procedures, principles more than precepts.

Today, in our cultural milieu, the place of theology in general and of Christology and soteriology in particular, is the servants' quarters, not, as in the period of Christendom, the throne. Its style will be more modest, more broken. Yet at its center is be a figure, as the author of Hebrews insists he always is, who is "suited to our need" (Heb. 7:26, NEB), and whom in all his humiliation Christians still rightly call "Teacher" and "Master" (John 13:13).

Whatever more he is—or was—he must be one of us. If Jesus is to be our Person, our Man, he must be a human being in every sense of the word. This is what we find in the New Testament. The early Christians began with a view of Christ that was uncomplicated and relatable. They certainly did not see Jesus to be of *merely* human significance, since he embodied what God was doing in their midst. But their earliest memory was fashioned into a simplistic Christology, perhaps the earliest, of "a man," Jesus of Nazareth, singled out by God, crucified and raised from the dead, as Peter's speech on the day of Pentecost recalls (Acts 2:22–24). "This Jesus God raised up, and of that all of us are witnesses. Being therefore exalted at the right hand of

Part I: Human

God, and having received from the Father the promise of the Holy Spirit, he has poured out this that you both see and hear" (Acts 2:32–33).

John Knox has made the point that as long as this primitive, "adoptionist" Christology prevailed, "the simple actuality of the humanity was in no sense or degree compromised. Not only could it be whole and intact, but it was also subject to no theological or mythological pressure of any kind."[1] But the pressure began soon thereafter, when the idea that the death of Jesus was according to "the definite plan and foreknowledge of God" (Acts 2:23) became translated as the preexistence of Christ. As soon as Jesus Christ was, or could be, represented as a preexistent being who had come down from heaven, then the genuineness of his humanity while he was on earth was open to question. Not that his followers actually questioned his humanity, for the memory was too strong. From the beginning of theological reflection on the significance of Jesus there was the insistence on his solidarity with humanity; otherwise his relevance for us would be undercut. Nevertheless, the threat to his humanity was there, precisely because of the story told about him to bring out the significance of his humanity for our salvation.

Son of Man

When we think of the humanity of Jesus, particularly in light of the Gospel accounts, the title or designation that seems most appropriate for consideration is Son of Man. The meaning of this biblical expression is complex and much debated by scholars, and when used comprehensively it embraces Jesus' identity and the totality of his work as does almost no other biblical concept. The great significance of this expression is that it is the self-designation most often used by Jesus, and that quite regularly. The phrase occurs seventy-two times in the Synoptic Gospels and thirteen in John's Gospel. All Son of Man sayings are christologically significant.

While the Synoptics generally associate the expression with sayings of Jesus about his mission, fate, and position beyond his resurrection, in the Fourth Gospel the situation is different. Here Son of Man sayings compete with the "I am" sayings and the self-designation "the Son." The expression Son of Man is always used in major theological statements. Apart from John 5:27, the Greek in each case is literally "the son of the man." Of the New Testament writings, only Acts 7:56 is an exception to the rule that

---

1. Knox, *Humanity and Divinity of Christ*, 6–7.

Son of Man (Part I)

Jesus alone utters the expression. John 12:34 (where the crowd asks Jesus to explain the meaning of the expression), like Luke 24:7, is only an apparent exception to the rule. The indefinite or undetermined form, "a son of man," occurs in Hebrews 2:6 (quoting Ps. 8:5) and in Revelation 1:13 (the exalted Christ) and 14:14 (an angel or Christ?).

In the Gospels, Jesus uses the term "son of man" in three different ways: (1) as a circumlocution for himself (speaking indirectly of himself as a man; see Matt. 8:20); (2) to speak of his vocation, specifically of his earthly mission and coming passion (see Mark 8:31); and (3) with reference to an eschatological figure who will bring God's judgment at the end of time (Mark 8:38). Scholars debate which, if any, of these three uses of the term can be ascribed to Jesus. Some scholars question Jesus' use of the term altogether, attributing all Son of Man sayings to the midrashic activity of the early church or to theological redaction by the evangelists (the gospel writers). It seems likely that the designation does go back in some way to Jesus, though it clearly underwent development by the later church, particularly the application of the second usage to Jesus' death and resurrection and the third to his future exaltation and coming judgment. Our concern at this point is primarily with the first usage. We will address the second under the title "Suffering Servant" (see Session 2) and the third when we discuss the vindicating role of the messianic eschatological judge (see Session 9).

The New Testament nowhere provides hints regarding the meaning of the expression "son of man," and there is no evidence for the determined form "the son of the man" before it appears in the New Testament. In the Septuagint (the Greek version of the Old Testament widely used at the time of Jesus and later by the New Testament authors) the expression appears only in the undetermined form, which, similar to the Hebrew original *ben 'adam*, conveys a generic meaning synonymous with "man" or "person," that is, with human being, or humankind in general (see Ps. 8:4; 80:17). In the Hebrew Bible, the expression occurs 108 times, 93 of which are in Ezekiel as God's way of addressing the prophet (see Ezek. 2:1, 3, 6, 8; 3:1 etc.). The Aramaic equivalent, *bar 'enash* (the expression Jesus would have used), could mean "the man," "a man," "somebody," or "mankind in general." It is used only once in the Old Testament (in Daniel 7:13), which speaks of "one like a (son of) man," meaning "one like a human." The saying in Daniel has had a decisive impact on the understanding of Son of Man in the New Testament, particularly on the usage related to the exalted Christ.

Part I: Human

It is now widely agreed that in Jesus' day the Aramaic expression was in general usage both as a noun (meaning "a human being") and as a substitute for the pronoun "I," the actual meaning depending on the context. The double meaning could express a generalization, meaning "one" or simply "a human," or it could be a self-reference associated with awe, modesty, or humility, depending on the context. A near parallel can be seen in Paul's way of speaking of himself in 2 Corinthians 12:2–3: "I know a person . . . who thirteen years ago was caught up to the third heaven." It is possible to understand the Gospel Son of Man sayings in accordance with this Aramaic idiom.

However, in the Gospels the term appears to be a title, and it refers exclusively to Jesus Christ. One explanation for this discrepancy is that the meaning of this term changed when the words of Jesus were translated from Aramaic to Greek. Jesus may well have used the term as a way of referring to human beings in general or to himself specifically. An example of this general usage is Mark 2:27–28, where Jesus defends the disciples for plucking grain on the sabbath by saying: "The sabbath was made for humankind, and not humankind for the sabbath; so the Son of Man is lord even of the sabbath." As long as Jesus' words circulated in Aramaic, it was possible to understand his words as having both a general reference and a more specific reference to himself. If intended generally, Jesus might have been suggesting that humanity in general, that is, each person, is lord of the sabbath, since the sabbath existed for his or her sake. When the Gospel writers translated the sayings of Jesus into Greek, however, the ambiguity was lost. The translators had to choose between the specific and the general and opted for a translation that could be understood as a christological title: "the Son of Man."

While expressions such as "The Son," The Son of God," "Christ," and "Lord" appear as titles in the Hebrew Bible and therefore were utilized by early Christians in hymnic material and in liturgical confessions, this appears not to have been the case with the Son of Man expression. So we wonder; if the title did not exist in Judaism before the time of Jesus and the early church, what caused the church to invent this title and apply it to Jesus? Why does the title occur almost exclusively on the lips of Jesus in the New Testament? Why is it so widely represented in the gospel tradition yet almost nowhere else outside of the Gospels? More specifically, why does belief in the Son of Man never appear in primitive creedal statements, liturgical formulas, and summaries of Christian preaching? No other title applied to Jesus by the early church displays such a peculiar history.

Son of Man (Part I)

Ultimately, the question of the genuineness of the individual Son of Man sayings must depend upon their content: are they understandable in the mouth of the historical Jesus or not? Naturally, the answer will depend upon the individual interpreter's idea of what Jesus believed and preached about himself, and what may be referred to the early church. It seems probable that the sayings about the risen and exalted Son of Man and his return as vindicating Judge, depending on Daniel 7:13–14 for their messianic and prophetic imagery, were created by the early church in the process of interpreting faith in the resurrection of Jesus. As indicated by 1 Thessalonians 4:15–17, this interpretation is early and reflects the same tradition expressed later in Mark 13:26 and especially in Matthew 24:30–31.

The uncomplicated way in which the expression is used in the Synoptic Gospels, amplified in the Fourth Gospel, indicates ongoing theological and editorial reflection in the Greek tradition, which transcends the purely idiomatic meaning it had in Aramaic. However much the Son of Man expression was developed later by the church, it seems reasonable to suppose that the usage of the expression in the Gospels originates with Jesus, in the way he spoke about himself. The slur on Jesus in Matthew 11:18–19 and the relegation of him to a status equivalent to that of John the Baptist make it unlikely that this saying was created by the church. Why should the early church have inserted a title connected with the Parousia (the return of Christ) into a context where Jesus is called a glutton and a drunkard? Seemingly, then, Jesus the parable maker used the enigmatic, figurative designation Son of Man to refer in a paradoxical way to himself as the lowly, disreputable messenger of the powerful, transformative kingdom of God.

Some Modern Implications of the Humanity of Jesus

While traditionally an over-emphasis on the humanity of Jesus tended to lead to positions that the church labeled eccentric or heretical, an over-emphasis on the divinity of Jesus led to positions that the church embraced as orthodox. Today, however, the suggestion that Jesus was not completely human is actually more destructive than doubts about his divinity. To say that Jesus was not God but like God says something important. But to say that Jesus was not human but like a human is to judge his entire life a charade.

What does it mean today—post Darwin, Marx, Freud, and the deciphering of the human genome—to insist that Jesus was completely human? To say, with the ancient church theologians, that Jesus was truly man but

Part I: Human

not a man, truly human but not a human being, is nonsense to a modern person. To say that the individual personality of the man Jesus was supplied by, or included in, the hypostasis or substance of the second person of the Trinity, so that what was human was assumed by this superhuman being, strikes us as threatening the very core of Jesus' manhood, his human personhood.

While emphasis on the humanity of Jesus is central to the classic creeds of Christendom, the patristic expression of what it meant for Christ to be human—spelled out in the astonishing doctrine of *anhypostasia* or "impersonal humanity," which saw Christ not as a human person but as a divine person who assumed human nature without assuming human personality—left him aloof and alien to the human condition. Today, when we think of a human being, we think not of a solitary visitor who may have entered completely the place where we are, but only as a visitor. Rather we think of one active in the nexus of biological, historical, and social relationships with fellow human beings and with the universe as a whole. If Jesus was like us, but whose genes and chromosomes were not shaped and transmitted by millions of years of evolution, he was not a member of the species *homo sapiens*, and hence not one of us. No one can just become a human unexpectedly; a genuine person can only come out of the organic human process, not into it.

As it turns out, this concern for Jesus' solidarity with the rest of creation, with the culture of Israel, the seed of David, and the rest of creation, is not only modern but also biblical. As every person participates in race, nation, or culture, Jesus was a son of Abraham. More importantly, he was a son of Adam, as all humans are, regardless of culture, nation, or race. There is no other conceivable way of being human. Not only is it impossible, by definition, that God should become human, it is also impossible, by definition, that God should "make" one so. A true human cannot be freshly minted. Such a being might look human, but he would not be human by virtue of not belonging to the social, chemical, and biological process.

The genealogies of Matthew and Luke were not intended to be set against the assertion of Jesus' heavenly conception, or vice versa. Rather they were asserting both. Matthew's first chapter is focused not on the birth of Jesus but on his origin. The fact that for Jews this lineage is necessarily traced through the male line places the genealogy in glaring contradiction to the accompanying narrative, which claims that Joseph was not genetically the father. The purpose of the nativity story is not to deny something at the level of flesh asserted in the genealogy, but to affirm something at the level of spirit, namely, the initiative of God in and through it all.

When the biblical authors ask, directly or indirectly, the identity of Jesus, they do not confine the answer simply to the immediate accidents of history and geography, but locate their understanding within the plan and purpose of God. Their approach to Jesus, while affirming his humanity, likewise affirms the divine initiative. In their view, God is doing a new thing, not only *in* Jesus, but also *through* him.

To recognize what newness meant to the early Christians, we need to recognize the two Greek words in the New Testament for "new"—*neos*, a reference to novelty, and *kainos*, meaning renewal. With occasional exceptions for stylistic effects, all theologically significant phrases, such as "new covenant," "new humanity," "new commandment," and "new Jerusalem," utilize *kainos* rather than *neos*. Biblically speaking, the "newness" God is doing always involves the re-creation of the old rather than its abolition. Rather than start from scratch, God's approach renews or remakes existing continuities.

Whatever God's "new creation" may mean, it does not involve starting anew with completely different material; rather, as Jeremiah learned from the potter's workshop (Jer. 18:1–11), it is to fashion new possibilities by remolding the old lump of clay. In the birth of Jesus, it is the Spirit of God at work once again, as in fashioning the first heaven and earth (Gen. 1:2), "overshadowing" the process (Luke 1:35). It is for this reason, not because his "matter" is different, that Mary is told that the child to be born to her will be called "Son of God."

It is important to recognize that if today, with our knowledge, we take the virgin birth literally, we are bound to distort it. For ancient peoples there was no suggestion that it involved the making of new matter—except in the sense that every child was a fresh gift from God. In the Lukan account of the birth (unlike Matthew's), there is no necessity to see the promise to Mary to mean more than that her son would be "great," like Elizabeth's (see Luke 1:15 and 32).

Assuming, as Luke and probably his contemporaries did, that the female contributed everything to the birth of a child and the male nothing, the perspective would have been that Jesus took the substance of his humanity completely from Mary his mother, activated in this case by the divine Spirit rather than by the male impulse. We now know that genetics works differently, and that even if human parthenogenesis were biologically possible, Jesus would have been female. Mary could not have supplied what specifically made him male. That being the case, the male genes would have been created and introduced by God. But is that what we are being asked to accept? If so, we have reached a point akin to that asserted by the defenders of conservative orthodoxy in the late nineteenth century when they said that God created rocks with fossils in them to look as though evolution were true. The dogma may have been saved, but the position was fundamentally untenable. Reading scripture this way, arguing dogmatically today for belief in a physical virgin birth, casts irreparable doubt on the genuineness of Jesus' humanity.

The view that the birth of Jesus required a special creation so that he could assume a sinless nature was until recently scarcely challenged, though it should have been, for such a view flies in the face of the biblical evidence. The Epistle to the Hebrews speaks of Jesus as a man "who in every respect has been tested as we are" (4:15), who was "subject to weakness" (5:2), who "offered up prayers and supplications, with loud cries and tears, to the one who was able to save him from death, and he was heard because of his reverent submission" (5:7). Such language surely points to a person of common nature with ourselves. For Paul, also, the solidarity of Jesus with our present human condition is of fundamental theological importance. Without questioning the sinlessness of Jesus, Paul makes it clear that this has significance only if Jesus really did share our nature. God sent his Son "in the likeness of sinful flesh" (Rom. 8:3), and "made him to be sin who knew no sin" (2 Cor. 5:21). For our sake he came under the curse and custody of the law (Gal. 3:13, 23), and in bearing the human likeness, he assumed the position of a slave to the powers of evil and death (Phil. 2:7–8).

For Jesus to become in every respect one of us, belonging to the human race, he must have been linked through his biological tissue to the origin of life on this planet and behind that to the whole inorganic process reaching back to the star dust and the hydrogen atom. How can we judge Jesus extraordinary if we cannot first judge him ordinary? The New Testament does not seem embarrassed by Jesus' natural connection with the rest of his fellow humans: "Is not this the carpenter, the son of Mary and brother of James and Joses and Judas and Simon, and are not his sisters here with us?" (Mark 6:3; cf. 3:31; also 1 Cor. 9:5; Gal. 1:19; John 2:12; Acts 1:14). This combination of witnesses is far stronger than for the virgin birth story, which on any natural reading of the words that Joseph "had no marital relations with [Mary] until she had borne a son" (Matt. 1:25), implies rather than rules out subsequent relations. It asserts that Jesus was Mary's firstborn son, not her only son (Luke 2:7).

While the significance of Jesus is not understood solely from the point of view of heredity and environment, these conditions are not abrogated in Jesus, any more that they are for ordinary Christians who, as children of God, "were born, not of blood or of the will of the flesh or of the will of man, but of God" (John 1:13). However, this is not to deny that at the level of nature they are so born. The one truth does not contradict the other. As many have stated, notably Donald Baillie: "It is . . . nonsense to say that [Jesus] is 'Man' unless we mean that He is *a* man."[2] No more docetism! That is the first factor in the distinctive situation of Christology today.

---

2. Baillie, *God Was in Christ*, 87.

Part II

Fully Human

IN THE PREVIOUS SESSION we took seriously the requirement that if Jesus Christ is to be anything for us at all, he must have been genuinely human, with the peculiarities and limitations of any unique individual. In this segment we address our reluctance to press this to the limit, for this hesitancy is connected with the desire to see him as extraordinary, something more than merely human. If Jesus is to be the Christ, he must point beyond himself. He must be a representative figure, standing for the highest and best in us all.

If that is true, what does it mean to say that Jesus Christ holds the clue to human nature, the norm of what human existence should be? It means speaking of him not simply as *a* "son of man" but as *the* Son of Man, as the archetypal man, the last or definitive Adam, the completely integrated self, the one who speaks fully when he says "I." Not only Christians but also people of other faiths seek such a person. Martin Buber, the Jewish philosopher, spoke knowingly when he remarked, "How powerful, even to being overpowering, and how legitimate, even to being self-evident, is the saying of 'I' by Jesus! For it is the *I* of unconditional relation in which the man calls his *Thou* Father in such a way that he himself is simply Son, and nothing else but Son."[1] Is it possible to see this ideal of normality and universality in any one individual, and if so, what relation does it bear on the Jesus of history?

Christians have tended to take as axiomatic that Jesus was complete and perfect in every respect. He must have had every desirable human

---

1. Buber, *I and Thou*, 66–67.

quality, he must have been everything a human could be, they assert, or he could not have been the Christ. Set on a pedestal, such a Jesus becomes unique not because he is normal but because he is abnormal. Paradoxically, what we want to say of him as *the* man undercuts his humanity. Such claims might have made sense to Christians in the past, but for many today such attributions makes Jesus unapproachable, an unreal figure of static perfection rather than a person of flesh and blood. So pervasive and damaging is this estimate that it is necessary to pay some attention to it.

What would it mean to say that Jesus Christ was a "perfect" human being? Would it mean that Jesus was "perfectly human," that is, "completely human," which makes good sense, or would it mean he was the perfect specimen of humanity, with no imbalance of any kind? Would he be attractive physically? Would he have been, as some describe him, the greatest philosopher, mathematician, doctor, politician, orator, painter, carpenter, engineer, physicist, athlete, even chess-player? If diagnosed today, would his IQ register as the highest possible? Would his health be perfect, his physique ideal?

If diagnosed, wouldn't he exhibit one particular blood type and the characteristics of a particular psychological type? And wouldn't he be right-handed or left-handed rather than ambidextrous? The norm for the Bible is that a person can be fully human without being odd, peculiar, or the complete Renaissance person.

Of course, even if Jesus were extraordinary, surely he would have exhibited normal human qualities. One cannot read the Synoptic Gospels without noting their emphasis on the humanity of Jesus (he is born; he develops physically, spiritually, and intellectually; he weeps, asks questions, needs sleep, is hungry, gets angry, suffers, and dies). Mark's Gospel, and even John's Gospel, which stresses mostly his divinity, presents grounds for the fears of those, including his family, who questioned his mental stability (Mark 3:21; John 7:20; 8:48, 52; 10:20).

As fully human, Jesus would have displayed a power not of omnipotence or omniscience but rather of character, a vision and determination that enabled followers to choose between alternatives. With his resolve and singleness of purpose, he risked becoming a fanatic. Most likely he would not have epitomized the ideal levelheaded man parents of a daughter might welcome as son-in-law. His qualities of justice and goodness probably relegated him to a minority type, such as the Hebrew prophets before him. It would be more true to say of him that he had nothing than that he had everything (Matt. 8:20; Luke 2:7), and rather than representing a Greek god, he more likely represented one who had "no form or majesty that we should look at him, nothing in his appearance that we should desire him" (Isa. 53:2). Given these qualities, it might not be proper for everyone to aim, in simple general terms, at being "like Jesus." To be the fully human, as we might claim of Jesus, is not to say that one has every human quality, but rather that one is the sort of person that transcends the individual. It is to see in Jesus what each of us could be, in our own unique way. What attracts us to Jesus is not that he represents the person who has everything, but rather that we find in him one in whom we glimpse a vision of the essential, the authentic.

In an evolutionary world, the idea of one person from the past who already has everything one person can have seems to place a limit on human potential. It represents a static ideal on which no advance is possible. Indeed, the claim that Jesus was "perfect" needs so much explanation and qualification that perhaps we should drop it. We can imagine him asking, "Why do you call me perfect?" as he asked, "Why do you call me good?" (Mark 10:18). The Epistle to the Hebrews, the only New Testament document to refer to Jesus' perfection, always uses of Jesus the verb "made perfect" (or "perfected"), never the adjective "perfect" (Heb. 2:10; 5:9; 7:28).[2] The author insists that Jesus "learned obedience through what he suffered" (Heb. 5:8), that is, through the circumstances of his life that affected him and changed him. This passage provides forceful evidence that Jesus was remembered as a man of like passions with ourselves who had to persevere in the same way as everyone else.

We need to recall that the church's images of Jesus come primarily through the Gospels, and though the Gospels provide us with numerous portraits of Jesus, they are not modern biographies; as such, they are not concerned to trace or record Jesus' human development. There is a tendency in some Christian circles to conclude that merely to approach Jesus with this interest is to be misguided. However, there is no reason for us not to raise this issue. In fact, not to do so leaves the impression that because the Gospels are not interested in Jesus' development, there was none, just as one might assume that their silence about his sexuality means that he was sexless. For us to interact with the scriptures on our terms, as

---

2. The sole occurrence of the phrase "a perfect man" (translated "maturity" or "mature person" in the NRSV of Ephesians 4:13) in the New Testament is not a description of Jesus but of humanity fulfilled in Christ.

twenty-first-century individuals, means we must bring our questions and concerns to the table, and not merely those of antiquity. The truth of Cardinal Newman's dictum applies to every human, including, we might add, to Jesus: "Here below to live is to change, and to be perfect is to have changed often." One of the notable contributions of Martin Luther to Christology is that against the stream of his heritage, he recognized not only Jesus' personhood but also that Jesus became a person through the normal processes of maturation and moral growth.

In this brief overview, one final question remains: "Was Jesus sinless?" According to every recognized religious and political standard of his day, Jesus was a "sinner," a law-breaker and outcaste. The charges at his trials, however trumped-up, stuck, and as a victim of crucifixion, he was viewed as cursed by God (see Gal. 3:13; Deut. 21:23). Yet within a generation of his death (in some cases far sooner), Christian authors were stating that he "knew no sin" (2 Cor. 5:21), that he was "without sin" (Heb. 4:15), and that "he committed no sin" (1 Pet. 2:22). This judgment held largely unquestioned until recently.

That judgment, of course, was theological rather than historical, for the latter is nearly impossible to prove. Can we say of anyone, beyond doubt, that they were always fair, kind, and loving, that in the secret recesses of their heart they never sinned? The contexts in which the New Testament speaks of Jesus as being without sin make the theological intent plain: In order to do away with sin, Jesus had, according to the sacrificial theory of the day, to be spotless and without blemish, whether as priest (Heb. 4:15; 7:26) or as victim (2 Cor. 5:21; Heb. 9:14; 1 Peter 1:19; 1 John 3:3–5). John Knox sums up what he deems as "the poignant dilemma" of the early Christians about the humanity and the sinlessness of Jesus: "How could Christ have saved us if he were not a human being like ourselves? How could a human being like ourselves have saved us?"[3]

As we have seen, both Paul and the author to the Hebrews insist that the humanity of Christ must be complete if his death was to impact our human condition. But each draws back at the point of total identification. They can think of Jesus as sharing our weakness, but not our sinfulness. Yet this presents them with a dilemma. Paul goes so far as to say that for our sake God "made him to be sin who knew no sin" (2 Cor. 5:21), yet qualifies it by stating that God sent Jesus "in *the likeness* of sinful flesh" (Rom. 8:3). The last thing Paul wants to do is deny that Jesus was really one of us.

---

3. Knox, *Humanity and Divinity of Christ*, 52.

Part II: Fully Human

Equally, the author of Hebrews treads carefully. Whereas in every other respect his argument requires that in order to be our high priest Jesus must totally share our condition ("since he himself is subject to weakness," Heb. 5:2), he goes on to make a virtue of Jesus' unlikeness to us, for such a high priest must be "holy, blameless, undefiled, separated from sinners" (Heb. 7:26).

The same dilemma appears when this author insists on the reality of Christ's temptations: "For we do not have a high priest who is unable to sympathize with our weaknesses, but we have one who in every respect has been tested as we are, yet without sin" (Heb. 4:15). We question the nature of such a temptation: Is one really tempted if one never consents? If Jesus was not subject to human temptation, if his choices are not different of degree but of kind from ours, such choices would be irrelevant to ours.

The question has been raised many times: Are we to say of Jesus that he was not able to sin (*non posse peccare*), or that he was able not to sin (*posse non peccare*)? If the former, his humanity would not be ours. He must have had the freedom to sin or not to sin, or he would not have shared *our* freedom. We might say, if we wish, that it was *morally* impossible for him to sin, or, as P. T. Forsyth put it, "He could be tempted because he loved; he could not sin, because he loved so deeply."[4] We cannot say, however, that it was *metaphysically* impossible for him to sin, namely, because he was God. His sinlessness, if historically valid, would need to have been the outcome of a genuinely *human* freedom.

The question remains, "Was Jesus that perfect?" The only honest answer is, "We do not know." All we can say is that this is how his followers remembered him. Of course, we must expect them to have remembered, and to have improved upon, idealized portraits. Additionally, we must expect doctrinal interests to have influenced the picture.

A third option remains, stated classically as a double negative: Jesus was not able not to sin (*non posse non peccare*). If "to err is human," and Jesus was truly human, this seems altogether possible to say about Jesus. However, Christians traditionally have avoided this possibility, and understandably so. To entertain this option places Jesus solely on the human side of the divine/human equation, meaning he would be part of the problem rather than of the solution. That need not be the case, however, particularly if we rethink our understanding of anthropology and soteriology, of "sin" and "salvation," a task incumbent on every generation of believers. If sin,

---

4. Forsyth, *Person and Place of Jesus Christ*, 303.

for example, were understood primarily as inauthentic human existence, spiritual bondage, or unrighteousness (disruption of one's relationship to God), it might be possible to view the human Jesus as sinless, and if salvation is understood as authentic human existence, spiritual freedom, and righteousness (proper relationship to God), it might be possible to view the human Jesus as savior.

Several factors remain for our consideration. First, the early Christians seemed to have retained a remarkable reverence for Jesus. However, they showed considerable reluctance to make him claim of himself, what they claimed of him—that he was "Lord," "Christ," and "Son of God." Conversely, they consistently put upon his own lips and upon no one else's, the mysterious and ambiguous title "Son of Man." In Mark's Gospel Jesus states explicitly, "Why do you call me good? No one is good but God alone" (Mark 10:18), a statement Matthew modifies (see 19:17). The gospel writers, clearly aware of the need to vindicate Jesus against Jewish attacks, nevertheless report Jesus as referring to his reputation as a glutton and a drinker (Matt. 11:16–19; Luke 7:31–35). They also report at least three incidents where he had his feet (or head) kissed, scented, and wiped with the hair of a woman, whether or not of doubtful repute. The lack of defensiveness with which they relate such compromising stories says a great deal. Yet they make no sweeping historical claims for his perfection, which he actually disclaims.

The astonishing claim of sinlessness attributed to Jesus by the church, for theological reasons, is actually sustained by the considerable testimony to the character of Jesus, whose goodness even Josephus, the first-century Jewish historian, apparently conceded. Perhaps theologian Emil Brunner's conclusion is fair. Acknowledging that the verdict "without sin" goes further than anything that can be grasped empirically, he adds, "we know of no situation which could shake the truth of these words."[5] The "perfect person," however, remains a judgment of faith, not of history.

---

5. Brunner, *Doctrine of Creation and Redemption*, 324.

Session 2

Servant (Son of Man, Part II)

Questions for Individual or Group Reflection: How do you interpret the healings and miracles attributed to Jesus? Should they be viewed parabolically, metaphorically, theologically, or literally? Explain your answer.

Important Biblical Verses and Passages: Mark 1:34; 2:15–17; 8:11–12, 31–38; 9:12, 31; 10:33–34, 45; Isaiah 42:1–4; 49:1–7; 50:4–9; 52:13—53:13; Matthew 8:16, 17; 9:36; 12:9–32; 14:22–33; 15:28; Acts 3:13

Technical Words and Concepts: Servant Christology; Servant Songs; Babylonian exile; Suffering Servant; Essenes; Qumran

THE EXPRESSION SON OF Man, widely applied to Jesus in the Gospels, appears to be the only title used by Jesus of himself. As previously noted, the title can be divided into three categories, as a way of speaking (1) about himself and his humanity; (2) about his vocation, specifically his earthly mission and coming passion; and (3) about his future exaltation or coming judgment. This session focuses on the ministry of Jesus, particularly in the designation of Jesus as Servant of God, compassionately obedient to his Father's will.

Many Son of Man sayings are set in the present ministry of Jesus. For example, the Son of Man (a) "has nowhere to lay his head" (Matt. 8:20; Luke 9:58); (b) "came to seek out and to save the lost" (Luke 19:10); (c) "has authority on earth to forgive sins" (Mark 2:10; Matt. 9:6; Luke 5:24); (d) "is lord even of the sabbath" (Mark 2:28); and (e) "came eating and drinking" (Matt. 11:19; Luke 7:34). Some sayings clearly predict the sufferings of the

Son of Man, and some are "apocalyptic," pointing either to the coming of the Son of Man or to a Day of the Son of Man (for the latter, see Session 9).

The depiction of Jesus as Servant of God in his ministry and passion is frequently associated with the Gospel of Mark, the first Gospel written and hence the most primitive. Finding numerous christological titles embedded in Mark, scholars note that beneath this collage lies a distinct and authentic portrayal of Jesus as a servant come to suffer in obedience to God. Mark presents Jesus as a person of action, using the term "immediately" over forty times in its brief format. He records mostly what Jesus did, and little of what he said. There is no Sermon on the Mount, for example, and relatively few parables. There is no genealogy and birth narrative, for these records would have little value for one whose worth is servitude. In addition, the Markan Jesus does not know the time of the end of the age (13:32), and he is not at liberty to assign seats of honor in his coming glory (10:40). He prays to the Father and submits completely to him, even to the points of death (14:36). For Mark, Jesus is God's Servant. In Luke's Gospel, by comparison, there is no saying about the ignorance of the Son (cf. Mark 13:32; Matt. 24:36), nor the saying where the Son defers to the Father to decide who will sit at his right and left hand (cf. Mark 10:40; Matt. 20:23).

Sixteen chapters in length, one-third of Mark's Gospel is devoted to Jesus' passion. Mark heightens the passion by inserting three passion predictions into the mouth of Jesus. Beginning with Peter's confession, they occur at Mark 8:31, 9:31, and 10:33-34. The first of these marks the turning point in Jesus' teaching about himself. Previously in Mark Jesus had made allusions to his role, but now the eyes of the disciple are opened. They learn that Jesus must suffer and die, something that strikes them as inconceivable, as indicated by Peter's attempted rebuke in 8:32. Most of us remember Jesus' harsh retort, where he calls Peter "Satan"—meaning "opponent" or "antagonist"—for viewing discipleship from a human perspective only. Jesus then goes on to teach his followers the cost of discipleship, that like him they too must suffer and die (8:34-38).

The third passion prediction (10:33-34) is the most detailed. Here what Jesus expects is predicted feature by feature, in six stages. These correspond so exactly with the course of the passion narrative and the Easter story, even down to details, that there can be no doubt that this prediction is a summary of the passion composed after the event. In the final prediction we are told that the Gentiles "will mock him, and spit upon him, and flog him, and kill him." These words echo Isaiah 50:6, where God's servant says: "I gave my back to those who struck me, and my cheeks to those who pulled out the beard; I did not hide my face from insult and spitting."

Isaiah 50:4–9 is one of four passages in the book of Isaiah that describes a character identified as the Lord's servant (see also Isa. 42:1–9; 49:1–7; 52:13—53:12). Modern scholars refer to these passages as the Servant Songs. When the New Testament authors depict Jesus, one of the Old Testament characters they find most persuasive is the Servant of the Lord, described by Isaiah as a figure whom God had chosen. God equips him with his Spirit so that he might bring justice to the nations (42:6). God will be glorified in him (49:3), and he is expected to bring salvation not only to Israel but also to the Gentiles (49:5–6). He suffers at the hands of evildoers (50:6–7), but is vindicated by the Lord (50:8–9). The fourth song explains that the servant's suffering is also his way to glory (52:13). His suffering is not for his own wrongdoing, but is the way in which he bears the sins of his people, thus bringing them salvation. He is without sin (53:9), yet it is God's will to make him suffer (53:10), thereby making "intercession for the transgressors" (53:12).

Isaiah closely connects the servant with the people of Israel, and God is said to address the servant as "Israel" in Isaiah 49:3. Applied to Isaiah 52:13—53:12, this identification would cohere with the Jewish conviction that no one could die vicariously for the sins of others, but only for oneself. The Babylonian exile is given this interpretation in Israel's prophetic literature, which viewed Israel's exile as punishment for its own disbelief, social injustice, and religious unfaithfulness. An alternative interpretation, based on the book of Job, views Job as Israel. According to this view, Israel is an innocent victim, and the exile the story of servant Israel's vicarious suffering on behalf of the nations of the world, including Israel's unrighteous enemies. Such an interpretation would prove useful to Christianity's emerging Christology.

Some scholars question the communal or corporate interpretation of Isaiah's Servant, insisting on an individual identity. Others take a mediating position, arguing that the Servant stands for "ideal Israel" and that this ideal eventually is represented by an individual, specifically the long-awaited Jewish Messiah, as the traditional Christian interpretation maintains. One of the arguments for this position is that the Servant must be distinguished from the people, as he is said to suffer in their place and to bear their sins. Echoes from Isaiah's songs in Jesus' words indicate that he understood his own role in light of the picture of this Servant of the Lord, particularly when he maintains that it is "written about the Son of Man, that he is to go through many sufferings and be treated with contempt" (Mark 9:12; cf. 14:49).

One of the most debated verses in Mark's Gospel is also the only verse where Jesus explains the purpose of his death, namely in 10:45: "For the Son of Man came not to be served but to serve, and to give his life a ransom for many." Is there an allusion to Isaiah 53 here? Though there are no clear verbal links, the conceptual links are significant. It seems evident that the Markan Jesus understands his mission as a fulfillment of the prophecies regarding Isaiah's Suffering Servant. Specifically, he will give his life on behalf of his people, to set them free from sin. We may also find a connection to the Servant Songs in Jesus' words at his Last Supper: "This is my blood of the covenant, which is poured out for many" (Mark 14:24). As the Suffering Servant dies for the people, so Jesus gives his life for them.

In contrast to Mark, who usually leaves implicit the identification of Jesus with the Servant of the Lord, Matthew makes it explicit. In fact, the lengthiest of Matthew's many quotations from the Old Testament is from Isaiah 42:1–4 (Matt. 12:18–21). Matthew understands the first Servant Song as a prophecy fulfilled in Jesus' healing ministry. He reads Isaiah 53:4 in the same light; when Jesus casts out demons and cures the sick, he fulfills "what had been spoken through the prophet Isaiah, 'He took our infirmities and bore our diseases'" (Matt. 8:17).

The latter of these quotations occurs in a summary statement regarding Jesus' activities. That is important because it shows that Matthew is not only more explicit than Mark; he also understands Isaiah's Servant as providing the paradigm for Jesus' entire ministry. Where Mark alludes to Isaiah's Servant Songs in order to explain Jesus' suffering and death, Matthew expands the application. He sees Jesus' public ministry, specifically his healing activity, as the fulfillment of Isaiah 53:4. In Matthew 12:18–21, Matthew uses Isaiah 42:1–4 to explain why Jesus did not seek fame and public adulation. Isaiah's song describes a humble servant, and this servant provides the model for Jesus' character.

Surprisingly, Matthew does not quote from the Servant Songs in connection with Jesus' death. He also tones down Mark's allusions to the Servant Songs (compare Mark 10:33–34 and Matthew 20:18–19), though like Mark, he includes the saying about Jesus giving "his life as a ransom for many" (Matt. 20:28), which appears to be inspired by the prophecy about the Servant's vicarious suffering in Isaiah 53:10–11.

Servant (Son of Man, Part II)

In Mark, the clearest identification of Jesus as Isaiah's Servant occurs at his baptism, when the heavenly voice declares that with Jesus he is "well pleased" (Mark 1:11; cf. Isa. 42:1). According to Matthew, the heavenly voice makes this allusion not only at Jesus' baptism (Matt. 3:17), but also at his transfiguration (Matt. 17:5). We might see an allusion to Isaiah 53:11 ("the righteous one, my servant, shall make many righteous") in Matthew 3:15, when Jesus prepares for his baptism by John by insisting that together he and John must "fulfill all righteousness."

The Origin and Development of Servant Christology

In the Old Testament and in the writings of ancient Judaism the expression "Servant of God," used religiously, was employed in a variety of ways, principally as (1) a self-designation of a pious worshipper or as an ascription in the plural of pious persons; (2) as a collective term for the nation of Israel; and (3) as a denotation of the Messiah. It is clear that at least certain sectors of Palestinian Judaism understood Isaiah's Servant Songs messianically during the first centuries BC and AD. While it seems that the concept "Servant of God" was thought of in some circles within late Judaism in a messianic fashion (this seems to have been a designation used by the Essenes, as the Hymns of Thanksgiving from Qumran suggest), a "suffering servant" conception of the Messiah had not yet been formulated, particularly due to the connection of the Messiah with the royal "son of David."

The New Testament explicitly calls Jesus God's "servant" in Acts 3:13, 26, and 4:27, 30, with both Isaian and Davidic nuances present. In five passages, quotations from the Servant Songs are applied to Jesus and to aspects of his ministry (Matt. 8:17; 12:18–21; Luke 22:37; John 12:38; Acts 8:32–33). Of these, only Jesus' quotation in Luke 22:37, Philip's text in Acts 8:32–33, and possibly Peter's statement in Acts 3:13 directly connect Jesus with a Suffering Servant concept as well as a Servant motif. In addition, the traditional formulations in 1 Corinthians 15:3–5; 11:23–25; Philippians 2:6–11, and 1 Peter 2:21–25, together with confessional fragments found in Romans 4:25; 8:32, 34; 1 Timothy 2:6; and 1 Peter 3:18, evidence either verbal or conceptual affinities to Isaiah 53.

Surveying the passages where Jesus is explicitly identified as God's Servant, where the Isaian Songs are applied to him or to aspects of his ministry, and where the language of confession is based on Isaiah 53, there is little doubt that early Christians thought in terms of Servant Christology—even of Suffering Servant Christology. And judging by the fact that such a conception exists in Paul's letters, principally (if not exclusively) in confessional portions, and later in the writings of the early patristic theologians only in prayers and liturgical formulations, it is reasonable to conclude that such a Christology stems from the first Jewish Christians.

In fact, the understanding of Jesus' ministry in terms of a Suffering Servant Christology is attributable to two factors, to Jesus himself and to the church's consciousness of Jesus as the Messiah. Someone within the Christian movement very early took the original step of fusing the concepts of Messiah and Suffering Servant, for it does not appear to have been done prior to the rise of Christianity. Luke 22:37 indirectly asserts that it was Jesus: "For I tell you, this scripture must be fulfilled in me, 'And he was counted among the lawless' [Isa. 53:12]; and indeed what is written about me is being fulfilled." In all likelihood, Jesus only allowed himself to be known as the Suffering Servant in his private teaching and not in his public preaching. Only to his disciples did he indicate that he viewed the fulfillment of Isaiah 53 as his divinely appointed task, and to them alone interpret his death as vicarious.

Having said this, a significant problem remains, to explain why the Suffering Servant theme and Isaiah 53, the only clearly redemptive Suffering Servant passage in the Old Testament, was not employed more explicitly in the canonical Christian writings. If such an understanding permeates the Christian message, why are there only three passages in the New Testament where the concept is mentioned directly, namely in Luke 22:37; Acts 8:32–33, and 1 Peter 2:21–25?

The explanation, if it exists, appears in Paul's letters. In 1 Corinthians 1:23 he says plainly that the proclamation of Christ as crucified was central to his message, while acknowledging that this was "a stumblingblock [a scandal] to Jews" and "foolishness to Gentiles." In Galatians 5:11 he speaks of "the offense [scandal] of the cross," which he considers to lie inherent in the Christian gospel. Trained as a rabbi, Paul was well acquainted with the reaction of the Jews to the Christian proclamation of a suffering Messiah (see also Luke 20:18; Rom. 9:33; 1 Pet. 2:8). Living in the Roman world, he was aware of the seeming absurdity and indignity of such a redemptive figure in the eyes of the Greeks. The muting of a Suffering Servant motif in the early church may indeed be due more to ideas current within Judaism and Greek religious philosophy than to ideas in Christianity regarding the nature of divine salvation. That this understanding of Jesus' vocation was firmly rooted in the consciousness of early Jewish Christianity seems beyond doubt. In view of the circumstances, it may even be considered surprising that the church proclaimed a redemption based upon vicarious suffering at all. Its continuance indicates the fixity of the Suffering Servant concept in the mindset of early believers.

Jesus as Healer and Exorcist

The classical creeds of the church—both the Nicene and the Apostles' Creed—are deficient in that they say nothing about Jesus' active ministry on earth. They go directly from his birth to his passion. In so doing, they overlook the portrait of Jesus' life and work in the Gospels. Jesus' task on earth, according to Matthew 20:28, was "to serve," something he accomplished through a ministry of "teaching," "preaching," and "healing" (Matt. 4:23; 9:35). According to Matthew, when Jesus heals the sick he fulfills the prophecy about the Suffering Servant in Isaiah 53 (Matt. 8:16–17).

In the world's religious literature, miracles are often attributed to people viewed as saints or mystics. How natural, even appropriate, it seems that persons who live selflessly and compassionately be endowed with healing ability. Often we hear stories of people tragically flawed, deeply wounded, compensated with paranormal power and healing ability. We call them "wounded healers."

The Gospels report that Jesus performed many wonderful cures, physically and psychologically, including on occasion extraordinary control over inanimate nature. In fact, during his lifetime Jesus was known primarily as a healer and exorcist. In Capernaum the inhabitants flocked to him, "and he cured many who were sick with various diseases, and cast out many demons" (Mark 1:34; cf. Matt. 8:16; Luke 4:41). His reputation was such that as soon as people heard that Jesus was approaching, they immediately brought to him those afflicted with illness (Matt. 14:34–35; Mark 6:53–55). The same scenario was repeated all over Galilee (Matt. 14:36; Mark 6:56).

However, Jesus' fame was based not only on his healing and on casting out demons. He was also the renowned physician of those despised and relegated to pariah status. They were symbolized by the "publicans and sinners," the tax collectors and prostitutes. Just as he did not avoid contact with contagious disease, Jesus did not shun social outcasts, thereby causing astonishment and even scandal among the general populace. He justified this association by identifying them with those who are ill and need the help of a physician (Matt. 9:12; Mark 2:17; Luke 5:31). Accepting the companionship of the despised was sufficiently well established and of common knowledge to endow Jesus with the contemptuous nickname "friend of tax collectors and sinners" (Matt. 11:19; Luke 7:34). His overriding concern was to assist those in the greatest spiritual need: "those who are well have no need of a physician, but those who are sick; I have come to call not the righteous but sinners" (Mark 2:17; cf. Matt. 9:12–13; Luke 5:31–32). The overriding concern of Jesus and his disciples was for the helpless and marginalized (Matt. 10:6).

The words most often used to describe Jesus' healing activity are "mighty works" and "signs." The former, used chiefly by the Synoptic Gospels, are connected primarily to the eschatological inbreaking on earth of God's rule or dominion (Matt. 12:28). The Gospel of John prefers to describe Jesus' deeds by the word "signs" (John 2:11; 4:54; 20:30), a term that calls attention to the spiritual significance of the "mighty works." Thus, when Jesus multiplies the loaves to feed the five thousand (John 6) or restores sight to a man born blind (John 9), the writer understands the individual work as a symbol of Jesus' continuing ability and willingness to feed his followers with the bread of life and to open the eyes of the spiritually blind.

Accounts of thirty-seven "miracles" of Jesus are included in the four Gospels. In Mark, the earliest Gospel, over 30 percent of the verses deal directly or indirectly with this activity of Jesus. The implication is that healings and exorcisms and other "mighty works" are central to Jesus' ministry, not peripheral. We should not think, however, that the Gospels exhibit interest in the miraculous for its own sake. Though Matthew and Luke occasionally heighten the Marcan account of Jesus' power to effect cures, neither retained, for example, two striking miracle stories of Mark, the healing of the deaf man with a speech impediment (Mark 7:31–37) and the restoration of sight to a blind man (Mark 8:22–26). In short, the canonical Gospels, unlike later apocryphal accounts, do not speak of a miracle worker who performs as many wonders as possible, but of one who refuses to perform mighty deeds merely for the sake of a spectacle (Matt. 12:38–39; Mark 8:11–12; Luke 11:29; 23:8–9).

The Gospels make clear that Jesus performed healings and exorcisms, not of his own power or ability, but as derived from a higher supernatural power. We also learn that he performed such deeds not to make an impression, gain an audience, or even to elicit faith. His motivation seems to have been threefold: (a) to demonstrate his compassion (Matt. 9:36; Mark 1:41).

Servant (Son of Man, Part II)

Even the account of the feeding of the multitude, the only miracle recorded in all four Gospels, is prompted by Jesus' compassion for the hungry, who had not eaten in three days (Matt. 15:32); (b) to reward faith (Matt. 15:28; Mark 2:5; cf. 6:5–6); and (c) to demonstrate the nearness of God's kingdom (Matt. 12:28). Note that Jesus interprets God's reign in terms of changed human lives, not cosmic or political change. In the Gospels Jesus sees himself as the one who, like physicians, psychiatrists, and spiritual healers, can bring about change within the hearts, minds, and spirits of individual human beings so that they can relate better to themselves, others, and the divine.

The following practical principles can be helpful when we evaluate Jesus healing ministry.

1. Whenever we speak of spiritual matters, we should avoid dismissive thinking. Reductionistic, one-dimensional thinking, whether religious, scientific, or philosophical, is limited and cannot ultimately explain reality adequately. When faith, fact, and logic align, then we have true understanding. Exorcisms and unexplainable healing take place today, as they did in antiquity.

2. Not only followers of Jesus but even enemies acknowledged that he possessed extraordinary power (Matt. 12:24; Luke 11:18).

3. All strata of the Gospels identified by literary criticism testify to Jesus' ability to perform healings and other deeds of power.

4. Just as some of Jesus' sayings were modified in the course of their transmission, so it is possible that on occasion non-miraculous accounts have been transformed into miracle stories. For example, scholars think that what was originally a parable lies behind the account of the miraculous withering of the fig tree that Jesus had cursed (Matt. 21:18–22; Mark 11: 12–14) or of the account of the coin in the fish's mouth (Matt. 17:24–27). In the Gospels, most miracle stories are told, not for their own sake, but to illustrate matters of faith and discipleship. In other words, their function is didactic. Like parables, the details are rarely primary. Notice, for example, how in its Matthean form the account of Jesus walking on the water (Matt. 14:22–33; cf. Mark 6:45–52; John 6:16–21) is expanded to include a lesson on discipleship (Peter's attempt to walk on the water) and a statement on Christology ("And those in the boat worshipped him saying, 'Truly you are the Son of God'").

Part II: Fully Human

5. It is also possible that occasionally early Christians transferred to Jesus stories of foreign origin. For example, the account of the demons going into a herd of pigs (Mark 5:1–17) is thought by some to be originally a non-Christian story appropriated by the early church and blended into an account of one of Jesus' exorcisms.

6. Ultimately, even the accounts of Jesus' healings point to a higher message. Though these deeds were motivated by compassion over human suffering, their deepest meaning lies in their testimony to the reality of God's love and power that Jesus brings into human life. Jesus' miracles are signs that in him, as in all who are wholly human, God is fully present for those in bondage and need, physically, emotionally, and spiritually.

Session 3

Teacher

Questions for Individual or Group Reflection: In your own words, explain what made Jesus a "master teacher." In your estimation, which of Jesus' teachings is most memorable? Which is most original or revolutionary in nature? Explain your answers.

Important Biblical Verses and Passages: Galatians 4:4–7; Mark 2:13; 8:35; 10:31; Matthew 5:1–16; 7:12, 29; 8:35; 10:31; 13:51–52; 28:18–20; Luke 6:20–26; 10:29–37; 14:26; 2 Samuel 12:1–4

Technical Words and Concepts: *abba*; parable; the Beatitudes; Jewish wisdom tradition; conventional wisdom; counter-order wisdom; proverb *(mashal)*; poetic parallelism; aphorism; sapiential; Q source; narrative proverbs *(meshalim)*; Septuagint; prophetic sage; wisdom "from below"; Levitical laws; Pharisees; Samaritans; eschatology/eschatological; Torah; Sermon on the Mount; first evangelist; antithetical sayings

HAD JESUS NO OTHER legacy, he would be remembered as one of the world's master teachers. "Teacher" was a title even his enemies were willing to concede to him. When they approached him with a testing question, they began by saying, "Teacher, we know that you are sincere, and teach the way of God in accordance with truth" (Matt. 22:16; Mark 12:14; Luke 20:21).

The Gospels use three Greek titles to describe Jesus as teacher. The most common is *didaskalos* (teacher, master), used of Jesus almost forty times. Luke also uses the word *epistatēs* (chief, master, lord), a term that in secular Greek would have been used for a headmaster. Sometimes the

Part II: Fully Human

Gospel writers employ the title Rabbi, the standard Jewish title for a distinguished and acknowledged teacher. When we put the three titles together, knowing that they all represent the word Rabbi, the customary word for an accepted teacher, we find that the four Gospels call Jesus "teacher" more than fifty times. The New Testament thus presents us with the picture of Jesus as a master teacher, a teacher par excellence.

All great teachers possess three qualities: (a) mastery of a subject, (b) mastery of communication, and (c) ability to practice what they teach. Jesus excelled in each—in knowledge, ability, and practice. Jesus did not come on the scene of first-century Judaism, however, to conform to anyone's preconceived expectations about sages, or for that matter, about prophets or messiahs. His subject, essentially, was threefold: he came to make known something about God, something about humankind, and something about their interrelationship.

In Jesus' day there was a vast human quest for God, wrapped up in piety and legalism (Judaism), and in idolatry and superstition (Gentiles). The Jews were monotheists and had a central temple in Jerusalem, dedicated to sacrifice and rituals. Much of their worship was motivated by duty and regulated by tradition. While there were undoubtedly devout priests and religious leaders, many were corrupt. Despite good rabbis and moral leaders, teaching excellent maxims and pure precepts, many were ineffectual (see Matt. 7:28–29). However good their intention, their efforts failed to reach the human heart.

Jesus began his teaching by speaking of God as Father, as one who could only be approached through spiritual worship (John 4:23–24). When Jesus revealed God's character as Love (John 3:16), all existing worship, whether pagan or monotheistic, came under question as misguided or inadequate. Under Jesus' guidance, for the first time worshippers could address the Creator of the world as *abba* (Mark 14:36; see Rom. 8:15; Gal. 4:6), meaning "Daddy" or "Father." A greater understanding of God, a more transformative perspective, has never been imparted.

His words, a mirror into the character of God, likewise penetrated the secrets of the human heart. According to John's Gospel, never did one understand human thought and motivation as Jesus. After spending time with Jesus, the Samaritan woman could but testify: "He told me everything I have ever done!" (John 4:29, 39). When the Samaritans came and heard for themselves, they too agreed (John 4:42). When Jesus spoke, people did not just listen; they followed! (Mark 2:13–14). Where did he gain such knowledge, ability, and wisdom? Surely not from parents, school, or other rabbis.

From what we know, there was not a single precept that Jesus did not exhibit in his own conduct. He enjoined meekness, humility, self-denial, temperance, gratitude, prudence, generosity, forgiveness, and deeds of mercy, not only to those who could respond in kind, but also to the unlovable, even to one's enemy. As known by his followers and remembered by tradition, his character was pure and blameless, his motive sincere, his compassion and love unbounded. No one before had seen such a human, but those who knew him would agree with Nicodemus: "Rabbi, we know that you are a teacher who has come from God" (John 3:2).

Jesus seems to have begun his teaching in the synagogues of Galilee, but before long, whether due to opposition by religious authorities or to popularity or both, by far the greater part of his teaching occurred outdoors. Such teaching requires an engaging style, otherwise he would not have gathered an audience, or retained it. In the Gospels we find him teaching in the streets and on the roads, sometimes using a boat by the seashore, holding the crowd spellbound. We find him engaged in technical arguments and discussion with the scholars of his day, even teaching the crowds gathered in the temple precinct at Jerusalem. He was equally effective amidst the crowds as within the intimate inner circle of his disciples. Such diversity of audience and setting required universal appeal.

To be arresting, universal in appeal, and intellectually intelligible requires another capacity, the ability to be permanently memorable. How did he accomplish this task? Through a combination of forms such as picturesque speech, paradoxical statements, puns, proverbs, and parables. Think of the Beatitudes (Matt. 5:1–16; Luke 6:20–26), statements if taken literally sound incredible, but that somehow haunt the mind and heart with the sense that, given time, they contain great truth: "Blessed are the poor, the hungry, the sorrowful, the persecuted." Each beatitude contradicts the world's standards, reverses worldly wisdom, turns life upside down. Or consider the statement that unless adults change and become like children, they will never enter God's domain (Matt. 18:3). One such sentence from the mouth of Jesus annihilates current standards of prestige and greatness. The great value of such sayings is their penetrating power, their ability to linger long after their first hearing. In many ways Jesus was the great disturber, not least in these thought-provoking paradoxes.

Part II: Fully Human

Along with his contemporaries, Jesus delighted in sharp contrasts and extreme statements, in hyperbole and exaggeration. His teaching was characterized, not by greys and halftones, but by bold contrasting colors. Note the colorful speech he used in Matthew 7:3–5 to point out ludicrous behavior: "Why do you see the speck in your neighbor's eye, but do not notice the log in your own eye?" Jesus uses extreme imagery to say in a powerful and memorable way what most people would express tritely as "Why are you acting inconsistently?"

By taking into account the presence of vivid hyperbole in Jesus' teaching, we can sometimes avoid misinterpreting the meaning of certain hard saying in the Gospels. For example, the passage in Luke 14:26 about the necessity of "hating" one's family in order to become a follower of Jesus is best understood in light of the use of exaggeration so common in the Middle Eastern culture of that time. Obviously, Jesus had no desire to increase the sum total of hatred in the world. An examination of the parallel statement in Matthew 10:37 shows that Jesus did not come to increase hatred but to increase love for God and loyalty to himself as their teacher.

A word of caution is appropriate, however, against attempting to find exaggeration in the teachings of Jesus where the statement is to be taken literally. We must be careful not to dilute uncompromising statements simply because we find them extreme or demanding. For example, Jesus' command to the rich man who inquired what he should do to inherit eternal life, "Sell all that you own and distribute the money to the poor . . . then come, follow me" (Luke 18:22), should not be taken as hyperbole. As the context makes clear, the questioner understood Jesus' words literally.

Wisdom Language and Imagery in the New Testament

The study of Jewish wisdom literature as found in the Hebrew Bible (Old Testament) and in the intertestamental literature provides readers of the New Testament with an important and intriguing perspective on Jesus and early Christianity. Following the resurrection of Jesus, when early Christians were looking for language and concepts to express their experience and understanding of Jesus, one of the most helpful resources was the Jewish wisdom literature. Of course, other parts of the Hebrew Bible were valuable, such as the prophets, the psalms, and the historical traditions of Israel, but the authors of the New Testament and the leaders of the early Christian communities saw in the wisdom literature, particularly in the books of Sirach and Wisdom, important resources for understanding Jesus and their new life in Christ.

In *Jesus the Sage*, Ben Witherington divides early Jewish wisdom into two major traditions: conventional wisdom (as found in Proverbs and Sirach) and counter-order wisdom (as found in Ecclesiastes and Job). He maintains that through his teaching and way of life Jesus modeled the latter tradition, particularly in his parables and aphorisms of reversal (as exemplified by his care for weak and marginalized individuals).

If we are correct in assuming that sages constituted a distinct class within Israel, primarily as teachers of Jewish youth, we may also assume that they used a characteristic mode of discourse. The introduction to the book of Proverbs (1:6) mentions four kinds of sapiential teaching that students must understand: (1) the *proverb* or *mashal*. This short, pithy statement, a basic similitude or likeness in which a given phenomenon is compared or contrasted alongside another, is expressed through the Hebraic feature of parallelism. There are three major types of parallelism. The simplest is called synonymous parallelism, where the second half of the line repeats the thought of the first with a slight variation (see Prov. 4:11). Antithetic parallelism contrasts ideas (see Prov. 10:7) while the third type, synthetic parallelism, advances an idea and moves it toward a new concept (see Prov. 16:31); (2) the *parable* (a saying or narrative conveying an important message hidden within a clever formulation); (3) the *"wise saying"* or aphorism (a general category or collection of sapiential instruction); and (4) the *riddle* (an enigmatic saying leading to reflection on the meaning of life and its inequities). While no pure riddles have survived within biblical wisdom literature, there can be little doubt that ancient sages coined enigmas and that the solving of riddles belonged to the essential tasks of the wise. All of the above use admonitions and warnings as powerful expressions of cultural truth.

The Jewish wisdom tradition profoundly influenced the New Testament community. Wisdom images and ideas appear in every layer of the New Testament, from the Letter of James, a document of early Christianity best understood as Jewish Christian sapiential writing, to the Gospels, which portray Jesus as a wisdom teacher, to the letters of Paul, where Christ is called the wisdom of God (1 Cor. 1:24). Wisdom traditions influenced the document called "Q," an early sayings source that circulated independently and is believed to have been used by the authors of the Gospels of Matthew and Luke. This source, whether oral or written, consisted mainly of Jesus' teachings. While drawing on diverse genres, the majority of the sayings in Q are wisdom sayings, which portray Jesus as a sage or teacher of sapiential truth.

The first three Gospels in the New Testament are called "synoptic" because they draw from one another and look at Jesus with similar eyes. In all three, Jesus is portrayed as a wisdom teacher, displaying a style of instruction similar to that of the sages, teaching disciples through parables (narrative proverbs or *meshalim*) and wisdom sayings (aphorisms) that tease the mind.

In the teaching of Jesus there is no feature more striking than his parables. Whether we consider their literary features or according to their influence in human life, they are incomparable. They have supplied inspiration to poets, artists, moralists, philosophers, theologians, and public speakers. Many expressions used commonly today come from Jesus' parables. Most of us know what is meant by "hiding one's lamp under a bushel" or "being a good Samaritan." No one had previously spoken of natural abilities as "talents" until Jesus told his parable of the talents; the original meaning of talent referred to a certain measure or weight of gold and silver.

The old definition of a parable as "an earthly story with a heavenly meaning" contains some truth, but one must beware against seeking elaborate allegorical meaning in every parable. The proper method of interpreting Jesus' parables is to make a thorough inquiry into the "life-setting" in his ministry when he first uttered the parable, and to seek out the main point it was intended to teach. Usually the details provide little more than background and should not be assigned allegorical meaning. An analysis of Jesus' parables reveals that most were intended to perform one of four functions: (1) to portray a human trait or character for our warning or example (in other words, to teach a form of conduct that Jesus' followers should either emulate or avoid); (2) to disclose a principle of God's providential rule in the world (that is, to reveal something of the character of God and God's dealings with humanity); (3) to depict a truth about how Jesus' followers are to relate to others and to society at large; and (4) to provide warning or preparation for the future (namely, to speak of future judgment and preparedness for entrance into God's kingdom).

Teacher
Jesus as Jewish "Prophetic Sage"

It is possible to argue that the Jesus tradition (Jesus material found in the New Testament and espoused by the first Christians) is the next logical development of the Jewish wisdom tradition. The New Testament draws on the entirety of that tradition, particularly on Sirach (Ecclesiasticus) and the book of Wisdom (Wisdom of Solomon), intertestamental books read by Christians familiar with the Septuagint (books found in Roman Catholic and Eastern Orthodox Bibles but excluded from most Protestant Bibles).

The Gospels introduce Jesus as a Jewish prophetic sage who communicates primarily in wisdom forms of utterance and who, like great Jewish sages before him, cross-fertilizes them with sapiential adaptation of prophetic and legal forms of utterance. What makes the category of "sage" most appropriate for describing Jesus is that he either casts his teaching in recognizable sapiential forms (aphorism, beatitude, or riddle) or else uses the prophetic adaptation of sapiential speech—the parable (narrative *mashal*). In either case, he speaks figuratively, addressing his audience with indirect speech. This teaching style makes Jesus enigmatic, particularly for modern people who value communication based on self-evident propositions and syllogistic logic.

The majority of authentic Jesus sayings are either aphorisms (*meshalim*) or parables (narrative *meshalim*), and it is these we briefly examine. It is important to note that Jesus never uses the classic prophetic formula, "thus says the Lord." The closest approximation of this formula is in a Q saying found in Luke 11:49: "Therefore also the Wisdom of God said." As this passage indicates, Jesus' chosen way to communicate is the way of a sage, persuading by indirect and figurative speech. Scholars estimate that around 70 percent of the sayings of Jesus represent some sort of wisdom utterance such as an aphorism, riddle, or parable. While the Gospels portray Jesus as speaking in parables (one scholar counted 247 in the Synoptic Gospels), they should not be seen as mere illustrations of Jesus' preaching; they were, in fact, his primary vehicle of proclamation. Their distinctive connection to Jesus' ministry is borne out by the fact that other than in the Gospels, the term "parable" appears nowhere else in the New Testament except in Hebrews 9:9 and 11:19.

We need to distinguish between proverbs, which are universally acceptable forms of communication, and aphorisms, which are enigmatic and innovative in nature. Whereas proverbs are associated with traditional wisdom, aphorisms are associated with counter-order wisdom. Jesus, like

Part II: Fully Human

Qoheleth (the author of the Old Testament book Ecclesiastes), represents the latter, for there is little in the Jesus tradition that is purely proverbial. Surprisingly, many major themes of proverbial wisdom are absent from the teachings of Jesus. For example, none of his proverbs urge the seeking of wisdom, nor does he declare that the fear of the Lord is the beginning of wisdom. Jesus utters no proverbs or sayings commending hard work, nor does he offer conventional patriarchal wisdom about women such as found in Proverbs, or much less in the misogynist evaluation in Sirach 25:24.

Jesus not only countered the wisdom of the world, he used a controversial technique: the influence of the poor and marginal. While others sought the aid of the wealthy and the powerful, Jesus pronounced blessing on the "meek," the "merciful," the "poor in spirit," and even on the persecuted. Jesus' aphorisms are said to represent "wisdom from below," for they regularly challenge prevailing assumptions, giving voice to the poor and marginalized rather than to the privileged classes. Numerous sayings illustrate the parameters of the possible implied in God's new social order. For example, we think of the aphorism, "But many who are first will be last, and the last will be first" (Mark 10:31), or the riddle, "For those who want to save their life will lose it, and those who lose their life for my sake . . . will save it" (Mark 8:35). Moreover, we notice the absurdity in the aphorism, "It is easier for a camel to go through the eye of a needle than for someone who is rich to enter the kingdom of God" (Mark 10:25). The saying, "The sabbath was made for humankind, and not humankind for the sabbath" (Mark 2:27), suggests that Jesus is appealing to creation theology, which is characteristic of Jewish wisdom thought. However, he turns his appeal into an aphorism of counter-order in that he stands on his own authority in making a pronouncement that challenges the Mosaic/Levitical cultic tradition. In the statement about new wine and fresh wineskins ("no one puts new wine into old wineskins; otherwise, the wine will burst the skins, and the wine is lost, and so are the skins; but one puts new wine into fresh wineskins," Mark 2:22), Jesus points to his own ministry and mission as representing the coming of a new order.[1]

The study of Jewish wisdom literature indicates that parables were not characteristic of the canonical sages. Rather, they seem to have been a prophetic phenomenon, or at least prophetic adaptations of a wisdom form of utterance (see, for example, the court prophet Nathan's parable of condemnation of King David in 2 Samuel 12:1–4, or the allegorical riddle in Ezekiel

---

1. Though these citations are from Mark, they appear in Matthew and Luke as well.

17:3–10). In Sirach we note a new development or understanding of the sage's role, the claim to be inspired as were the prophets: "I will again pour our teaching like prophecy" (24:33).[2] Similarly, in Wisdom 7:27 the sage informs his audience that when the spirit of wisdom passes into people's souls, she makes them "friends of God and prophets." Here the sage is seen as the one who delivers the prophetic word. Like these predecessors, Jesus seems to have viewed himself as a Jewish prophetic sage, appropriating various traditions in his role as teacher.

When we think of Jesus' parables, we ordinarily think of the Prodigal Son or the Good Samaritan, classic stories about how God relates to humans and how they should relate to one another. However, many, if not most of the parables, are distinctly eschatological in nature. These parables have a prophetic element, in that they tend to reverse conventional values rather than reinforce them. Though many reflect "wisdom from below," the source is "from above," for the means of the expressed counter-order is the inbreaking eschatological kingdom of God.

The parable of the yeast (leaven) in Matthew 13:33 (also Luke 13:20–21) is misleading as translated in the NRSV: "The kingdom of heaven is like yeast that a woman took and *mixed in with* three measures of flour until all of it was leavened," since the original Greek speaks of yeast that is "hidden in" the measures of flour. Could this story be about Jesus' mission, about how he is planting (hiding) the kingdom message in his audience through his *meshalim*? The woman kneading the dough may also be seen as an allusion to wisdom. In either case, the parable reflects an eschatological optimism about how things will finally turn out.

The parable of the Good Samaritan (Luke 10:29–37), one of Jesus' most beloved parables, has been called an "example story" rather than a comparative *mashal*, since it appears only in Luke, and only Luke contains example stories (10:30–37; 12:16–21; 16:19–31; 18:10–14). Furthermore, the parable exhibits clear marks of editorial activity (10:29, 36–37). Despite Luke's editorializing, this story likely goes back to Jesus, who intended it not as an example of "proper" behavior but as a counter-order *mashal*, a parabolic portrayal of how the inbreaking of the kingdom of God transforms people and reorders their thinking. The focal point of the story cannot be the Samaritan's good deed of kindness or compassion, since the Samaritan exceeds all bounds, "not merely ethnic bounds, but even the

---

2. This statement is unexpected, given the common Jewish belief that prophecy had ceased during the Restoration Period, following the classical prophets.

suggested bounds in the Old Testament of what compassion would look like."[3] What we have here is an ethnic reversal, used to challenge current attitudes regarding ritual standards. The notion of a "good Samaritan" was a contradiction in terms for a traditional Jew, but such reversal is typical of Jesus the sage, "who seems to specialize in oxymorons like good leaven, light burdens, and here a good Samaritan."[4]

The underlying issue in this parable is ritual holiness. There is surely some degree of contrast here between the Samaritan and the priest and Levite, the latter paragons of holiness and virtue in Jewish society. Both Jesus and the Jewish religious leaders wished to spread holiness throughout the land, but they disagreed on procedure. The Pharisees wished to apply Levitical laws to everyday life of ordinary Jews, but the net effect of their program was to further divide and separate Jews from Samaritans, Gentiles, and others. Jesus by contrast stressed an intensification only of the basic moral demands of the Old Testament such as fidelity in marriage, honoring parents, and loving neighbor, coupled with a benign neglect or outright dismissal of the more divisive of the ritual requirements. The net result was conflict over holiness between Jesus and the Pharisees.

Perhaps what the passage represents is an apologetic for the scandalous behavior of Jesus and his disciples, who broke Levitical laws by associating with tax collectors and sinners. The Pharisees, together with "priests and Levites," would have viewed Jesus and his followers as ritually unclean and therefore, like the Samaritan, outcasts (cf. John 8:48). Jesus seems to be asking, not "who is my neighbor?" (Luke's editorial question in 10:29) but "how is one a neighbor?" If that is Jesus' primary concern in this passage, then his answer to the question is not "show compassion," but "demonstrate lavish compassion." As we know, the Samaritan not only acts compassionately, he becomes personally involved in the restoration of the victim, seeing him through to full health and wellbeing.

The parable, then, is eschatological at its core, for it teaches that when God's kingdom breaks into human lives and situations, it results in shocking patterns of behavior, where old prejudices die and new ways of life emerge. In this case Jesus is not relinquishing but rather intensifying the basic moral demands of Torah, exemplifying fully what it means to love one's neighbor. For Jesus, compassion trumps ritual holiness as a weightier matter of the law.

3. Witherington, *Jesus the Sage*, 195.
4. Ibid, 194.

Teacher

The primary purpose of this and other parables is not simply to instruct, but more importantly to move the listener/reader to decision or action. As a sage, Jesus taught to persuade, but never to coerce. Furthermore, he taught more by example than by prescription. His supreme achievement as a teacher was that he exemplified in himself all that he taught.

Matthew's Gospel, written during the eighth decade of the first century, some ten years after the cataclysmic destruction of Jerusalem and the temple by the Romans in AD 70, provides a significant understanding of Jesus not only as teacher but as master teacher, and provide textual support for a training school for Jewish Christian scribes. Indeed, throughout this Gospel one finds an emphasis on pedagogy not found in the other Gospels. For example, the end of the Sermon on the Mount makes clear that the first evangelist (the author of Matthew's Gospel) wishes to distinguish between Jesus the sage, who teaches as one who has independent authority, and "their scribes" (7:29), that is, Jewish teachers. In summary passages of Jesus' ministry, Matthew cites "teaching" ahead of preaching and healing as the chief task of Jesus (4:23; 9:35; and 11:1). This is significant when one notes that in Matthew's Markan source (Mark 1:39) there is no mention of teaching and no parallel to Matthew 9:35. In the Lukan parallel to Matthew 11:1, instead of "teach," one reads "after Jesus had finished all his sayings." When one examines the style of Jesus' teaching in Matthew, wisdom language predominates. Jesus offers beatitudes, aphorisms, parables, and wisdom discourses. In short, Matthew portrays Jesus as a Jewish sage. In 26:18 Jesus refers to himself as "The Teacher"; the assumption is that the reading audience knows who "the Teacher" is, and that those who hear are disciples.

Many scholars suggest that the statement in Matthew 13:52 provides a clue to how the evangelist saw himself: "Therefore every scribe who has been trained for the kingdom of heaven is like the master of a household who brings out of his treasure what is new and what is old." This uniquely Matthean saying indicates as much about the audience for whom this Gospel was intended as it does about the author. The evangelist is one scribe showing other scribes the proper content and form of their teaching before they are sent out to make further disciples chiefly by teaching (cf. 28:19–20). Whereas Mark views the disciples as hardheaded and obtuse, not understanding the parables of Jesus, Matthew's inner circle of disciples understands even the more enigmatic wisdom teachings of Jesus (13:51).

Part II: Fully Human

Several additional passages reveal Matthew's purposes and aims in producing this Gospel. In Matthew 16:17–19, Peter is given the keys of the kingdom, explained as binding and loosing (in 18:18 the entire church is given this authority). One way to interpret this imagery is as referring to the teaching authority of the church, in this case, the commissioning of scribes with authority to teach, transmit, and interpret the Jesus tradition. Matthew 10:24–25a, the first commissioning scene in Matthew's Gospel, states that a disciple is not to be above "*the* teacher," but rather is called to be *like* his teacher. This passage, unique to Matthew, prepares readers for the culminating scene in 28:18–20, where the evangelist summarizes various wisdom and pedagogical themes, particularly obeying commandments and teaching others, two tasks of disciples.

Thus at crucial junctures in Matthew's Gospel—at the end of the first discourse (7:28–29); at the first commissioning of the disciples (10:24); at Caesarea Philippi, when Peter is granted the keys (16:19); at the close of the chapter on parables (13:52); and at the Great Commission that ends the book (28:19–20)—Jesus is portrayed as Teacher and the disciples as teacher-scribes (for information on Jesus as divine Wisdom incarnate, see Session 10).

At the conclusion of the Sermon on the Mount we find these remarkable words: "the crowds were astonished at his teaching, for he taught them as one having authority, and not as their scribes" (Matt. 7:28–29). A central feature of Jesus' preaching and teaching was the degree of authority with which he spoke. Rabbis (scribes), as teachers of Torah, derived authority from scripture. The prevailing approach of Jesus' day, used by rabbis, was to quote previous rabbis. Scribes never spoke solely on their own authority, for they derived their authority ultimately from Moses, whom they viewed as mediator of God's law.

Earlier in the Sermon, in the antithetical sayings of Matthew 5:21–48, Jesus quoted traditional Jewish legal statements, believed to be based upon the Torah of Moses ("you have heard that it was said"), only to intensify or surpass their original meaning ("but I say to you"). Unlike the scribes of his day, Jesus appealed to his own authority. This approach embodied a claim that rivaled and surpassed that of Moses. Scribes may have challenged one another in debate, but Jesus challenged the Law of Moses. To this, there is no Jewish parallel.

How are we to explain the authoritative nature of Jesus' teaching? While we cannot provide a final answer, the only reasonable explanation must be based on Jesus' claim of an immediate relationship to God, in the strict sense of being unmediated. When Jesus spoke of God as "Father," this intimacy was not theoretical but personal in nature: Jesus *knew* God as Father. In addition, Jesus was able to communicate to others the assurance of what he taught. Building on this important foundation, he was able to translate religious experience into transformational action, into *doing*, and not simply into hearing (Matt. 7:24–27).

For Jesus, the essence of God's will is practical, meaning it is to be manifested both privately and publicly (Matt. 22:36–40). The Christian ethic, then, is based on sincerity (on inward attitudes and motivation, Matt. 6:1–4), but it flows forth into social responsibility, as demonstrated in "the Golden Rule": "In everything do to others as you would have them do to you; for this is the law and the prophets" (Matt. 7:12).

The important element in the ministry of Jesus is that he not only lived according to the highest standards, but that he inspired others to follow his example.

Session 4

Prophet

Question for Individual or Group Reflection: If Jesus viewed his mission as prophetic, did he understand his role eschatologically or non-eschatologically (that is, did he see himself as pivotal in God's end-time transformation of history or more as a social reformer, advocating an alternative social vision)? Explain your answer.

Important Biblical Verses and Passages: Deuteronomy 18:15, 18; Malachi 4:5; Matthew 11:2–19; Mark 1:15; Luke 4:18–21; 7:16; 17:20–21; John 5:46; Hebrews 1:1–2; 2 Corinthians 5:17

Technical Words and Concepts: prophecy; messianic age; eschatological prophet; election; War of the Jews against Rome; kingdom of God; Day of the Lord; teleological; doctrine of two ages; Zion; realized eschatology; social prophet; the New Israel

AT THE START OF the first century AD, prophecy as a profession no longer existed in the Jewish world. In fact, Jewish prophecy had died out several centuries earlier, and in Jesus' day, it existed only in the prophetic writings of the Hebrew scriptures. The lack of the prophetic element was replaced by the expectation that in the messianic age the spirit of prophecy would be restored and the final prophet—the eschatological Prophet—would appear to fulfill all prophecy, in preparation for the anticipated Golden Age on earth. The expectation of such a prophet with a specific task to perform at the end of time was widespread at the time of Jesus. This expectation was associated with the words of Moses in Deuteronomy 18:15: "The Lord your

God will raise up for you a prophet like me from among your own people; you shall heed such a prophet." This prophet was expected to bear an intimate relationship to the Messiah or possibly be the Messiah.

Ideas regarding the exact nature of this prophetic activity were varied, as was the identity of the expected figure. Speculation centered around Elijah as the coming prophet (see Mal. 4:5), while others awaited the return of Enoch, Moses, Ezra, or Jeremiah.

The Gospels reflect these Jewish expectations. Here we find that John the Baptist is viewed as the eschatological Prophet, in the sense of being the forerunner not only of the Messiah but also of God. We read in Zechariah's hymn of praise (Luke 1:76) that the Baptist will be called "the prophet of the Most High" [God], for John "will go before the Lord [God] to prepare his ways." The angel's announcement to Zechariah indicates the same conception of the coming prophet: "With the spirit and power of Elijah he will go before him . . . to make ready a people prepared for the Lord" (Luke 1:17). While John the Baptist did not think of himself as the Prophet of the end time in the sense of one preparing the way for God (see Matt. 11:2-6; John 1:19-23; 3:25-30), John's disciples clearly saw him in that role.

When Jesus appeared, the masses immediately placed him in the prophetic category: "A great prophet has arisen among us!" (Luke 7:16; see also 24:19; Mark 6:15; 8:28; John 4:19). Whether Jesus ever thought of himself or was considered by others to be *the* eschatological prophet like unto Moses, there can be little doubt that the way Jesus is presented in the Gospel of John is intended to indicate that he is the fulfillment of Deuteronomy 18:15-19 (see John 1:17 and 5:46). In Acts 3:22 and 7:37 we note that Deuteronomy 18:15 and 18 are directly referred to as being fulfilled in Jesus. Likewise, the opening words of the Epistle to the Hebrews, while not explicitly Mosaic, are clearly based on a view of Jesus as the Prophet of eschatological consummation: "Long ago God spoke to our ancestors in many and varied ways by the prophets, but in these last days he has spoken to us by a Son" (Heb. 1:1-2).

Most scholars today accept the idea that Jesus viewed his mission as prophetic, but they are deeply divided as to whether he saw this role eschatologically or non-eschatologically. The key question concerns whether Jesus viewed himself as playing a pivotal role in God's end-time transformation of history or more as a social reformer, advocating an alternative social vision. It is not pedagogically acceptable to commingle eschatological and non-eschatological perspectives of Jesus. Either his mindset was eschatological or it was not, and for that reason modern scholarship does not allow fence-sitting on the matter.

First-Century Jewish Eschatology

As a first-century Palestinian Jew, Jesus belonged to a world where religion (theology) and politics went hand in hand. The theology was Jewish monotheism, a doctrine forged through centuries of subjugation and persecution, going back to the Babylonian exile. First-century Jews held their monotheism passionately. Theirs was not an abstract theory about the existence of one God. They believed their God, Yahweh, was the only God, and that all others were idols. A corollary of monotheism was "election," the belief that the Jews had been chosen by this one God, making what happened to Israel of universal significance. Many Jews of Jesus' day believed that God was about to vindicate them, understanding this act as having global implications, as the means of divine judgment and/or mercy upon the rest of the world. Monotheists currently suffering oppression would naturally view the present state of affairs as temporary.

Monotheism and election together gave give birth to eschatology, a perspective that views history as purposeful and therefore as moving toward a climactic resolution or restoration, at which time everything would be made right. First-century Jewish eschatology claimed that Yahweh would soon act within history to vindicate his people and to establish permanent justice and peace. This belief included the great promises of forgiveness articulated by biblical prophets, notably Isaiah, Jeremiah, and Ezekiel. The so-called post-exilic writings spoke of a restoration still to be described, a liberation they described as a new exodus.

E. P. Sanders, in his classic text *Jesus and Judaism*, maintains that before the outbreak of the War of the Jews against Rome in AD 66, "common Judaism" held the following hopes for the future: the restoration of the tribes of Israel; the conversion, destruction, or subjugation of the Gentiles; the renewal of Jerusalem, including a new or rebuilt temple; and the purification of God's people and their worship.[1] Whatever one makes of his idea of a common Judaism, surely the beliefs Sanders highlights were widespread among Jesus' contemporaries, as was apocalyptic eschatology in general.

---

1. Sanders, *Jesus and Judaism*, 279–303.

Jesus as Eschatological Prophet

According to Sanders, Jesus was an apocalyptic prophet standing in the tradition of Jewish restoration theology. He shared the beliefs common in Judaism, together with this prevailing understanding of Israel's story and hope. Having established the essential Jewishness of Jesus on this topic, Sanders finds primitive Christianity to be a movement in continuity with Jesus' hopes and expectations: "The most certain fact of all is that early Christianity was an eschatological movement."[2]

Biblical support for that contention can be found in the well-known fact that, with the exception of Philemon, 2 John, and 3 John (all three of which are brief and nearly devoid of theology), apocalyptic eschatology or some obvious trace of it appears in all first-century Christian documents. For instance, 1 Thessalonians, the earliest extant Christian writing, is full of apocalyptic expectation. As A. T. Robinson recognized, this letter is a "challenge" for anyone who denies that Christianity began amid apocalyptic enthusiasm.[3] Since Jesus was the point of origination for what became Christianity, one might reasonably infer that he was an apocalyptic figure. If within a year or two of Jesus' death Paul persecuted the followers of Jesus because of their eschatological proclamation, that leaves precious little time in which the followers of a noneschatological Jesus could have developed an entirely new eschatological perspective without a precedent in the preaching and actions of Jesus. The conclusion seems obvious: Eschatology was pervasive at the beginning of the Christian movement because it was central to Jesus and his mission.

In keeping with this understanding, it follows that Jesus of Nazareth might have viewed his mission as prophetic, announcing, like John the Baptist before him, God's coming kingdom. But Jesus, it seems, went beyond John's verbal role, embodying in his person and his ministry the presence of that kingdom. For Jesus, the all-encompassing rule of God was near, which, when it came in its fullness, would restore Israel's role as "light to the nations" and challenge evil in all its manifestations, political, social, and economic. The coming kingdom of God was not a new sort of religion, a new moral code, or a new soteriology (a doctrine about how one might go to heaven after death). Nor was it a new sociological analysis, critique, or

---

2. Sanders, "Jesus: His Religious Type," 6.
3. Robinson, *Jesus and His Coming*, 104–17.

agenda. It was about Israel's story reaching its climax, about Israel's history moving toward its decisive moment.[4]

Understanding Jesus as "eschatological Jewish prophet" announcing the inbreaking of God's culminating kingdom is controversial in current biblical scholarship, in part because of a debate on the meaning of the term "eschatology" (typically defined as "the study of last things"). In addition to the idea of "the end of the world," much emphasized by current evangelical Christians but essentially a non-Jewish view,[5] at least three biblical possibilities regarding eschatology can be maintained:[6]

1. An *apocalyptic* meaning, in which eschatology truly signifies a time in the future when the course of history will be changed to such an extent that one can speak of an entirely new state of reality on earth; it concerns a cosmic cataclysm and a new age followed by utopian bliss. This view is generally associated with "end-time" events such as the coming of a messianic age, the vindication of Israel or the elect, and sometimes a last judgment and resurrection of the dead. This is not what I believe Jesus had in mind, though biblical memory suggests that he seemed to envision the occurrence of something cataclysmic.

2. An *historical/political* meaning, in keeping with the spirit of the Old Testament pre-exilic prophets, who spoke of the "Day of the Lord" (a day of judgment) as referring to an event or a cluster of events within history, such as the military conquest of Israel or Judah by a foreign empire. Here "end" means "an end of statehood" and newness "a restoration of statehood."

3. A *teleological* meaning, understanding the concept of eschatology in the sense that the "end" it envisions is associated with ultimate purpose, hope, or an ideal vision. This view seems to capture what Jesus meant when he came proclaiming the good news of God, saying, "The time is fulfilled, and the kingdom of God has come near; repent, and believe in the good news" (Mark 1:15). That kingdom, surely, concerned the final destiny of the Jewish people.

4. Borg and Wright, *Meaning of Jesus*, 31–35.

5. Jewish eschatologies did not typically involve "the end of the world." The disappearance of the material world is not part of the expectation. The exception may be 2 Peter 3:10–12.

6. G. B. Caird, in *Language and Imagery of the Bible*, 243–71, examined the variety of uses given to the concept of "eschatology" by modern scholars and discovered seven different senses in which the term is used.

What adds to the biblical confusion is that various understandings of eschatology lie superimposed one upon another in the New Testament. There were some within the early church who clearly expected the "end of the world" in their generation, including the resurrection of the dead, the last judgment, and the "new heavens and new earth." Where did this expectation arise? Was it grounded in Jesus' own expectation, or should the church's expectation of the "last things" be understood as a post-Easter development, a deduction based upon the Easter event itself?

As is well-known, "resurrection" in Judaism was an event expected at the end of time. To some within the early church, the fact that Jesus' resurrection had occurred was an indicator that the general resurrection must be near: Christ was the "first fruits" of those to be raised from the dead (1 Cor. 15:23). Moreover, first-century Christians did not think about the imminent coming of the kingdom or talk about the end of the world in a general way. Rather, they spoke of the imminent end of the world only in connection with the return of Jesus. It is important not to exaggerate the extent to which the early church was an "end-time" community. Despite the explicit statements affirming an imminent end, it is not clear that this was an essential expectation (except, perhaps, in the book of Revelation). Though the letters of Paul and the Gospel of John contain explicit references to the end, clearly the emphasis of both authors is on the present rather than on the future, acknowledging the present as the time when the reality of God can be known in a decisive way.

The belief in two ages, a characteristic of Jewish eschatology, is found in the thought of the apostle Paul. In his writings, the present evil age is giving way to the coming age of justice and peace, so that the end of the one is the beginning of the other. It is not altogether clear to which of the three eschatological categories of biblical meaning this view belongs. Defining and cataloguing such a concept involves a mixture of subjective and objective evaluation. How, for instance, do we understand Isaiah's vision in Isaiah 35:1–10? Read literally, it describes a complete reversal of nature, a final kingdom of justice and peace such as envisioned in the first meaning of "eschatology." Read contextually, however, the vision applies to the restoration of Zion (the kingdom of Judah), and can be viewed as an example of the second meaning of eschatology. Such an understanding, read through Paul's "two-age" understanding of eschatology, applies in the present and can refer to the third meaning of eschatology, namely to the spiritual newness Christian believers experience as the result of the death and resurrection of Christ. We recall the well-known reference in 2 Corinthians 5:17, where, according to Paul, the Christ-event itself signifies the passing of the old age and the inception of the new: "everything old has passed away; see, everything has become new!"

Some scholars, particularly church-based theologians concerned to extricate Jesus from error and from the troubling possibility that his expectations were disappointed, have toned down or reinterpreted many of the eschatological prophecies in the Gospels and thereby disassociated Jesus from failure as a prophet. The British scholar C. H. Dodd ingeniously read the Synoptic texts so that they give us "realized eschatology," meaning that we should view the kingdom as having already come in Jesus' ministry. John Dominic Crossan dissociates Jesus from a large number of biblical traditions about him and from the violent expectations of John the Baptist, occasioned by the last judgment. Crossan's Jesus hopes instead for a utopian future of justice and egalitarianism, a future inaugurated not by the last judgment but by social renewal. N. T. Wright passionately promotes a Jesus who used eschatological metaphors to prophesy what actually came to pass in the first century: his own resurrection, the coming of the church, and Jerusalem's violent demise.

New Testament scholar Dale Allison disagrees, arguing persuasively that Jesus placed himself as the central figure in the eschatological end-time drama. For Allison, the historical Jesus was not a poet speaking metaphorically about judgment; rather he lived and thought apocalyptically. Citing profusely from the Gospels, Allison concludes that Jesus envisaged, as did many other Jews in his time and place, "the advent, after suffering and persecution, of a great judgment, and after that a supernatural utopia, the kingdom of God, inhabited by the dead come back to life, to enjoy a world forever rid of evil and wholly ruled by God. Further, he thought that the night was far gone, the day at hand."[7] The belief of early Christians in the imminence of the end, according to Allison, originated not from the church's post-Easter expectations, but with Jesus himself.

This is not to say that Jesus was an apocalyptic extremist, or that he had only eschatology on his mind. Part of the reason that Jesus so fascinates and inspires is that he embodied in his own person the extremes of human experience. On the one hand, Jesus announced and made real the eschatological presence of the God of Israel: Satan has fallen like lightning from heaven and the demons are being routed; the lame walk and the blind see;

---

7. Allison, *The Historical Christ*, 95.

lepers are cleansed and those in poverty are cheered with good news. The long-awaited kingdom of God has arrived; the bridegroom is here. The old world is gone; the new world has come.

That, however, is only half of the story. Paradoxically, the joyful Jesus is familiar with sorrows and acquainted with grief. He has nowhere to lay his head; respected leaders assail his teachings and behavior; John the Baptist, whom he hails as more than a prophet, is arrested and beheaded; his own companions misunderstand him, betray him, and abandon him. Pagan soldiers whip him, mock him, and nail him to a cross of execution. His end is physical torment and mental anguish, loss of life and loss of meaning. So the tradition gives us a Jesus who "knows how to laugh loudly and to wail miserably, a Jesus who knows the presence of God and the absence of God."[8]

If Jesus had pretended to know only the blessings of the future age, we should turn our backs on him, for we would know his faith to be a hopeless flight from the pain of living. And if he had focused exclusively on the tribulation to come, we would dismiss his hope as inconsequential, the distance between him and God as too great. But by announcing not only tribulation present and future but also salvation present and future and then by living into both, Jesus commends himself to us.

Marcus Borg represents a growing number of modern scholars who challenge this understanding of Jesus, envisioning instead a non-eschatological Jesus, whose role, if interpreted prophetically, should be limited to that of a social prophet engaged in radical social criticism. According to this model, Jesus was a counter-cultural revolutionary who opposed the domination systems of his day both in person and through an alternative community of disciples, chosen to represent the New Israel of God. In Borg's view the kingdom of God represents a this-worldly social vision—a vision that empowers Christians and defines the church's ongoing role in society—rather than an other-worldly eschatological vision imposed from above and occasioned by a church raptured from this earth, an interpretation popular in many American fundamentalist and evangelical circles today.

Viewing Jesus as a deeply Jewish but non-eschatological figure, Borg challenges another vital element in the popular image of Jesus, namely that Jesus understood himself to be the Messiah. According to Borg, the pre-Easter Jesus consistently pointed away from himself to God; his message

---

8. Ibid., 117.

was theocentric, not christocentric, meaning that he was centered in God and not in messianic pronouncements about himself.

Whether Jesus conceived of his person and work in strictly messianic terms is uncertain (see Session 6), but what is more plausible is that he felt himself to be the central actor in a great drama that would usher in the coming kingdom, even if achieving this end involved his own submission to death as the supreme act essential in establishing that kingdom.

The Prophetic Motif in Luke's Gospel

The prophetic aspects of Jesus' ministry appear central in Luke's Gospel, more so than in the other Gospels. Luke's original material (designated by scholars as "L") reflects an early interpretation of Jesus as prophet (Luke 7:16), and only in Luke does Jesus speak of himself as a prophet (Luke 4:24; 13:33). The same idea is expressed in Luke 24:19: "Jesus of Nazareth, who was a prophet mighty in deed and word"; and in Acts (also written by the author of Luke's Gospel), Jesus is the prophet like Moses whom Moses promised (Acts 3:22–23). In material uniquely Lukan, Jesus defines his ministry with strong affinities to that of the prophets, as he appropriates for himself the prophecy of Isaiah 61:1–2 and claims that the Spirit of the Lord is upon him to proclaim God's message (Luke 4:18–21). In the discourse that follows, Jesus explicitly uses a prophetic paradigm to explain his own action, comparing himself to Elijah and Elisha (Luke 4:25–27).

Luke's "travel narrative" (Luke 9:51—18:14), an expanded account of Jesus' journey to Jerusalem, may be compared to Deuteronomy's account of Moses' journey toward Canaan, an account that focuses on Moses' instructions to his people, rather than on his itinerary. Similarly, the journey to Jerusalem serves Luke as a useful framework for Jesus' instructions, which include unique information and exclusive teachings such as the parable of the Good Samaritan (10:29–37) and of the Prodigal Son (15:11–32). Like Moses, Jesus brings a prophetic message of repentance to a rebellious people.

When Jesus responds to the warning regarding Herod's intention to kill him, he asserts, "It is impossible for a prophet to be killed outside of Jerusalem" (13:33). Elaborating on this statement, Jesus exclaims: "Jerusalem, Jerusalem the city that kills the prophets and stones those who are sent to it! How often have I desired to gather your children together as a hen gathers her brood under her wings, and you were not willing!" (13:34) Jesus appears to identify his own attempt to gather Jerusalem's children with the sending of the prophets in the past. Jesus is not only the prophet that has to die in Jerusalem, but is also the head of all the prophets sent to her.

Luke's use of prophetic motifs is ambiguous, for while he paints Jesus as a prophet and his career as prophetic, at the same time, Jesus is more than a prophet. As Jesus himself indicates, John the Baptist was more than a prophet (7:26), yet the least in the kingdom of God is greater than John (7:28). When the disciples tell Jesus the verdict of the crowds—that Jesus is a prophet—Jesus apparently wants them to understand him differently (9:18–20). Jesus later compares himself to the prophet Jonah (11:29), then adds that something greater than Jonah is present (11:32).

As an eschatological prophet, Jesus brought the entire package of prophecy to bear on his task, meaning that through his work and ministry he believed he was inaugurating and embodying the works of the kingdom. Possessed as he was by such a conviction, Jesus was a living embodiment of all that he taught and did. In this respect, he was more than a prophet.

We need not see God's kingdom as a strictly "end-time" phenomenon, however, for in a spiritual sense the kingdom is found in whole nowhere, but in part everywhere. Jesus' first sermon, as recorded in Luke 4:18–21, singles out the marks of the kingdom. In this passage Jesus takes the scroll of the prophet Isaiah and finds the place where it is written: "The Spirit of the Lord is upon me, because he has anointed me to bring good news to the poor. He has sent me to proclaim release to the captives and recovery of sight to the blind, to let the oppressed go free, to proclaim the year of the Lord's favor." After reading he said, "Today this scripture has been fulfilled in your hearing." This passage reveals the manifesto of Jesus, who understood himself as embodying the hopes of the long-awaited Jubilee, which decreed the emancipation of land, slaves, and debts at the end of the seventh sabbatical, an appropriate image of what current Judaism envisioned as the coming reign of God. According to Luke's Gospel the kingdom Jesus envisioned is already here, "within us" or "in our midst" (Luke 17:21).

While the kingdom could be envisioned as embryonically present in Jesus, we need not say it was fully present in him. As Jesus made clear in his parables, the kingdom is an expanding (unfolding) phenomenon. Like yeast in dough, the kingdom grows continuously until all is leavened (Matt. 13:33; Luke 13:21). Each age must announce its coming and commit fully to its hopeful vision. In every age, all who seek the kingdom are citizens and every messenger holy.

Part III

God's Human

IN THE FIRST TWO units we spoke of Jesus as *a* man and as *the* man, as human and as fully human. "Why speak of him thus at length?" some may ask. Why should it be so necessary to stress this man's genuine humanity? Would anyone think to spend so much time insisting on the humanity of Gandhi, or Socrates, or Abraham Lincoln? The reason is that the statements that Jesus was a human being like everyone else and that he was in some sense *the* fully human person (in that he gave us a vision of what humanity is and can be) are rendered problematic by the claim that he was more than this—that he speaks to us of humanity and of divinity because somehow he represents both. For many, even this depiction falls short, for how could he be genuinely human if all the time "underneath," as it were, he was really God?

The pressure to say "divine" things about Jesus is somehow inseparable from saying that he is "the Christ." For most Christians, the mystery of the Christ is once the clue to the meaning of human history as well as to the meaning of God at work in it. In the words of the church's creeds, Christ is "truly God and truly man"; he represents simultaneously the reality of the human and the divine. Yet the starting point for the classic debate on Christology in the fifth century, which culminated at Chalcedon (451) and fixed its shape for the next fifteen hundred years, was determined not by scripture or by experience but by the controversy over the doctrine of the Trinity, which had reached its resolution at Nicaea (325). With Christ established there as a distinct person or hypostasis of the Trinity, fully God in every sense of the word, this was the feature that could not be questioned,

Part III: God's Human

not his existence as an individual, historical person. This starting point—his divinity—separates us from ancient schools of Christian thought more than anything else, doctrinally or dogmatically, primarily because Trinitarian theology was determined more by medieval philosophical logic than by scripture or experience.

If the christological foundation is based on one individual substance, and that divine, it means one cannot introduce another substance (human) without finding oneself with the impossible exercise of trying to place two billiard balls on the same spot. Either the divine displaces the human (as in the doctrine of *anhypostasia* mentioned earlier), or the human consists of two individuals side by side. If one begins with the metaphysical bias in favor of divinity over against humanity, Christ may have had two equal natures (even though in practice one was more equal than the other), but the person who had these natures was firmly on the divine side of the line. However, if one does not conceive of the preexistent Christ as a divine "being" but as something more like "the self-expressive activity of God," then it is possible—at least christologically—to recognize Jesus as human in the fullest possible sense, while also God's Word to the world (to this we shall return in the following units).

Insofar as the functions for which the church theologians allege that Jesus required a second, divine nature, they need not be evidence for us, as for the New Testament, of divinity, but of what is possible *with* God to any person wholly open to the divine. The biblical response to the healing of the paralytic is typical: "The crowds . . . were filled with awe, and they glorified God, who had given such authority to human beings" (Matt. 9:8). The farthest Matthew's Gospel goes, with its heightening of the supernatural, is to have Jesus say in Gethsemane, before his arrest, "Do you think that I cannot appeal to my Father, and he will at once send me more than twelve legions of angels?" (Matt. 26:53). There is no suggestion here that Jesus could rely on them because he was God. Nor is there any suggestion that he was able to do these things because he was a "divine man" (*theios anēr*) in the later Hellenistic tradition. Even in the great prayer of John 17, when Jesus makes plain his awareness of oneness with the Father, there is no hint that one part of his person is speaking, or that what he is saying might not be true of his whole person. When he faces the final agonies on the cross, he offers no excuse for his weakness, nothing to suggest, as later apologists contrived, that while he suffered in his human nature, his divine nature was immune because it still reigned in heaven.

Part III: God's Human

The christological approach we propose in this unit is not that of a superhuman person with two natures, divine and human, but of a human person of whom we speak using two sets of languages. The one is natural, scientific, and descriptive. The other is supernatural, mythological, and interpretive. The former views the course of events in the categories of evolutionary cosmology, the latter in terms of "events" such as Creation and Incarnation. Thanks to the profound contributions of the past several centuries, there is now substantial agreement about how these two ways of speaking and thinking are related. We need not force the "events" of the latter into the former, as if the supernatural penetrates the natural by special creations, interventions, or acts of God. We no longer need to view the supernatural as a parallel, superior, causal sequence, but rather as an interpretation, in terms of "myth" or a second "story," of the same process studied by science and history. Creation and Fall are not particular events in the historical past, but ways of giving theological expression to processes and experiences that are ongoing. Similarly, we are coming to view the Parousia or Second Coming not as a decisive, once-and-for-all event in the historical future, whether near or remote, but as a mythological way to clarify what it means to see all things "new" in the kingdom of God. In each case what the myth does is to focus and clarify in a single dramatized picture the realities obscured by the relativities and continuities of the historical process.

Take, for example, the biblical event called the Exodus. To see this event as mere history (as *chronos*, as historical, as one event among many in the history of the Israelites), is to miss its biblical portrayal as paradigmatic (as *kairos*, as historic, as decisive for interpreting God's meaning for history). Yet continuity in the processes of nature and history does not mean that all moments are of equal significance. There are Rubicons, however insignificant the stream. The crossing of the "sea of reeds," which has become for us the "Red Sea" (Exod. 15:22), may have been another such stream or swamp. Yet if the Exodus proved to be simply myth, in the popular sense, an event of insignificance or one that never happened, then it would be difficult to celebrate it as the supreme example of the mighty acts of God as Lord of history. The same applies to the Incarnation or the Resurrection. These words belong to the mythological story, but it is of the essence of this story that the events it interprets belong equally to the historical series.

Nevertheless, to insist on equivalence between these stories, on precise correspondence between natural and supernatural events, is to confuse the stories and to minimize their meaning and uniqueness. Until the nineteenth century, it did not really matter whether the mythological story of the first human (Adam) was confused with the scientific story. After Darwin, the distinction became vitally important. Had this distinction not occurred, the deeper theological meaning of the account would have been lost. Similarly today, with regard to Jesus, it has become vitally important to discriminate between what we say "according to the flesh" and what we say "according to the spirit." Previous generations may not have been forced to distinguish that the virgin birth is not there to provide gynecological information, any more than the story of the Fall provides specific information about primitive anthropology. Thankfully, we embrace a broader perspective today. It is clear now to many Christians that the doctrine of the Incarnation is not biological but theological in nature. Thus understood, the doctrine provides information not on the level of flesh but on the level of spirit, affirming the entire genesis of Jesus Christ as act and initiative of God.

According to this view, Jesus is wholly and completely human, but a person who speaks truth not simply of humanity but of God. He is not a person plus, a person fitted, as it were, with a second engine, for that would mean he was not human in any genuine sense, but a person who in all he says and does is the personal representative of God. Because he stands in God's place, he *is* God to us and for us.

This conception of Jesus as the one who is transparent to God, who allows God to show through, who speaks of God because he does not speak of himself, is reflected in all Jesus is and does in the Gospels. Listeners sensed he spoke "with authority" and "not as the scribes" (Matt. 7:29) because he stood *in loco dei*, as God's representative. Ernst Fuchs addresses this understanding of the historical Jesus by stating that Jesus' "conduct is neither that of a prophet nor of a teacher of wisdom, but of a man who dares to act in God's stead."[1] Because he "lived God," people saw in Jesus "the human face of God."

What Jesus claimed for himself in the way of titles—Son of God, Christ, Son of Man—is notoriously uncertain and much debated. Perhaps he might more truly be represented as claiming nothing for himself, but everything for what God was doing through him. He was condemned for blasphemy (Mark 14:64; John 19:7), for "making himself God" (John 10:31–38), but precisely for speaking without every saying "Thus says the Lord." Even in Mark 14:61 it appears that Jesus' original reply to the

---

1. Fuchs, *Studies of the Historical Jesus*, 23.

question, "Are you the Son of the Blessed One?" is more likely to have been "You have said so." In the Matthean (26:64) and Lukan parallels (22:70) and in the reply to Pilate in all four Gospels (Matt. 27:14; Mark 15:5; Luke 23:3; John 18:37) the answer is ambiguous. By overruling the law, in forgiving sins, in subduing the spirits and the powers of nature, he steps, in the eyes of his contemporaries, into the space reserved for God. When he invites people to come to him for life and for rest (Matt. 11:28–30), he does so as God's representative. In his parables, he justifies his conduct by the way God acts. Indeed, his entire life is a parable of God, a representation of God in the human drama. His vocation is not to usurp or replace God—Jesus' utter dependence on the Father remains unquestioned (Mark 14:36)—and certainly not to "play God" by lording it over others, manipulating their lives. Precisely the opposite; his vocation is to identify with them in suffering, serving love. It is to place himself entirely at their disposal. As John's Gospel interprets it, there is no need to look beyond Jesus: "Whoever has seen me has seen the Father" (John 14:9). To make the reality of God present; this is the essential mystery of Jesus.

The climax of the discussion in John 14 is stunning—and unexpected: "Very truly, I tell you, the one who believes in me will also do the works that I do and, in fact, will do greater works than these" (John 14:12). Like Jesus, the Gospels call us to participate in God's work by representing Jesus Christ to the world.

Session 5

Son of God

Questions for Individual or Group Reflection: Explain how first-century Jews and Jewish Christians would have understood the term "Son of God." How does Mark's Gospel use the term? What is its use in John's Gospel? If Jesus used this term or the simpler term "Son" as a self-designation, discuss the range of meanings he might have intended.

Important Biblical Verses and Passages: Exodus 4:23–24; Jeremiah 31:9; Hosea 11:1; 2; Samuel 7:14; Psalm 2:7; 82:1, 6; 89:26–29; Deuteronomy 32:8; John 1:14, 18; 10:31–39; Matthew 5:9; 11:25–27; 27:38–43; Luke 20:36; Mark 1:1, 11; 9:7; 14:61–64; 15:39; Acts 8:36–38; 1 John 4:15; Romans 1:3–4

Technical Words and Concepts: Son of God; divine sonship

THE TITLE "SON OF God, "like "Son of Man," is complex and capable of several meanings. Like the phrase "Son of Man," which we take to mean "a human being," but which for most first-century Jews would have meant someone divine, the term "Son of God" today is probably at odds with how most Jews in the first century would have understood that expression. In our way of thinking, a "son of God" would be a god and the "Son of God" would be God, but for most first-century Jews the term "Son of God" would have meant someone human. Generally speaking, they would have understood divine sonship to mean (1) being related to God in some special way and (2) being commissioned by God to fulfill some vocation.

The origin of the concept lies in ancient oriental religions, in which kings were thought to be begotten of gods. This belief was prevalent in Egypt, where rulers (Pharaohs) were considered to be sons of the sun god Re. In Babylonia and Assyria kings were viewed as endowed with divine power. In the New Testament period the title was used of Roman emperors.

Divine Sonship in the Old Testament

The Old Testament attributes divine sonship to a range of subjects, particularly the chosen nation of Israel, their kings, and persons with a special commission from God, such as angelic beings and possibly also the Messiah. This manner of speaking of God as father to the chosen people of Israel appears in several important texts. In Exodus 4:22 and Jeremiah 31:9, God calls Israel his "firstborn son"; in Exodus 4:23 and Hosea 11:1, his "son." Correspondingly, in Deuteronomy 32:6, 18 and Jeremiah 3:4, God is called the people's "father," and in Deuteronomy 14:1; 32:5, 19 the Israelites appear as "children" of God. In Isaiah 1:2 and 30:1 the Israelites as a whole are called "sons" (children). The plural form may also designate a special group, such as the pious or priests. In these texts the designation expresses both the idea that God has choses this people for a special mission and that this people owes God absolute obedience.

This is also true of the way God addresses kings, as representatives of the chosen people. Thus, the primary passage of the Israelite ideology of divine kingship says of Solomon: "I will be his father, and he will be my son" (2 Sam. 7:14; cf. Ps. 89:26–29). In this ideology the conception of divine sonship is meant to indicate a special relationship between the king and God, but certainly not deification. This also applies to Psalm 2:7, where God says to the king, "You are my son; today I have begotten you." In this passage, much cited by early Christians as a reference to Christ, sonship refers to the king's election and commissioning by God. The use of the word "today," a reference to the king's coronation day or its anniversary, rules out a mythological or preexistent connotation. The primary thought in these texts is the same as that in the designation of the people as "children" or "sons" of God. The king is son of God because the nation is.

Scholars raise the question whether the Messiah bears this title in late Judaism, particularly since the New Testament identifies Messiah with Son of God (Matt. 16:16; Mark 14:61; Luke 1:32). As biblical scholarship demonstrates, the Synoptic designation of Jesus as Son did not grow out of his messianic office, and it could simply be that the connection between Messiah and Son of God (which occurs only in a few passages) simply resulted from the fact that early Christians saw in Jesus both figures at the same time, but from two different points of view. In any case, we must carefully distinguish between Messiah and Son of God in the New Testament (note that Luke follows a better tradition when he separates the high priest's question concerning the messianic claim from that concerning the claim to be the Son of God; Luke 22:67–70). Messianic usage of the expression outside the New Testament from this period does occur in the Dead Sea Scrolls, indicating that the connection might have been emerging at the time of Jesus, but in the postbiblical Jewish literature as a whole, "son of God" designates either the pious or the suffering righteous (Wis. 2:18–20), while the plural designates the elect people. Obviously, Son of God was not a common messianic title in Judaism, if at all.

In some Old Testament passages angels are called "sons of God"; they too are commissioned by God. In Genesis 6:2–4 angels are said to marry human women and become the fathers of the Nephilim (people of gigantic stature whose superhuman power was thought to result from divine-human marriage). In Job 1:6 and 2:1, as in Deuteronomy 32:8 and Psalms 29:1 and 89:6, angels make up the court of God. In Psalm 82:6, a reference to the members of the heavenly "divine council" (Ps. 82:1) but possibly also to human rulers and even to humanity as a whole (note its quotation by Jesus in John 10:34), God addresses his audience in the memorable words: "You are gods, children of the Most High, all of you."

In conclusion, the Old Testament and Jewish concept of the Son of God is not essentially characterized by the gift of a particular power or by a substantial relationship with God by virtue of divine conception, but by the idea of election to participation in divine work through the execution of a particular commission, and by the idea of strict obedience to the God who elects.

Divine Sonship in the New Testament

As the evidence in the Synoptic Gospels makes clear, Jesus understood his relationship to God as one of sonship. But what kind of sonship did Jesus imply or claim? Was it intimate to the point of being qualitatively and radically unique? The answer requires a distinction between what Jesus said (or as least is represented as saying) about his sonship and what others say about him in this connection.

In the Synoptics we find Jesus speaking absolutely of "the Son" but never of "the Son of God." In an important Q passage, Jesus refers to the Father, identified as "Lord of heaven and earth," and claims that a unique and exclusive knowledge of the Father is possessed by the Son, whom he tacitly identifies as himself: "All things have been delivered to me by my Father; and no one knows the Father except the Son and anyone to whom the Son chooses to reveal him" (Matt. 11:25-27; Luke 10:21-22). Of the few Synoptic passages in which the earthly Jesus calls himself "Son" (in addition to Mark 13:32 and Mark 12:6 and its parallel in Matthew 21:37), the genuineness of this Q passage is strongly doubted. The fact that the "Son" designation occurs primarily in this problematical passage may be the reason why many New Testament scholars deny that Jesus ever used the title. The problem is compounded by the presence of the Johannine character of the saying (it has been called the "Johannine thunderbolt in the Q tradition"), so foreign to the Synoptics. But according to the influential New Testament scholar Joachim Jeremias, the use of the definite article "the," which makes this image sound ontological, is really generic in Greek idiomatic usage, as in Luke's parable of "the" faithful and prudent manager (Luke 12:42) or Matthew's parable of "the" sower (Matt. 13:18; cf. Mark 4:3). Unlike in Greek, the English idiom requires the indefinite article: "As only *a* father knows his son, so only *a* son knows his father."[1] Thus understood, the Q saying is a parable drawn from the intimate knowledge that a father and a son alone have of each other, which Jesus is using to describe the *abba* relationship to God that he claims for himself, and ideally for every human being.

In another passage, Jesus refers absolutely to "the Son" and acknowledges limits to his knowledge over and above the Father with respect to the end of the age (Mark 13:32). Also, in the parable of the vineyard and the wicked tenants, the owner sends to the tenants "my son" and they kill him. Yet neither here nor elsewhere in the Synoptic Gospels does Jesus ever say openly, "I am the Son of God" (see, however, Matthew 27:43).

Interestingly, three times the Synoptic Gospels present Jesus as referring to the divine sonship enjoyed by others here and hereafter: "Blessed are the peacemakers, for they shall be called the sons of God" (Matt. 5:9); "love your enemies . . . and you will be sons of the Most High" (Luke 6:35); those who participate in the coming resurrection from the dead "cannot die anymore, because they are like angels and are children (sons) of God, being children (sons) of the resurrection" (Luke 20:36).

---

1. Jeremias, *Central Message of the New Testament*, 23-26.

Part III: God's Human

According to the Synoptic Gospels, Jesus spoke of God as "my Father" (Matt. 11:27; 16:27; Luke 22:29). He not only spoke like "the Son" but also acted like "the Son" in knowing and revealing God, in challenging the divine law and its application, in forgiving sins, in being the one through whom others could become children of God, and in acting with total obedience as the agent of God's final kingdom. Jesus came across as expressing a unique filial consciousness and as laying claim to a unique filial relationship with the God whom he addressed as "Abba." This clarifies the charge of blasphemy brought against him at his trial (Mark 14:64); he had given the impression of claiming to stand on a par with God.

Whether Jesus ever called himself "the Son of God" (see Matt. 27:43), in the Synoptic Gospels others called him by this name, but only in exceptional cases, and then due to supernatural knowledge. He is recognized as such by Peter, to whom "flesh and blood" had not revealed it (Matt. 16:17), by Satan (Matt. 4:3, 6), and by demons (Mark 3:11; 5:7). Otherwise it is only the divine voice at his baptism and at his transfiguration that addresses him as "Son".

The oldest complete Gospel, Mark, provides a complicated view of Jesus, presenting Jesus as God's servant and as God's representative. Both aspects are ingeniously combined in the idea that Jesus is the Son of God. For Mark, Son of God is the foremost title for Jesus. The first verse, which may serve as the Gospel's title, reads: "The beginning of the gospel of Jesus Christ, the Son of God" (Mark 1:1). The surviving manuscripts are divided between those that include "the Son of God" and those that lack it. The use of the expression Son of God in the title, whether original or not, certainly is in keeping with Mark's intention, since the title appears strategically at key events in the life of Jesus, including his baptism, transfiguration, trial, and crucifixion. The confession by the Roman centurion, "Truly this man was [the] Son of God" (Mark 15:39) is significant on several levels, including its strategic location. The title serves Mark's bookend technique, bringing the recognition of Jesus' true identity full circle, from the announcement by God at the baptism (1:11), the beginning of Jesus' ministry, to the announcement by a pagan Roman soldier at the crucifixion, the end of Jesus' ministry. The confession of Jesus as God's Son by the centurion is indicative of what would happen to the Christian movement during the first century. Its message would not find fertile soil among Jews, but it would be embraced principally by those outside Judaism, by Gentiles as represented by this Roman.

Son of God

As we know, faith in Jesus as the Son of God was a central tenet of the early church and therefore also of early Christian writers. Shortly after the resurrection, the expression "Jesus is the Son of God" emerged as an early creedal statement, and it seems to have been used in the earliest baptismal liturgy, traces of which appear in Acts 8:36–38, where Philip baptizes the Ethiopian eunuch after the eunuch makes the confession, "I believe that Jesus Christ is the Son of God."[2] Likewise in 1 John 4:15 the statement: "God abides in those who confess that Jesus is the Son of God" appears to come from an ancient creed of the church. The existence of such a formula in the early church is further demonstrated in Hebrews, where the author designates Jesus "Son of God" in the context of "let us hold fast to our confession" (Heb. 4:14). We also find evidence of faith in the Son of God in the Pauline confessional passage in Romans 1:3–4, believed to have been taken from an ancient church creed. In this context, the title seems intended to convey the elevation of Jesus to a position of transcendent status and to denote a uniquely close connection with God. This brings us to ask whether Jesus understood himself to be the Son of God, and if so, what this self-designation would have meant to him?

It seems clear on the basis of the Old Testament and later Jewish views that there was little ground for the early church to designate Jesus as Son of God. If, as many have argued, the first Christians did not derive the Son of God designation from his messianic role, and if Jesus consciously avoided, if not actually rejected, the title "Messiah" for himself, the obvious solution is that this designation came from Jesus himself. The conviction that in a unique way he was "God's Son" must belong to the very heart of what we call the "self-consciousness" of Jesus. If Jesus preferred the title "Son of Man" to "Son of God," it is because the former expresses most clearly what is important to him in the latter. That is, "Son of Man" points to the complete identity of Jesus' will with that of the Father as expressed in his obedience to the divine plan, but unlike "Son of God," it is not so likely to be misunderstood as sacrilegious by the disciples and the people.

There is another reason for Jesus' reserve in using the title Son of God. While the term expresses Jesus' experience of complete unity of will with the Father, this is more than simply the prophetic consciousness of one who knows himself to be God's instrument, more even than the compulsion the apostle Paul describes when he declares: "woe to me if I do not proclaim the

---

2. Even if verse 37, omitted by some manuscripts, is an interpolation, it is clearly an early addition.

gospel!" (1 Cor. 9:16). God not only acts through Jesus, but with him. Thus Jesus can presume to forgive sins, an act interpreted as blasphemy by the scribes, who saw that this meant a conscious identification with God: "Who can forgive sins but God alone" (Mark 2:7). Jesus does carry out God's plan as does a prophet or apostle, but in so doing he experiences oneness with the Father. This experience is Jesus' secret, and herein lies the explanation as to why he speaks of himself as the "Son" so infrequently. Even in antiquity, ordinary human understanding would consider such "Son consciousness" or "Son identification" to be unacceptable, whether on religious or psychological grounds.

Therefore, in the few Synoptic passages in which Jesus speaks of himself as the "Son of God" or simply as the "Son," two aspects appear: first, the obedience of the Son in fulfillment of God's will, and second, the profound awareness that as Son he is related to God as no other person is. If the expression "Son of God" seemed appropriate to Jesus to describe his experience from his baptism onward, his understanding of the title must have come from Old Testament usage. There the people of Israel and their king bore this name as instruments chosen to fulfill God's redemptive plan for the world. The connection between Jesus' consciousness of sonship and this Old Testament view becomes clear if we remember that this consciousness expresses itself as obedience. On the other hand, precisely in executing this obedience Jesus had also a new experience, bound to himself uniquely, of the complete unity of will with the Father. While the Old Testament "Son of God" concept offered no parallel to this experience, the model, like "Son of Man" and "Suffering Servant," expresses the idea of representation, central to Jesus' mediatorial self-understanding.

As suggested above, Jesus' baptism seems to have marked the beginning of his awareness that he stood in a unique Son-Father relationship with God. Thus, Jesus' baptism experience introduces for us an understanding of the whole life of Jesus—and of all Christology. Who is Jesus? At this point, the answer is revealed: "You are my Son, the Beloved" (Mark 1:11). From this moment Jesus never loses consciousness of his oneness with the Father and of his clearly defined task. The temptation account shows this immediately: "If you are the Son of God . . . ," says Satan. But Jesus resists temptation, for he knows that because he is God's Son, he cannot be a religious miracle worker or a political messiah. As "Son" he must utilize divine power only through total obedience to his divine commission. It is no accident that the words from heaven at the transfiguration repeat those of the heavenly voice at the baptism (Matt. 17:5). The awareness of divine sonship does not leave him even in Gethsemane, although he must once again guard his obedience against temptation (Matt. 26:39). Only in the moment of death does he cry out, "My God, my God, why have you forsaken me?" (Matt. 27:47), yet even here, the exclamation is fully understandable only on the basis of his sonship.

Divine Sonship in the Gospel of John

In the New Testament the central terms "the Father" and "the Son," whose origin is parabolic language, are drawn from human relationships. Nowhere does Father-Son terminology have greater prominence than in the Fourth Gospel. In John's prologue, the original parabolic foundation of the christological language often appears beneath the theological surface. In fact, where sonship language is first introduced, at the climax of the prologue, it is specifically in the form of a simile from human relationships: "the glory as of a father's only son" (John 1:14). There are no articles in the Greek, and yet translators and interpreters regularly supply them. The simile was already a familiar one for describing Israel in relation to God (Exod. 4:22; Jer. 31:9). Glory (*doxa*) and image (*eikōn*) were used as equivalents in late Judaism to mean "reflection," as by Paul in 1 Corinthians 11:7: man is "the image and reflection [glory] of God." The idea behind John 1:14 is almost certainly that Jesus Christ is the reflection of God, or as we might say colloquially, God's "spitting image."

Nowhere in the New Testament are we closer than in the Fourth Gospel to the fundamental Hebraic use of sonship to designate not an absolute status or title but a functional relationship marked by character (this comes out clearly in the dialogue in 8:31–47). To be a son is to show the character, to reproduce the thought and action, of another. To claim, therefore, to be a son of God is a sign of fidelity, not blasphemy, as the Jews suppose (see 10:31–39). This discussion, which places Jesus on the same metaphysical level as every other son of God, yet attests him functionally unique, presupposes a thoroughly Hebraic way of thinking. John's Gospel grounds the highest and most intimate union Jesus has with God in the utter faithfulness and obedience he displays as loyal Son. For John, Christ Jesus is "God the only Son" (1:18) because as human he is utterly transparent to the Father, who is greater than he is (14:28) and indeed than all. In reality the emphasis in John's Gospel, where "sonship," the dominant christological category, is usually seen as the main support for an ontological representation, is the same conception of filial obedience the Synoptics use to represent Jesus at his baptism and temptation. For the Gospels as a whole, Jesus' connection with the Father is in terms of the relationship of sonship and servanthood prefigured in the Old Testament. Sonship is enacted not by deeds of power but through filial trust and obedience. This conception of the one who allows God to show through, who is transparent to God and thus speaks of God because he does not speak of himself, is reflected in all Jesus is and does in the Gospels.

Who is Jesus? Again, it is important that we not read back Nicene categories into first-century Christianity. Just as Word and Wisdom, like Spirit of God, were personified as agents of God's relationship to the world, so Son of God stands for the representative of God's will and character, the one who truly embodies what God is and does, and in whom God's authority is vested. The Synoptic Gospels do not portray God's "Son" as an individual superhuman being of preexistent substance but rather as one who stands, or rather is called to stand, in that relationship. In contrast with the prophets, who were sent as God's servants, Jesus is the son in whom all is vested, the representative who stands in and acts for God.

In this capacity Jesus is seen throughout the New Testament as the expression and agent of God's purpose from the start. He fills a role prepared for him from the foundation of the world (John 17:24), though in this respect he is no different from the elect in general (Matt. 25:34; Eph. 1:4). But as the Son, Jesus is uniquely the reflection of God's person and character (Heb. 1:3). It is thus entirely natural that Paul and others should see in him the preexistent wisdom, power, and image of God (1 Cor. 1:24; 2 Cor. 4:4; Col. 1:15–20). It is natural also that John should view Jesus as the creative Logos who from the beginning was with God and who was God (John 1:1–3), portraying him as speaking as one who was before Abraham (John 8:58), and who shared the Father's glory before the foundation of the world (John 17:5). But none of these affirmations, however exalted, are intended to suggest that Jesus was not fundamentally human, with all the antecedents of every other human, who was yet called from the womb to embody this unique role. As Son, he is not of this world, and yet, as the man from Nazareth, he is born and bred completely within a local human situation, with parentage open to inspection—and insinuation (John 6:42; 7:27; 8:41).

Session 6

Messiah

Questions for Individual or Group Reflection: Whether Jesus ever thought of himself as the Jewish Messiah (that is, as "King of the Jews"), it is clear that the authors of the Synoptic Gospels did so. What did the concept "Messiah" mean (a) to first-century Jews? (b) To the disciples of Jesus? (c) To Jesus? (d) To the Gospel writers? What does the concept mean to you?

Important Biblical Verses and Passages: Micah 5:2; Matthew 2:1–12; 19:28; 20:20–23; Luke 1:32–33; 2:4, 10–11; 4:16–21; Isaiah 61:1–2; Psalm 72:1–17; Ezekiel 37:21–28; Mark 8:27–30; 15:2–5, 26; John 6:15; 10:7–18; 18:33–37

Technical Words and Concepts: Christ; Messiah; anointed one; Davidic ruler; Dead Sea Scrolls; Messiah of Aaron; Messiah of Israel, the good shepherd; King of the Jews

THE SINGLE MOST COMMON descriptive title applied to Jesus in the early years of the Christian movement was the term "Christ." In Greek, the language of the New Testament, the word "Christ" is a title, a translation of the Hebrew word for "messiah." Saying "Jesus Christ" means saying "Jesus is the Messiah." The Greek word "*Christos*" is simply a translation of the Hebrew *mashiah*, meaning "anointed one." In modern parlance the word "messiah" is roughly synonymous with "Savior," though in scholarly usage it is more specific than that. It is used in the Old Testament both for kings and high priests, who were in fact anointed, and metaphorically with reference to prophets. As used in the Hebrew Bible, the title had no future or eschatological connotation. In the postexilic period, when there was no longer a king on the throne, the term as applied to a king came to refer to the one who would restore the kingship of David and usher in the eschatological age. In order to grasp the importance that the first Christians attached to "Messiah" as a title, we have only to remember that this word has functioned as *the* christological title for Christians from New Testament times until today.

In the oldest Christian document, 1 Thessalonians, Paul repeatedly calls Jesus "Christ," in a way that suggests that within twenty years of Jesus' death and resurrection this comprehensive title for Jesus was widely used and taken for granted by early Christians. But by this time the title had almost completely lost its original significance, and was essentially functioning as Jesus' second name (see 1 Thess. 1:1, 3; 5:23, 28). In a notable pre-Pauline confessional statement (1 Cor. 15:3), which also goes back to the early church, the term "Christ" seems no longer to be associated with messianic significance and to function largely as an alternative name for Jesus. In his letters Paul uses "Christ" 270 times, sometimes alone, other times in combination with the name "Jesus" as "Jesus Christ"(meaning "Jesus Messiah") or "Christ Jesus" (meaning "Messiah Jesus"). While the former fixes the word "Christ" as a proper name, the latter suggests that Paul is still aware of the title's original meaning.

The author of Mark, deeply rooted in a Jewish worldview, begins his Gospel by making it clear that Jesus is the Messiah (Mark 1:1). Readers living in the Greco-Roman world would not recognize "Christ" as a name; for most of them it was not even a meaningful title. Crafting the story of Jesus as Mark does, his intention, according to the Jewish understanding of the Messiah, is radical and misguided, for he ties Jesus' messiahship not to power but to suffering, not to victory but to death. Mark shows a messiah whose mission is to die. He thereby interprets messiahship in a radically different way from the common Jewish expectations of a political leader who would restore the kingdom of Israel.

Matthew follows his predecessor Mark in beginning his Gospel by identifying Jesus as the Messiah, but he elaborates Mark's reference to "Jesus Christ," not with "Son of God" but with "son of David, son of Abraham" (Matt. 1:1). The phrase "son of David" makes clear that Matthew understood the term "Christ" to mean "Messiah of Israel." As Matthew's readers realized, Abraham was the father of the Jews, and David their greatest king, whose descendant was to resume his rule, enthroned in Jerusalem and reigning over a sovereign state of Israel as God's anointed. This son of David would be the Messiah. Matthew's narrative portrays Jesus as thoroughly Jewish and therefore as the ultimate fulfillment of the hopes of the Jews, as his genealogy makes clear. In the infancy narratives, Jesus is announced as the fulfillment of the messianic prophecy from Isaiah 7:14 (Matt. 1:23). He is born in Bethlehem, in fulfillment of the prophecy from Micah 5:2 (Matt. 2:6). The magi from the East come to see the king that is born (Matt. 2:1–12). But Matthew portrays Jesus as much more than a conventional Messiah. As Emmanuel (Matt. 1:23), Jesus represents the presence of God among his people and is appropriately the object of worship (Matt. 2:11; 14:33; 28:9, 17).

In Luke's Gospel, "Messiah" is also an important title, second only to the title "Lord." In the infancy narrative, the angel Gabriel draws on central messianic themes when he tells Mary that Jesus will be given the throne of his ancestor David (1:32; cf. 2 Sam. 7:12–13, 16) and that he will reign forever (Luke 1:33; cf. 2 Sam. 7:13, 16; Ps. 89:4, 29; 132:12; Isa. 9:7). Other messianic themes include that Jesus is born in David's city, Bethlehem (Luke 2:4, 11), thereby fulfilling the messianic prophecy in Micah 5:2. Jesus is introduced as the Messiah by the angels in the field (Luke 2:11) and confessed as such by Peter (Luke 9:20). At his resurrection, Jesus' mission is explained in terms of messiahship (Luke 24:24, 46). Luke also repeatedly makes use of the messianic theme that Jesus is the son of David (Luke 1:32, 69; 2:4, 11; 18:38, 39). The theme is obviously important to Luke, who includes Jesus' genealogy to establish that Jesus is descended from David (3:23–38).

The Messiah in Ancient Judaism

By a ritual act of symbolic anointing with oil, Old Testament kings were installed (1 Sam. 9:16; 10:1; 2 Sam. 2:4; 1 Kgs. 1:34, 39). Hence, a king would be called "the Lord's anointed" (1 Sam. 16:6; 24:6; 2 Sam. 1:14; Ps. 2:2) or simply "the anointed one." The practice of anointing kings at their investiture was extended to the ceremony for the ordination of the Aaronic priesthood. As in the case of the kings, the high priest's head was anointed with oil (Exod. 29:1–9; Lev. 4:3; Ps. 133:2). However, the title "anointed one" is not reserved for kings and priests; anyone to whom God assigns a special mission concerning the people of Israel can bear the title. Even a foreign pagan king, Cyrus, bears the title "messiah" when God commissions him with a special task (Isa. 45:1). Prophets also were considered anointed by

Part III: God's Human

God, even though no actual rite of anointing is mentioned. Elijah was commanded to "anoint" Elisha prophet, an event accomplished by throwing his mantle over him (1 Kgs. 19:16, 19).

In Isaiah 61:1–2, an important passage central to Jesus' self-understanding, a prophetic author knows himself to be empowered by the divine Spirit and sent to encourage the exiled and oppressed Israelites: "The spirit of the Lord God is upon me, because the Lord has anointed me; he has sent me to bring good news to the oppressed, to bind up the brokenhearted, to proclaim liberty to the captives, and release to the prisoners; to proclaim the year of the Lord's favor" (cf. Luke 4:16–21). Even the ancestors of Israel, viewed as having a prophetic role, could be called "anointed ones" (Ps. 105:15). During Israel's monarchic period, however, the central figure, the one special divinely commissioned person, is the king, considered the representative of God in a special sense. The idea is that God is the true king of Israel and that the earthly king exercises this divine function in his place.

When we examine the messianic consciousness at the time of Jesus, what the term "messiah" meant to first-century Palestinian Jews, the key to the widespread understanding of "messiah" was the promise that God made to David in 2 Samuel 7, that God would "be a father" to the king, and that David's kingship would last forever. This covenant with David is celebrated in Psalms 89 and 132.

Israel's Royal Psalms, in particular Psalms 2, 72, and 110, nurtured this early messianism. The reference to the divine begetting of the king (Ps. 110:3) and to divine sonship (Ps. 2:7) were part of the symbolic court language used to describe the king as God's representative. The eternal priesthood "according to the order of Melchizedek" (Ps. 110:4), promised to the king, was probably part of the hereditary ideology of the Canaanite kings of Jerusalem, exemplified in the priest king Melchizedek of Genesis 14. The eternal and universal reign of the king was partly an optimistic wish for long life and many victories and partly a reflection of the permanent greatness promised the Davidic dynasty. Psalm 72 expresses the ideal of the king as savior, as one who governs with justice and who intervenes on behalf of the poor and the needy. He is victorious over his enemies, who are also the enemies of his people. However, nowhere is the king represented as a future eschatological deliverer. As the reigning successor of David, he is heir of the covenantal promises made to David.

As it turns out, descendants of David did rule for a long time, for some four centuries, but in 587 the Babylonians defeated the nation of Judea and destroyed its capital city of Jerusalem, along with the temple built by Solomon, and removed the Davidic king from his throne. It was probably first during the Babylonian exile, when the throne of David no longer existed, that the Jews postponed God's promise to the distant future, a time when Israel's redemption would be realized in an earthly setting, but in a final way. During the exile the prophet Ezekiel conferred upon the future king the very characteristics that also later described the figure of the Messiah. According to Ezekiel 37:21–28, the whole kingdom of Israel will one day be united under David, who will rule eternally.

During the postexilic period, the Davidic line no longer ruled, and this made a profound difference in messianism. Now there could be no ideal king until the indefinite future, when the Davidic throne would be restored. It is in this period that we may begin to speak of the Messiah in the strict sense. The hope of the eschatological appearance of a Davidic ruler became particularly active as Jewish nationalism developed under the rule of Greece. During this time there is no clear evidence that the Messiah was viewed as a transcendental figure whose mission would extend beyond history. Some Jews, including the prophet who wrote Zechariah 9:9–10, expected him to be a peaceful king, but still one who would play a political role. Others—by far the majority—expected him to be a warring ruler who would conquer all Israel's enemies. The Psalms of Solomon, written around the middle of the first century BC, emphasize this latter view. Psalms 17 and 18 of this book call the expected king, a descendant of David, "Messiah." These messianic hopes were widespread among the Pharisees of Jesus' time.

The noncanonical book of 1 Enoch, particularly the section called the Similitudes (chapters 37–71), dated to the first century AD (some scholars date this material near the end of the century, while others earlier, to the time of Jesus), speaks of the coming Son of Man, viewed as an angelic being, as God's Messiah. More commonly, though, the term "messiah" was used to refer not to a divine angelic being, but to a human being. We know from the Dead Sea Scrolls, for example, that some Jews expected two messiahs—one priestly (the Messiah of Aaron) and the other political (the Messiah of Israel), the former considered as superior to the latter. The priestly ruler would be an authoritative interpreter of scripture and would rule the people as a sage, explaining God's laws and enforcing them as necessary. The Dead Sea Scrolls also speak of an eschatological or messianic prophet who would usher in the end-time.

In Jesus' day, however, the more common understanding of messianism did not involve an angelic judge or an authoritative priest, but a different kind of ruler, a mighty warrior and skilled politician. He would overthrow the Roman oppressors and reestablish both the monarchy and the nation. It appears that some Jews, especially those with an apocalyptic mindset, anticipated that God would personally intervene in the course of history to restore the kingdom through a messiah. They conceived this future kingdom as a kingdom of God, a utopian state in which there would be no evil or suffering. There is no question that the first Christians identified Jesus as the promised Messiah. Indeed, there is good reason to think that Jesus' first followers, during his lifetime, hoped—indeed believed—that that he might be this anointed one.

Jesus as Messiah

The question whether Jesus had a messianic self-consciousness is one of the major problems for understanding both his life and teachings. If Jesus saw himself as the eschatological prophet anointed with the Spirit, as promised in Isaiah 61:1–3 (cf. Luke 4:16–21; 7:20–22), we might say that in that sense he would be the Messiah. However, there is little proof that Jesus ever directly described himself as messianic prophet who would usher in God's kingdom.

Three Synoptic passages are especially important for our consideration: Mark 14:61–62 and parallels, Mark 15:2–5 and parallels, and Mark 8:27–30. We begin with the first, in which the question is most clearly stated. During the trial of Jesus, the high priest Caiaphas asks him, "Are you the Messiah, the Son of the Blessed One?" Caiaphas obviously asks the question in order to set a trap; whatever answer Jesus gives will be to the high priest's advantage. Caiaphas probably expects an affirmative answer, for he knows that Jesus appeared with a particular claim about himself. If Jesus gives an affirmative answer, Caiaphas could turn him over to the Romans as a political rebel, as one guilty of treason. On the other hand, a negative answer from Jesus would discredit him among the people. How did Jesus answer? According to the most obvious interpretation, he answers with an unmistakable affirmation: "I am." But note that the parallel texts in Matthew and Luke read differently. On the basis of the Greek, Jesus' reply signifies an affirmative answer. But the corresponding Aramaic expression (the language that Jesus spoke) suggests an indirect answer, even a veiled denial: "You say so, not I." If we may understand his answer to the high priest's question in this way, then Jesus neither clearly affirmed nor clearly denied that he was the Messiah. In addition, in the following verse Jesus adds another sentence to his answer, one in which he clearly ascribes to himself a role that does not agree with that of the Messiah. His saying about the Son of Man sitting on the right hand of God and coming again with the clouds of heaven is not derived from the concept of the Messiah. The Son of Man is a heavenly being, not an earthly king who will conquer the enemies of Israel and exercise earthly sovereignty. Matthew's version seems to have translated the Aramaic original more faithfully than the other Synoptic writers. The correct translation of Jesus' answer is probably, "You have said so. But I tell you . . . ," followed by the statement about the Son of Man. Luke's version also preserves the memory that Jesus refuses to answer directly. Jesus' rejection of the Messiah title need not mean he rejects the concept altogether, but only the political and military expectation associated with it.

In Mark 15:2–5 and parallels, Jesus stands before Pilate, who asks him, "Are you the King of the Jews?" Pilate thereby translates the designation "Messiah" into Roman terminology. The Synoptics agree in his answer, "You say so." Here also it is possible that Jesus intends an evasive answer. The dialogue about "My kingdom is not from this world" that follows Pilate's question in John 18:33–37 could point in this direction. It is important to note that in all accounts Pilate does not find Jesus guilty. Could he have said, as in Luke 23:4: "I find no basis for an accusation against this man," if he had understood Jesus' answer to be an affirmation?

The third text having to do with Jesus' attitude toward the title Messiah is the well-known scene in Caesarea Philippi (Mark 8:27–30 and parallels). In Mark 8:29 Peter confesses, "You are the Messiah." According to the usual interpretation of this passage, Jesus accepts Peter's proclamation, particularly when viewed through the Matthean lens (Matt. 16:16–20). However, Matthew's redaction attributes material to Jesus about Peter's being the "Rock" on which the church will be grounded, material that originally was not part of this context. As Mark's Gospel shows, Jesus neither affirms nor denies Peter's messianic claim. Saying nothing at all about the Messiah, Jesus goes on to speak instead of the Son of Man, adding that he must suffer many things. It is difficult to connect suffering with the Jewish messianic expectation. A crucified Christ was even more alien and scandalous, as Paul indicates in 1 Corinthians 1:23.

Part III: God's Human

In Mark's account, when Jesus speaks of suffering, Peter confirms his Jewish bias about the Messiah, rebuking Jesus for such an idea. Jesus' response, "Get behind me, Satan," seems extreme, for Jesus considers Peter's conception of the Messiah as a satanic temptation. For an explanation, we recall Jesus' temptation in the wilderness after his baptism, where Satan tried to impose upon him the role of a political messiah. According to Matthew's account of the temptations of Jesus, the third individual temptation and therefore the climax and meaning of the whole scene has to do with the nature of his mission and ministry: what kind of messiah will he be, a political messiah or a suffering one? The extraordinary vehemence with which Jesus rejects this view indicates how deeply the temptation of Peter affects him. He does not wish to be the king of Israel in this way; his conviction is that he must fulfill his task through service and suffering, and only thus to effect his role in the inauguration of God's coming kingdom.

Jesus knew very well that his disciples had the secret hope that he would assume the political messiah's seductive role. The arguments of the sons of Zebedee concerning their rank in the future kingdom is enough to show what thoughts were in the heads of the disciples (Mark 10:35–40; Matt. 20:20–23). Their desertion of Jesus when he was arrested, and their flight, was due not only to understandable fear on their part but also the result of disappointment that Jesus did not resemble the expected messianic king. It is also possible to understand Judas's betrayal of Jesus as due not simply to greed but also to messianic disappointment.

The three Synoptic passages we have examined agree that Jesus demonstrates an attitude of extreme restraint of the title "Messiah." This is confirmed by the fact that in almost no passage in the Synoptics in which the expression "Messiah" appears does Jesus apply it to himself; it is always others who speak of him as the Christ.[1] The Gospel of John yields the same conclusion. Besides the dialogue with Pilate in which Jesus emphasizes that his kingdom is not of this world, the writer reports in 6:15: "When Jesus realized that they were about to come and take him by force to make him king, he withdrew again to the mountain by himself."

We come now to a further question: Is there anything in the Jewish conception of the Messiah that Jesus would apply to himself? This question changes our conception dramatically, for it requires us to see that while

---

1. Only one passage seems to contradict this, Jesus' answer to the Samaritan woman in John 4:25–26. But here the author may well be inserting the designation "Messiah," familiar to him, and attributing it to Jesus.

Jesus rejected the Jewish understanding of the title, he had his own understanding of the title, which he no doubt firmly embraced. As noted earlier, Jesus viewed his mission as prophetic, announcing God's coming kingdom. At least one aspect of the Jewish conception of the Messiah can be reconciled with Jesus' consciousness of his calling: the title expresses continuity between Israel's historic role and his own. The messianic title represents the fulfillment of the role of mediation that God's chosen people should have realized. The task of mediation lies behind most of the christological titles originating in Judaism, and thus is a common element in the messianic and other eschatological figures. But it finds particularly powerful expression in the title "Messiah": the idea that the Messiah comprehends and fulfills the mandate of Israel. The fact that the Messiah fulfills the task of Israel is central to Jesus' understanding of his role; the conception of how the Messiah does this is not applicable to Jesus. Despite all its inadequacies, therefore, the idea of the Messiah is important to the extent that it establishes continuity between the vocation of Jesus and the mission of the chosen people of Israel.

There are many sayings of Jesus that indicate he thought of his task as carrying out the role of Israel. One must ask further if Jesus could not accept some elements of the Jewish conception of the Messiah with regard to his future, eschatological work. His citation of Psalm 110 in his answer to the high priest (Mark 14:62 and parallels) suggests that he probably expected future rule over the world. The fact remains that in his answer to the high priest, Jesus described his future work not as that of the Messiah but as that of the Son of Man, speaking of his role at the end in terms of Daniel's transcendent figure (see Session 9).

Despite his reluctance to accept the title Messiah, Jesus clearly interpreted his person and activity messianically. However, both he and his followers reinterpreted the messianic figure. Behaving in an unregal and unwarlike fashion (see Mark 10:42-44 and Luke 22:24-27), Jesus never promised, let alone tried, to free the people from foreign domination. Nor did he announce the imminent lordship of Israel over the nations (see Isa. 2:2-3; 25:6-9; Mic. 4:1-2). For Jesus the signs of the kingdom differed from that national hope. Ezekiel's language about God's promise to care for the flock through a Davidic shepherd-king to come (Ezek. 34:23-24; 37:24-25; see also Mic. 5:2-4) found an echo in Jesus' parable of the lost sheep (Matt. 18:12-14) and eventually in John's Gospel, which identified Jesus as the "good shepherd" (John 10:7-16; see 21:15-17; 1 Pet. 2:25; 5:4). But this shepherd would lay down his life for his sheep (John 10:11, 15, 16–17). This constitutes a major readjustment in the notion of Messiah.

Given the fact that Jesus did little or nothing during his life to make anyone think that he was the Messiah, and that his behavior seemed the opposite of what Jews expected a messiah to be, it is surprising that the first Christians conceived of him in this manner. He was neither a priestly messiah nor a political messiah, and he did nothing to set up a sovereign state or drive the Romans out of the Promised Land. Why, then, did his followers designate him by a title that suggests he had done these things?

The best explanation is that the followers of Jesus called him Messiah after his death "because they were calling him this before his death."[2] Despite Jesus' reserve, his disciples, even during his earthly life, seem to have thought of their master as in some sense the Davidic Messiah. Otherwise, their post-Easter identification of Jesus as the Messiah, enthroned at the resurrection (Rom. 1:3–4; Acts 2:36; 2 Tim. 2:8), makes no sense. At a later point, Christians began to think in these terms, arguing that the Hebrew Bible predicted such things (see Psalm 22 and Isaiah 53). However, these passages were not about the Messiah; in fact, the word never appears in them. To say that the resurrection caused his disciples to call Jesus the Messiah explains nothing, since at the time there was no common Jewish belief concerning an earthly messiah who must die and rise again. The resurrection could act as a catalyst and could be interpreted as the enthronement of the Son of David only if the disciples already harbored some idea of Jesus as Davidic Messiah. That even his adversaries interpreted Jesus' actions and claims in some royal messianic sense during his lifetime seems confirmed by the charge on which he was brought before Pilate: being "King of the Jews" (Matt. 27:37; Mark 15:26; John 19:19).

As an apocalyptic Jew, Jesus did not think that God's future kingdom would be won by a political struggle or a military engagement. God alone would be responsible for the kingdom's realization, and once it arrived, Jesus believe he would be its king. Bart Ehrman supports this interpretation ingeniously. First, the disciples clearly thought and talked about Jesus as the Messiah during his ministry. Yet this belief was not based on Jesus' actions, which seemed unmessianic to an extreme. So if nothing in Jesus' actual deeds would make anyone suspect that he had messianic intentions, why would his followers have thought about him in these terms? "The

---

2. Ehrman, *How Jesus Became God*, 117. This segment is adapted from Ehrman's discussion on pages 112–24.

easiest explanation is that Jesus told them that he was the messiah."[3] Next, the disciples had to understand what Jesus meant by "messiah" within the broader context of his apocalyptic message. Jesus had told his disciples that they would be seated on twelve thrones ruling the twelve tribes of Israel in the future kingdom (Matt. 19:28; Luke 22:30). And if he was the leader of the disciples now, he certainly would be their leader then. Jesus must have thought that he would be the king of the kingdom that God would inaugurate on earth. And what is the typical designation for the future king of Israel? Messiah. It is in this sense that Jesus must have taught his disciples that he was the Messiah.

According to all accounts, Jesus spent the week leading up to his arrest in Jerusalem preaching his apocalyptic message (Mark 13; Matt. 2425; Luke 21). The crowds were growing, and some were accepting his message. That's when the Jewish leaders decided to act. They did so by hiring an insider, Judas Iscariot, one of Jesus' disciples. According to the Gospel accounts, they hired Judas to lead the authorities to Jesus so that they could arrest him in private, away from the unruly crowds. If in fact such a relationship was established with one of Jesus' disciples, Ehrman proposes, it must have been to use Judas as a witness against Jesus, to betray him with "insider information." If Jesus never publicly proclaimed himself to be the future king of the Jews, and if his actions were not revolutionary or seditious, then why, when the authorities arrested him and handed him over to Pontius Pilate, was he charged with treason? The simplest answer is that this is what Judas betrayed. Judas had been one of the insiders to whom Jesus disclosed his vision of the future, that he would be king in God's coming kingdom and the disciples would all be rulers. This, Judas told the Jewish authorities, was what Jesus was actually teaching in private. It was all they needed to arrest and charge him; and then they turned him over to Pilate, a Roman governor who knew how to deal with troublemakers. There was no such thing as due process, trial by jury, or the possibility of appeal. In the provinces of Rome, away from the capitol, "justice" usually meant swift and violent justice. The charge was that Jesus called himself "King of the Jews," and either he admitted it or he refused to deny it. Pilate did what governors typically did in such cases. He ordered execution by crucifixion. The evidence that Jesus really thought of himself as "King of the Jews" is the fact that he was killed for it.

---

3. Ibid., 119.

Session 7

Savior/High Priest

Questions for Individual or Group Reflection: When you think of Jesus as Savior or as High Priest, do you focus on a specific function of his life (and death) or on the entirety of his life and ministry? When so doing, do you focus on his humanity, his divinity, or both? Can Jesus be Savior without being divine? Can he be Savior without being human? Explain your answers.

Important Biblical Verses and Passages: Philippians 3:20; Matthew 1:21; 5:40; 12:1-8, 28; 1 Corinthians 5:7; Acts 5:31; 10:38; Luke 2:11; John 4:42; Genesis 14:17-20; Psalm 110:1, 4; Mark 12:35-37; 1 Timothy 2:5-6; Hebrews 1:1-4; 2:9-18; 4:14—5:10; 6:20; 7:1-28; 9:15

Technical Words and Concepts: Savior; Pastoral Epistles; Aaronic priesthood; Levitical priesthood; Eucharist; paschal lamb; Ichthys; Mediator; high priest, Priestly Christology, Sadducees; Talmud; Hasmonean rulers; Melchizedek; *menus triplex*; Teacher of Righteousness; Elohim; Day of Atonement

Jesus as Savior

Given the popularity of the title "Savior" in later Christianity, particularly in pietistic circles, it is surprising to discover that in the early church this designation is missing from the most ancient of the early Christian writings. With the exception of one Pauline passage (Phil. 3:20), the title occurs relatively late in occasional passages in the Gospels of Luke and John and otherwise almost exclusively in the Pastoral Epistles (2 Tim. 1:10; Titus 2:13) and 2 Peter.

In the Old Testament the title originally referred to God. The Psalms and Isaiah give God this title most often, but it may be traced through the whole Old Testament. The title also distinguishes individual leaders such as Moses, who delivered the people from their oppressors. In connection with this task, the Messiah is seen as the coming Savior who will finally and permanently save his people (Isa. 19:20). Because this designation corresponds to the function the Messiah is expected to fulfill, one wonders why Jesus is not called Savior more often. Neither by himself nor by others was he ever called Savior during his lifetime, probably because the title was not used to refer to a specific function of Jesus but rather to his entire work: Jesus is Savior because he saves his people from their sins. This is how Matthew explains the name "Jesus" (Matt. 1:21).

Nevertheless, the title Savior definitely presupposes Christ's work of atonement. Jesus is often called Savior in writings that bestow this title also upon God (see Jude 25; 1 Tim. 1:1; 2:3; 4:10; Titus 1:3; 2:10; 3:4), indicating that even when God is called Savior, after the Old Testament pattern, the foundation of all divine salvation is the atoning work of Christ.

Unlike his cousin John the Baptist, Jesus was not born into a priestly family and could not claim Aaronic or even Levitical priesthood. However, his celebration of the Passover, his institution of the Eucharist (the Lord's Supper), and his crucifixion at the time of the Passover soon led Christians to apply sacrificial language to his death. Paul, when writing of Christ as "our paschal lamb" who "has been sacrificed" (1 Cor. 5:7) and whose blood atones for sin (Rom. 3:25; see 1 John 2:2), apparently took over traditional formulations. By virtue of his sacrifice, then, the first Christians addressed Jesus as Savior. But in the New Testament, from his birth to his future return, Jesus shows himself to be Savior. Often the title is combined with "Lord," as in "the knowledge of our Lord and Savior Jesus Christ" (2 Peter 2:20; see 1:11; 3:2, 18). In Acts 5:31 the title is combined with Leader. In Luke's infancy narrative the angel tells the shepherds: "To you is born this day in the city of David a Savior, who is the Messiah, the Lord" (Luke 2:11), and when Simeon receives the child Jesus in his arms, he praises God because "my eyes have seen your salvation" (Luke 2:30). Paul, speaking of Christ's present exalted status, states in Philippians: "Our citizenship is in heaven, and it is from there that we are expecting a Savior, the Lord Jesus Christ" (Phil 3:20). John refers to Jesus not only as Savior of some but more significantly as "Savior of the world" (John 4:42; 1 John 4:14), with global implications.

A full theological development of Jesus as Savior came later, during the period of expanding Christianity. In connection with other important titles added to the name Jesus, Savior later became part of the ancient Ichthys (IXTHYS) creed: "Jesus Christ God's Son Savior," an acrostic where each Greek letter represents a christological title or name.

Jesus as High Priest

There is no question that the New Testament writers view Christ as Savior; sixteen times they call him by this title. But is he also priest? Absolutely! The Pastoral Epistles, citing an earlier confessional statement of the church, recognized "one mediator" between God and humanity in the man Christ Jesus, "who gave himself a ransom for all" (1 Tim. 2:5-6). In the New Testament the title Mediator, a legal term designating an arbitrator or guarantor, has priestly connotations, since Jesus is seen, by his sacrifice on the cross, to be the mediator of God's new covenant with humanity (Heb. 8:6; 9:15; 12:24).

Applied to Jesus, the concept High Priest is closely related to that of Suffering Servant. Nevertheless, we devote a separate chapter to the title High Priest because its application to Jesus in early Christianity has a completely different historical origin, and also because it has aspects that are foreign to the Servant of God concept. Furthermore, we are dealing with a more complex christological conception than that of Prophet or Servant of God because the title High Priest extends beyond the historical work of Jesus to his present work.

Like the Servant concept, Priestly Christology is muted in the New Testament. The reason, at least in part, may be due to the widespread antipathy among the Jewish populace toward the corruption associated with the office of the high priest, supported by the Sadducean ideal of a priest-king dominion. From Jewish literature of the time, including the Assumption of Moses, the historian Josephus, and the Talmud, we learn that the Hasmonean rulers, successors of the Maccabean revolutionaries in the second and first centuries BC, adopted the title "High Priest of the Most High God." In so doing, they applied the title used of Melchizedek in Genesis 14:18, undoubtedly in an attempt to legitimize their reign. At the height of their power, during the reigns of Simon (142–134 BC) and

Savior/High Priest

John Hyrcanus (134–104 BC), it may well have seemed to many that they deserved the ascription. But such illusions were completely dispelled by the conduct of later Hasmonean rulers. Eventually intense antagonism toward such a claim arose.

The Essene covenanters at Qumran (the community that produced the Dead Sea Scrolls) continued to respect the priesthood of the biblical Melchizedek, expecting he would have a significant role in the messianic age, even while they denied the legitimacy of the Hasmonean-Sadducean assertion. But the Pharisees and other rabbinical teachers stood in such opposition to Sadducean priestly claims that they downplayed the supremacy of the biblical Melchizedek in the Genesis narrative and disparaged his inclusion in the messianic hope. In such a situation, it is not surprising that a Priestly Christology would be downplayed in the New Testament as well. The earliest Christians were guided by their remembrance of Jesus' negative attitude toward the priesthood and temple rituals, and his own ministry in relation to them. In addition, Jesus did not expressly speak of himself in terms of a priest. Taking their cue from him, they downplayed that role as well, though the concept figures prominently in the Christology of several New Testament books, primarily Hebrews.

Later Christians found in the Old Testament priestly function a basis for recognizing in Jesus the *munus triplex* (triple office) of anointed prophet, priest, and king. Present in the writings of patristic and medieval theologians, this theme of Christ's "triple office" was developed by John Calvin (1509–1564) and articulated by other Protestant and Roman Catholic thinkers, including Cardinal John Henry Newman (1801–1890) and the documents of the Second Vatican Council (1962–1965).

The high priest is an essentially Jewish figure. The tribe of Levi became a priestly class, within which Aaron and his sons were distinguished from the other Levites. Thus in the Hebrew scriptures the Levitical priesthood is set apart to offer sacrifice and to mediate in a cultic way between God and human beings. At first glance it might seem superfluous to devote a session to this concept, as it does not appear initially to be christological. Rather the expected Jewish redeemer seems to be an anti-establishment figure, at odds with a cultic system that appears ineffective or obsolete. Yet there are traces in Judaism of a connection between the awaited Messiah-king and the high priest. We begin with the mysterious Melchizedek, the priest-king of Genesis 14:17–20 and Psalm 110:4.

PART III: GOD'S HUMAN

Genesis 14 tells how Abraham freed his nephew Lot from Chedorlaomer, king of Elam, and his allies. When Abraham came back from the battle, the Canaanite King Melchizedek of Salem (Jerusalem?) met and blessed him, and Abraham gave him a tenth of the spoils. Genesis tells us nothing more about this mysterious king before whom Abraham humbled himself in this way. For this reason the figure of Melchizedek very early stimulated the imagination of the Jews. We read in Psalm 110:4: "You are a priest forever according to the order of Melchizedek." This psalm, cited in the New Testament more often than any other Old Testament passage, addresses the words to a Davidic monarch, most likely at his enthronement. Verse 4 confers on a king the high priestly functions of this high order. As the mysterious king of ancient Canaan was also a priest, so the newly enthroned king is said to perform a priestly office, higher than any actual priesthood, one that will not pass away because it is eternal. Insofar as the idea of kingship is the basis of messianism, and insofar as Psalm 110 connects this kingship with an ideal priesthood, we have here the starting point for a messianic formulation of the figure of the high priest.

When Jesus quotes Psalm 110 in Mark 12:35–37, he clearly presupposes that the king addressed in the psalm (the king who is at the same time a priest forever according to the order of Melchizedek) is to be understood as the Messiah. Not only was there messianic interpretation of Psalm 110 at the time of Jesus, there was also speculation in ancient Judaism that associated Melchizekek, if not with the Messiah (due to its anti-Christian polemic, later Judaism tended to devaluate the figure of Melchizedek), at least with other eschatological figures such as Shem, the archangel Michael, the Original Man, Adam, and Metatron.

In this connection we mention the Dead Sea Scrolls and the Qumran sect, whose "Teacher of Righteousness" is given eschatological characteristics, including priestly designation. Likewise we find in this community evidence that there existed within sectarian Judaism prior to and contemporary with early Christianity a messianic hope that included priestly features. One scroll (the Manual of Discipline) presents a doctrine of two messiahs, one priestly and the other Davidic, the priestly messiah being superior to the royal one. Another scroll (the Damascus Document) presents the concept of a singular messiah, who would fulfill both priestly and royal functions. Most intriguing in this context is the figure of Melchizedek in the fragmentary scroll 11QM, which presents Melchizedek as a heavenly being, the angelic leader of the heavenly hosts (Elohim) that execute eschatological judgment on the hosts of evil in the end-time. The name Melchizedek, as found in the Dead Sea Scrolls, may also be another name for the archangel Michael, perhaps also an allusion to the angel of Exodus 23:20-21, since the expression "my name is in him" in reference to a single angel is unexpected.

We conclude that Judaism knew of an ideal priest expected to fulfill in the last days all the elements of the Jewish priestly office. Because of this office, the high priest is the ideal mediator between God and humanity. From the Hasmonean period to the time of Jesus, the weaker the correspondence between the reality of the actual priesthood and the ideal expectations, the stronger became the Jews' hope for the end when all would be fulfilled. This hope included also the concept of priest, so that the figure of a perfect high priest of the end time moved ever nearer that of the Messiah.

Although we cannot be sure whether Jesus conceived of himself in priestly terms, in his ministry he clearly questioned the validity of the temple cult. Even if the cleansing of the temple (Matt. 21:12-13; Mark 11:15-19; Luke 19:45-48; John 2:13-23)[1] meant only its purging and not its rejection, there are numerous sayings of Jesus—such as that in Matthew 12:6 ("something greater than the temple is here")—that suggest he took a critical attitude toward its continuation. A genuine saying of Jesus about the disappearance of the temple quite likely underlies the accusatory words brought against him at his trial (see John 2:19; cf. Mark 14:58 and parallels). In John's interpretation of this saying, Jesus actually appears as one who takes the place of the temple (John 2:21). Whether or not Jesus conceived of his task as John interprets it, it seems likely he was convinced that his coming brought into question the continuation of the high priestly office.

When Jesus answers the high priest in Mark 14:62, he combines references to Daniel 7 and to Psalm 110: "You will see the Son of man seated at the right hand of the Power and coming with the clouds of heaven." The expression "seated at the right hand" is inseparably connected with the thought of the priest-king after the order of Melchizedek (see Ps. 110:1). We must not miss the significance—and the irony—that the evangelists (the Gospel writers) intend by having Jesus apply to himself a saying about the eternal High Priest precisely when he stands before the Jewish high priest and is questioned by him concerning his claim to be the Messiah. While

---

1. In John's Gospel the cleansing of the temple takes place at the start of Jesus' ministry, unlike the Synoptics, where it occurs at the end.

not claiming overtly to be an earthly, political messiah, Jesus is claiming covertly to be the heavenly Son of Man and the heavenly High Priest.

Priestly Christology in the Epistle to the Hebrews

The Letter to the Hebrews develops an intricate analogy and contrast between Jesus and the role of the Jewish priesthood, especially that of the high priest on the Day of Atonement. For the writer of Hebrews, Jesus is *the* Priest in an absolute and final sense, the fulfillment of all priesthood. As the "great high priest" (Heb. 4:14—5:10), Jesus was not born into the Levitical class but was appointed a priest "according to the order of Melchizedek" (Heb. 5:6, 10). He enjoyed two essential qualifications for priesthood: divine authorization (Heb. 5:4) and solidarity with those whom he represented (Heb. 4:15; see 2:17–18).

The seventh chapter is at the heart of Hebrews. It uses scriptural proof (Genesis 14 and Psalm 110) to describe Jesus as the true High Priest. Whereas other Christians at this time sought to prove by means of the Old Testament that Jesus was the Messiah expected by the Jews, the writer of Hebrews seeks to show that Jesus fulfills absolutely the high priestly function of the Jews. The writer seeks justification in the Old Testament for the idea that the priesthood of the former covenant is not final but must be replaced by a new priesthood, realized in Jesus Christ. He does so by showing the superiority of Melchizedek, who points to Jesus, over the Levites, the priests of the former covenant. Using a Jewish theory of ancestry, he argues that Levi, the ancestor of the Jewish priesthood, is the descendant of Abraham. Since Levi already existed in the "loins" of Abraham when Melchizedek met him (Heb. 7:10), what happened to Abraham therefore happened also to Levi. That Abraham received a blessing from Melchizedek is a sign of his inferiority to Melchizedek, since he who blesses is superior to him who is blessed. Therefore Levi and the whole Israelite priesthood that stems from him are inferior to Melchizedek. As one who blesses and receives the tithe, Melchizedek is the true high priest. Since Christ realized this true priesthood, he is finally the true High Priest, the actual mediator between God and humanity. For the writer of Hebrews, Jesus not only set aside the Levitical priesthood; he replaces and fulfills it. He does so by virtue of being at the same time sacrifice and sacrificer.

The Christology of the Epistle to the Hebrews is paradoxical throughout. The author, as perhaps no other early Christian theologian, had the

Savior/High Priest

courage to speak of the man Jesus in shockingly human terms, although at the same time he emphasized perhaps more strongly than any other the deity of Christ. The letter, more sermonic than epistolary, begins with one of the highest christological statements in all scripture, for it presents Jesus as Son, in contrast with all previous and partial revelations of God, whom God appointed "heir of all things, through whom he also created the worlds. He is the reflection of God's glory and the exact imprint of God's very being, and he sustains all things by his powerful word" (Heb. 1:2–3). Here Jesus is depicted as God's preexistent representative and divine heir, the agent of his purpose alike in creation and redemption. Yet if we ask who it is that fills this role, the whole point of the argument is that it is no divine or angelic being but a human being, one who totally shared the human condition (Heb. 4:15). Furthermore, in the midst of preexistent language, we read the apparently "adoptionist" term "appointed heir" (Heb. 1:2). And such language is characteristic of the letter as a whole. Nowhere in the New Testament more than in Hebrews do we find such a wealth of expressions that support an adoptionist Christology—of a human Jesus who becomes the Christ. For example,

- Jesus has *become* superior to the angels (1:4);
- because he has loved righteousness and hated wickedness, God has *anointed* him above his companions (1:9);
- God has *crowned him* with glory and honor because of the suffering of death (2:9);
- Jesus was *made* the pioneer of salvation and *perfected* through sufferings (2:10);
- Because, like Moses, he was faithful to the one who *appointed* him, Jesus is deemed "worthy" of more glory than Moses (3:2–3);
- Christ was *appointed* high priest by the one who said to him, "today I have begotten you" (Heb. 5:5);
- Jesus *learned obedience* through what he suffered (5:8);
- Jesus, *having been made perfect*, became the source of salvation (5:9);
- Jesus is *designated* high priest by God (5:10);
- Jesus is *appointed* a Son, who *has been made* perfect forever (7:28).

Part III: God's Human

These examples are astonishing for one who stresses the eternal pre-existence and post-existence of Christ more than any other New Testament writer. Adoptionism and incarnationism are generally held to be opposite extremes in Christology, yet here the author holds them together without any sense of tension or discrepancy.

A good example of the author's paradoxical language is Hebrews 2:17: "Therefore he had to become like his brothers and sisters in every respect." Later doctrine took this to mean that the Logos (the preexistent Word of God) had to be made human from having been something different (a heavenly, divine being). But is it possible that Jesus was ever anything but human? For the author, it seems essential that a consecrating priest and those who are consecrated all be of one "stock" (Heb. 2:11, REB),[2] sharing "flesh and blood" (Heb. 2:14). What was necessary was that the likeness that Jesus shared with God, the same "image" and "likeness" that Adam and Eve and their progeny share with God (Gen. 1:26–27), express itself in "merciful and faithful" service to God (Heb. 2:17) to the end. "For we do no have a high priest who is unable to sympathize with our weaknesses, but we have one who in every respect has been tested as we are" (Heb. 4:15).

Our understanding is crucial also to the interpretation of Hebrews 5:7-8: "In the days of his flesh, Jesus offered up prayers and supplications, with loud cries and tears, to the one who was able to save him from death, and he was heard because of his reverent submission. Although he was a Son, he learned obedience through what he suffered." On the presupposition of a heavenly figure coming in from the outside, this is interpreted to mean that, although Christ was the eternal Son of God, he condescended to suffer a life of humanity, like all other human beings. But if we take this language representationally, it means that Jesus' call to the unique role of living as God's Son, that is, as God's personal representative, did not exempt him from having to suffer to the end; precisely the contrary, it required this of him.

A final example involves the combination of negatives in Hebrews 7. The author observes of Melchizedek that he has no father or mother and no lineage. Having neither beginning nor end to his life, he is like the Son of God (Heb. 7:3). Is the author suggesting that Christ, as an eternal being, was inserted into the human scene without father and even without mother? This would be eccentric by any standard. But it is clear from what

---

2. Other translations use "Father," NRSV; "origin," RSV; "family," NIV; the original Greek is ambiguous, stating simply, "are all of one," as the footnote in the NRSV states.

Savior/High Priest

follows that he envisions no such thing. The Levites, as descendants of Abraham, were considered as having existed in the loins of Abraham when Melchizedek met him and received tithe of him (Heb. 7:10). Jesus, however, was not of that stock. But this does not mean that he was of no stock. On the contrary, Jesus stemmed from Judah (Heb. 7:14), and belonged to this tribe (Heb. 7:13). Our writer could have passed over this latter piece of information in silence, particularly if he wished to present Jesus as a priestly Messiah, but he mentions it as essential because it was a vital part of Jesus' continuity with the stream of human heredity and environment.

We note also a further point involved in Hebrews' formulation of the High Priest concept, the notion of "perfection." Jesus as the High Priest brings humanity to its perfection. As Jesus Christ is made perfect by the Father (Heb. 2:10; 5:9; 7:28), so the High Priest makes his human brothers and sisters perfect (Heb. 2:10–12; 10:14). The expression *teleios* and words from the same Greek root play an important part in the Christology of Hebrews. Since the task of the High Priest is to be Mediator between God and humanity, his crowning work is the perfection of humanity. For this reason *teleios* refers both to what is "perfect" and to that which is "complete." As in the injunction to perfection in Matthew 5:40, "Be perfect," the meaning, as the parallel "Be merciful" in Luke 6:36 clarifies, has more to do with moral maturity and with fulfilling one's ethical potential than with some biological or psychological standard.

In order to lead humanity to its completion, the High Priest too must go through the various stages of a human life. It is true that Hebrews thinks primarily of the final phase of that life, the passion, as "completion." But in connection with its emphasis on the necessary humanity of the High Priest, "made perfect/complete" necessarily takes into account Jesus' life in its entirety. The most important confirmation of Hebrews' conception of Jesus' full humanity is the statement that he "learned obedience" (Heb. 5:8). This expression, however comprehended, presupposes inner human development. Such growth is also attested in Luke's summary statement in 2:52: "And Jesus increased in wisdom and in years, and in divine and human favor." The word "learned" in Hebrews 5:8 means "leaning obedience through suffering." It reminds us of the same expression in Philippians 2:8: "obedient to the point of death, even death on a cross."

Hebrews is not so much interested in Jesus' *becoming* human as in his *being* human. That is what really characterizes the high priestly office. Jesus must be able to suffer with us in order to suffer for us. In Hebrews 6:20

we find another designation that expresses the relation between the High Priest and the faithful: Jesus is a "forerunner" on our behalf. The expression is not far different from the idea in the writings of Paul (Rom. 8:29; 1 Cor. 15:20) and in the book of Revelation (1:5) that through his resurrection Jesus has become the "firstborn" of the dead.

Another unique feature of Hebrews is the emphasis on the High Priest remaining in the Holy Place and there continuing his work in the present. This is also the meaning of Jesus being a priest "forever" (6:20; 7:3). This expression is the major theme of the second half of Hebrews 7. It corresponds to another major theme of "once for all" (9:12; cf. 10:12, 14). As High Priest Jesus thus fulfills a double office: that of the once-for-all act of atonement, and that of the extension of this work continually into eternity. Actually it is not a double function, but only one, for everything rests on the one act of sacrifice: "but he holds his priesthood permanently, because he continues forever" (Heb. 7:24). Hebrews thus considers the present lordship of Christ as a high priestly office. The idea that Christ intercedes for us in the present is central to Christian belief. It is characteristic also of Paul's writings, and even more so of the farewell discourses of the Gospel of John, particularly of chapter 17, known as the "high priestly prayer."

In summation, we learn from Hebrews that Jesus' priesthood according to the order of Melchizedek is superior to the Levitical priesthood and hence to all other priesthood. The efficacy of his sacrifice, his mediation of the new covenant, the perfect consistency between his human life and cultic activity, his divine impetus, and his direct appointment by God make Jesus High Priest par excellence.

Part IV

God in Christ

HAVING SPOKEN OF JESUS as God's representative on earth, as the one who is God to us and for us, we take the next step, from mortal humanity to eternal divinity, from a divinely commissioned human to a divine hypostasis,[1] a heavenly agent or being sent to earth "for us and our salvation." Such language, of which the New Testament is full, represents an entire range of statements about Jesus as the Christ. These cluster around the concept of preexistence—of an eternal, heavenly being who enters the conditions of our history and humanity to dwell within it from the outside. This is apparently so fundamental a statement of Christian doctrine as virtually to be a definition of "incarnation."

Yet John Knox, writing both as a New Testament scholar and as a Christian, declares flatly, "We can have the humanity without the preexistence and we can have the preexistence without the humanity. There is absolutely no way of having both."[2] If that modern, logical way of thinking is true, it appears to pose an irreconcilable contradiction or an ultimate choice for modern Christology. It may mean that we shall have to think of preexistence as a way of speaking that, like the language of virgin birth, we need no longer take literally or descriptively. However, since such language is deeply embedded in the New Testament presentation of Christ,

---

1. The term "hypostasis" comes from the Greek and refers to the essence or substance of something. In the context in which we will be using it, the term refers to a feature or attribute of God—for example, Wisdom, Spirit, Shekinah (divine glory) or Logos (divine logic or reason)—that comes to acquire a distinct existence apart from God.

2. Knox, *Humanity and Divinity of Christ*, 106.

Part IV: God in Christ

it is worth exploring what the New Testament writers had in mind when they used it, and whether they saw it as the threat to the humanity of Jesus that we see. It is basic, also, to the understanding of how they saw God in Christ. This will be our task in the four sessions that comprise this unit, to see through their eyes rather than ours.

Before doing so, it may be useful to distinguish between the concepts of virgin birth and preexistence. Whereas these have become fused in Christian teaching, originally they were separate and alternative ways of giving expression, in terms of the "second story," to the divine significance of Jesus. Curiously, the New Testament writers who speak most of preexistence (Paul, John, and the author to the Hebrews) say nothing of virgin birth, while the virgin birth story as such says nothing of preexistence. On the contrary, the virgin birth accounts presuppose that Christ is brought into existence as son of Mary and Son of God simultaneously by the creative act of the Holy Spirit (Luke 1:35). In Luke's genealogy, the link between Jesus and God is established not by preexistence but by the line of human descent ("son of Seth, son of Adam, son of God," Luke 3:38).

The New Testament writers combined, in a way that seems to us extraordinary, the story of the virgin birth (which presupposes no human father) and the genealogies (which presuppose Joseph as father), and held them together apparently without tension. We find the same phenomenon with the preexistence and humanity of Christ. The two are set side by side, seemingly without any sense of the antithesis that Knox articulated so acutely. In the case of Paul and John it is possible to reduce, if not to resolve, the dilemma. Of Paul we might say that he had so little interest in the historical Jesus, that he never really felt the problem (but see Gal. 4:4; Rom. 8:3). Of John we might say that he presents a quasi-docetic Christ, whose humanity is little more than a veil (but see John 1:45; 6:42; 7:12; 8:40; 9:24; 10:33). However, in my estimation, neither of these assessments are valid, as a study of the texts makes clear. What is clear is that there is no comparable escape route in the case of the author of Hebrews. Scholars agree that this person stresses the divinity and the humanity of Christ more unequivocally than any other New Testament writer does. Furthermore, the stress on the humanity is such that any hint that Jesus was not completely human ("one who in every respect has been tested as we are," 4:15) would be fatal to the theological argument that requires its insistence.

Yet none of these authors is naïve. Indeed, they are the three most sophisticated theologians in the New Testament. The usual argument is that the dilemma is more acute to modern thinkers. The biblical authors were content, we are told, simply to hold both affirmations as equally valid, with no attempt to harmonize them. They laid the foundations of New Testament Christology, and it was left to others to resolve the tension. Yet this position, particularly for the author of Hebrews, seems untenable. Surely this text, in which we find such a stark combination of opposites—divinity and humanity, preexistence and adoptionism, being and becoming—surely this writer of such subtlety and sensitivity must have appreciated the tension, let alone the contradiction, between the diverse statements made concerning genuine temptation and sinlessness.

Searching to explain this dilemma, New Testament scholar John A. T. Robinson discovered an explanation through inter-religious dialogue with a Buddhist monk on the difference between Hindu and Buddhist understandings of reincarnation. Hinduism speaks of continuity of a person's individual soul (*atman*), which after death reenters the world in a new body (whether animal or human), retaining its identity and theoretically memory of the previous state. The Buddhist concept (of incarnation rather than reincarnation) sees the individual's temporary self (*anatman*) negated and dispersed by death—there being no spiritual or physical continuity of the individual self. The self, reunited with its source, releases emanations into the world to reappear in new configurations or individuals. Thus, the Buddha can become incarnate in and be the source of enlightenment to countless other individuals, and a Tibetan lama can become incarnate in a particular successor, not in the sense that his soul-substance is exclusively reborn in that individual, but in the sense that a special portion of his spirit, as it were, finds embodiment in the one designated to be its inheritor.

We have here an analogy to the biblical concept that "a share of one's spirit" can rest upon another, such as the spirit of Elijah resting upon Elisha (2 Kgs. 2:9–15), or of John the Baptist possessing "the spirit and power of Elijah" (Luke 1:17), not in the sense that he was literally his reincarnation, but in the sense that he embodied his role (see Matt. 11:14; 17:11–13). In addition, one might find here an explanation of how Paul and John see the spirit of Christ released by the death of Jesus to dwell in the body of his followers. Of course, there are very real differences. The Hebraic tradition, and particularly the Christian, sees eternal life not in the negation of the individual in an impersonal nirvana but in the transcendence of the individual in the supra-personal communion of saints.

Part IV: God in Christ

Regarding the preexistence of Christ, is what takes flesh in Jesus an individual divine person or a divine power or activity? According to the presuppositions that would determine the theology of the patristic period, preexistence meant the prior existence in heaven of an individual hypostasis or person who in the fullness of time came into expression (became embodied) in the human nature taken from the Virgin Mary. This person, whom the early and medieval theologians called the Logos, was in their understanding already in the fullest sense the second person of the Trinity. At the incarnation he did not become an individual; he became human, without, of course, ceasing to be divine. As a being from eternity, he did not start like us but became (was made) like us by sharing our life. It is this concept that is so difficult (if not impossible) for modern thinkers to combine with the humanity of Jesus, being, like the rest of us humans, a genuine product of the evolutionary process.

Biblical scholars generally agree that this hypostatization of the Logos in ontological terms stemmed from the personification in ancient Judaism of an attribute of God, along with similar personifications of the Wisdom of God and the Spirit of God. There was also a tradition in late Judaism that God had a being who served as God's principal agent, a kind of vizier to God. In some ancient Jewish texts this is a heavenly or angelic figure, in others, a biblical hero such as Moses, Enoch, or Melchizedek. Whereas the initial claims of early Christians were that God had raised Jesus from death and installed or exalted him as the universal Lord, through whom all now were to be reconciled with God and to whom now all were to submit, this soon entailed the belief in Jesus' preexistence, especially the belief that somehow he was also the one through whom God had created the world and through whom God was now redeeming the world (2 Cor. 5:19). Even more novel was the conviction that God now required Jesus to be given the sort of reverence otherwise reserved for God alone (Phil. 2:9–11; John 5:22–23).

Although we do not know precisely how the earliest believers thought about preexistence and incarnation, likely they adapted this "chief agent" category and posited Jesus in such a capacity. They also expanded this category in novel ways, as we shall see.

Session 8

Spirit/Angel of the Lord

Questions for Individual or Group Reflection: When we think of the Incarnation, we think of a preexistent being incarnate in human flesh. And that brings us to the doctrine of the virgin birth, found in the nativity stories of Matthew and Luke. What role does the virgin birth play in the Gospels? Why is there no account of this event in the earliest (Mark) or the latest Gospel (John)? How do you interpret the virgin birth? How essential is it to your faith? What problems or difficulties does it present to you as a modern person?

Important Biblical Verses and Passages: Joel 2:28–29; Acts 2:16–18; 10:38; Matthew 12:22–29; John 7:39; 20:22; 1 Corinthians 10:4; 15:24, 26, 45; Colossians 2:18; Revelation 20:13–14; 22:8–9; Genesis 1:26–27; 3:5; 6:2–4; 16:7–13; Romans 8:38; Exodus 3:2–6; Galatians 4:14; Philippians 2:6–11; Isaiah 45:22–23; 2 Corinthians 8:9

Technical Words and Concepts: Yahweh; hypostasis; Palestinian Judaism; Hellenistic Judaism; Holy Spirit; "spirit person"; Paraclete; *charismata*; Spirit of Christ; Angel Christology; angelology; angelomorphic language; Nephilim; Angel of Death; Beelzebul; The Evil One; Angel of the Lord; The Christ Hymn; Second Adam; Adam Christology

AS IS WELL KNOWN, during the Intertestamental Period the Jewish emphasis on God's transcendence became increasingly elevated, probably in response to the exilic experience in Babylon. Fearful of offending deity, intentionally or inadvertently, rabbinical Judaism taught that the divine name YHWH (Yahweh) was forbidden to all except the high priest, who should only speak it in the temple in Jerusalem on Yom Kippur. Since the destruction of the temple in AD 70, most Jews never pronounce Yahweh but instead substitute Adonai ("my Lord") during prayer and while reading scripture, and HaShem ("the Name") at other times. We find here evidence of a long standing practice whereby attributes of God became personified, leading to the development in Judaism of the belief in a series of intermediaries that stand between God and the world, mediating God's activity and will to the world. Foremost among these intermediary beings are hypostases (Wisdom, Shekinah, Word) and angels, of which Judaism knows a great many, each with particular individuality.

One of the major features of late pre-Christian and non-Christian Judaism is the widespread speculation about such intermediary beings between God and humanity. In Palestinian Judaism (Jews in ancient Palestine), particularly in its apocalyptic writings, angels were accorded an extensive and significant role as intermediaries between heaven and earth. In Hellenistic Judaism (ancient Jews in the Greco-Roman Diaspora) there was a clear tendency to hypostasize the Name of God (Yoma), the Glory of God (the Shekinah), and the Word of God (Memra), and in rabbinic Judaism the Torah came to be regarded almost as a divine being independent of God. Likewise, this line of argument leads to the question whether the Spirit of God was hypostasized in pre-Christian Judaism, particularly in connection with the role given to Wisdom in the Jewish wisdom literature, where wisdom is said to have existed before the world was made, dwelt with God, and acted as God's agent in creation (Prov. 8:22–31; Sir. 1:4, 9; 24:4; Wis. 8:4–6; 9:9-10).

If pre-Christian Judaism already thought in terms of divine hypostases and intermediaries, did such speculation provide precedent for a Christian doctrine of Jesus as divine mediator? If so, do we have here also an explanation of the doctrine of incarnation, namely, that Jesus Christ was considered as the incarnation of one of these intermediary beings? In this session we will focus on two such possibilities, whether the Spirit of God was regarded as a divine hypostasis at the time of Jesus and whether pre-Christian Jewish angelology enabled some Christians to identify Jesus with an angel. Such questions become pertinent when we recognize how strong was the tendency in early Christianity to think of Jesus in Spirit or angel terms. Paul for one seems to have identified the risen Christ with the Spirit (1 Cor. 15:45) and it is possible to argue that Paul equated Jesus with an angel (see Gal. 4:14), likely with the Angel of the Lord. It is also arguable that the Johannine Paraclete functions as a link between Christ (the first Paraclete) and the Holy Spirit.

Spirit of the Lord

In the Old Testament, the concept of "spirit" (*ruah*) denotes power, whether of the wind, of the breadth of life, or of ecstatic inspiration. In particular, Spirit of God denotes divine power. In some instances there can be talk of a spirit sent by God, but in general it denotes the divine presence on earth (Ps. 139:7; although see 104:30, "when you send forth your spirit" and 143:10: "let your good spirit lead me on a level path"). Generally speaking, Spirit of God means God in effective relationship with and within creation; to experience the Spirit of God is to experience God as Spirit.

In postexilic Judaism, whether in the later books of the Old Testament or in ancient Judaism, we find texts representing the Spirit of God as a distinct hypostasis (see, for example, Isaiah 63:10: "but they rebelled and grieved his holy spirit"). In Wisdom of Solomon the issue becomes more complex, particularly because the author is also connected with Wisdom as hypostasis: "Who has learned your counsel, unless you have given wisdom and sent your holy spirit from on high?" (Wis. 9:17). The rabbinic habit of quoting scripture with the words, "The Holy Spirit says," may be a literary way of emphasizing the inspiration of scripture, a way of speaking indirectly rather than directly of God's action or immanence. In rabbinic writings the Spirit is preeminently the Spirit of prophecy. But this is a role that belongs almost entirely to the past, for in rabbinic thought we find that Haggai, Zechariah, and Malachi were the last of the prophets and that thereafter the Spirit had been withdrawn. There is, nevertheless, the hope that in the end-time the Spirit would be poured out (see Joel 2:28–29; cf. Acts 2:16–18). Yet more striking is the way in which the Spirit is subordinated to Torah: the Spirit inspired Torah, and Torah is the voice of the Spirit, but that also means that the Spirit does not speak apart from Torah. Thus tradition in Judaism is safeguarded. Why the Spirit faded in prominence in ancient Judaism is easily explainable, but whatever the reason, most pre-Christian Jewish writers preferred other concepts and phrases to "Spirit." For the explanation of developments within Christianity we have to look to the inner dynamic of Christianity itself.

Part IV: God in Christ

Some scholars characterize Jesus as "spirit person," meaning he was a deeply mystical individual. This view, however, seriously downplays how Jesus is viewed in the Gospels. Jesus was more than one who mediated the sacred to others. In the Gospels, Jesus is more than deeply religious, more than a spiritual person. No doubt he was deeply spiritual all his life, including as a youngster and adolescent. But according to the Gospels, that changed at his baptism, when the Spirt descended upon him (or into him), and from that moment on he became Spirit-powered, even Spirit-driven. The Synoptics agree that this heavenly anointing was immediately followed by a period of testing, into which Jesus was driven by the Spirit that had come upon him (Mark 1:12; Matt. 4:1; Luke 4:1). Matthew and particularly Luke emphasize that the whole of Jesus' ministry, including his healing and preaching, was in the power of the Spirit; and not only his ministry, but his entire life, beginning with his conception, was a manifestation of the Holy Spirit (Matt. 1:18, 20; Luke 1:35). More noticeable are the developments in John. Like Mark, John describes Jesus' spirit in very human terms (Mark 2:8; 8:12; John 11:33; 13:21)—language avoided by Matthew and Luke. But whereas Matthew and Luke describe Jesus' death in terms of his human spirit (Matt. 27:50; Luke 23:46), John uses a deliberately ambiguous phrase (he "gave up his spirit," 19:30, thereby anticipating the giving of the Spirit in 20:22), which seems to equate Jesus' spirit with the Holy Spirit. Evidently the Fourth evangelist has moved beyond the confines of the earlier Prophet Christology to a higher Logos Christology. Even though John sees Jesus as the incarnation of the eternal Logos (John 1:14), he is unable to dispense with the earlier picture of Jesus as a man indwelt by the Spirit.

There are good grounds for tracing back to Jesus himself several statements that demonstrate his awareness of being indwelt by the Spirit. We may note particularly the Q statement recorded in Matthew 12:28 and Luke 11:20: "But if it is by the Spirit of God that I cast out demons, then the kingdom of God has come to you." This was evidently Jesus' explanation for his success as a healer, and it is in terms of empowerment by the agency of the Spirit of God. Similarly, there is clear evidence that Jesus thought of himself as one in whom Isaiah 61:1–2 was being fulfilled: "The Spirit of the Lord is upon me..." (see Luke 4:21: "Today this scripture has been fulfilled in your hearing"). The same emphasis is also a memory of the earliest Jerusalem community. In Acts 10:38 Peter reminds Cornelius "how God anointed Jesus of Nazareth with the Holy Spirit and with power."

Spirit/Angel of the Lord

If the testimony of the New Testament writers on the relation between the earthly Jesus and the Spirit of God is clear enough, what of the relation between the exalted Christ and the Spirit of God? If the earthly Jesus was indwelt by the Spirit, by his resurrection he become a dispenser of the Spirit. That is the message of Luke-Acts and of John, the only New Testament books to provide such a comparison. In Luke-Acts, Jesus' relation to the Spirit seems to follow three stages: first, at his conception, when he was the creation of the Spirit (Luke 1:35); second, when he was anointed with the Spirit at his baptism (Luke 3:22); and third, when on his exaltation to the right hand of God he was granted the ability to pour the Spirit on others (Acts 2:33). So too the Fourth Gospel presents the glorified Jesus as the one who bestows the Spirit, as the one who sends the Paraclete (John 7:39; 15:26; 20:22). The biblical witness is clear: by virtue of his resurrection and exaltation Jesus the Spirit-filled human becomes Lord of the Spirit, giver of the Spirit.

In 1 Corinthians 15:45 the relation between the exalted Christ and the Spirit is expressed as an equation: "The first man, Adam, became a living being; the last Adam became a life-giving Spirit." The "last Adam" is obviously Christ, but it is equally obvious that the "life-giving Spirit" is the Spirit of God; the parallel with 2 Corinthians 3:6: "the Spirit gives life," puts this beyond dispute. Here too we recall the familiar observation that in Romans 8:9–11 three phrases are more or less synonymous: "Spirit of God dwells in you"; you "have the Spirit of Christ"; and "Christ is in you," just as in 1 Corinthians 12:4–6 "the same Spirit, the same God, and the same Lord" are all equivalent expressions to describe the source of the diverse *charismata* (spiritual gifts).

For Paul, as for the early Christian believers, it would not be true to say that the exalted Christ was the Spirit. "Spirit of Christ" in one sense means the Spirit who indwelt the earthly Jesus, but it must also denote the Spirit of the exalted, living Christ. In Paul's thought the categories "Spirit of God" and "exalted Christ" overlap. Each defines and limits the other, but neither wholly absorbs the other. With John the distinction between the Son as the sender of the Spirit and the Spirit who is sent is not clear either, for he seems to understand the coming of the Spirit as fulfilling the promise of Christ's return (see John 14:15–26) and also to envision the "other Paraclete" as the presence of Jesus when Jesus is absent. While some of the details are ambiguous, the New Testament writers agree that the life of Jesus cannot be adequately understood apart from his indwelling by the

Spirit, and that with the resurrection a transformation took place in the relationship between Jesus and the Spirit. This means that Jesus' risen life is different from that of believers who follow him: the last Adam becomes not just living spirit but life-giving Spirit. Though in some sense the life-giving Spirit and exalted Christ merge in Paul's thinking—the Spirit can now be thought of as the Spirit of Christ—in another sense Spirit and Christ remain distinct. It is presumably this uncertainty that pushed later Christian thought in a Trinitarian direction.

Angel Christology

Initially, the possibility of an Angel Christology, meaning that Jesus pre-existed in angelic form or became exalted to angelic status at his resurrection, seems farfetched. Does orthodox Christian thought allow for such an option? Is such a possibility even biblical? Can angels become human, or humans, angels? In their study of Christology, biblical scholars traditionally gave little if any credence to such ideas; angelology was deemed unimportant and irrelevant for understanding the origin and nature of early Christian views of the risen Christ.

However, we know with certainty that second and third century Christian theologians such as Tertullian, Epiphanius, and Justin Martyr used angelomorphic language (language attributing forms and functions of an angel to a person or being, even though the figure may not be considered to have the nature of an angel) to describe Christ. Nevertheless, in the past most scholars regarded this phenomenon as a historical curiosity from early Christian times, more reflective of the religious vocabulary Jewish Christians inherited from Judaism than of their actual view of Christ. They dismissed the question by pointing to New Testament passages that contrast Jesus with angels (for example, Heb. 1–2; Col. 1:15–20, 1 Peter 3:22; 1 Tim. 3:16; 5:21; Rom. 8:28–29), or that disparage their worship (Col. 2:18; Rev. 22:8–9).

Recent scholarship has taken a new approach, with radically different conclusions. Rather than starting with specific New Testament passages, asking whether Christ is there presented as an angel, scholars are now beginning earlier, examining angelology in the Hebrew Bible, in postexilic Judaism, and with Jewish writings of the New Testament period, to determine whether Jewish angelology assisted early Jewish Christians in coming

Spirit/Angel of the Lord

to terms theologically with their understanding of Christ, particularly his preexistence and/or exaltation.

Scholars now recognize more fully how prohibitions worked in antiquity. Examining passages that prohibit the worship of angels or that contrast Jesus with angels, they discover that these contain evidence not so much of conformity to set standards in behavior or belief, but rather indirect evidence of the propensity of the practice and belief they condemned in the popular culture. Understood in this way, admonitions against the worship of angels in the New Testament likely indicate not the paucity but the prevalence of their worship by ancient Jews and by Jewish Christians. Why establish rules prohibiting activities that no one performs? When we examine the Ten Commandments, for example, we notice that they were delivered, not in a monotheistic context, but in a polytheistic one. The first commandment does not say, "You shall believe that there is only one God." Rather it states, "You shall have no other gods before me." The commandments, as stated, presuppose the existence of other gods, recognizing that they are in fact being worshipped, or at least acknowledged. The commandments do not rule out the existence of the other gods. They simply state that these gods are not to be worshipped.

By the time of Jesus, most Jews considered themselves monotheistic. This did not mean, however, that they did not believe in the existence of other gods. They certainly believed that there were other superhuman divine beings with godlike powers, including angels and archangels. These were viewed as extraordinarily powerful beings, above humans in the scale of existence, yet not the equals of the ultimate God. In the New Testament we find Jewish Christians speaking of these as principalities, dominions, powers, and authorities—unnamed divine beings in the heavenly realm who are active as well on earth (see Eph. 6:12; Col. 1:16). These divinities stood in a hierarchical scale, some more powerful than others. Jewish texts even name certain great angels: Michael, Gabriel, and Raphael.

In ancient Jewish literature (up to and including the first and second centuries AD), we find a proliferation of angelic intercessors and intermediaries, to the extent that they constitute practically an obsession. The foundation for such speculation and fascination seems to be biblical. Passages about divine beings who beget semidivine beings (such as the reference to Nephilim in Genesis 6:2–4), and fascination with mysterious individuals such as Enoch, Abraham, Moses, Jacob, Elijah, and the quasi-human/quasi-divine "son of man" figure in Daniel 7, to whom God gives the kingdoms of the earth, led to a vast literature that told of humans who became angels and angels who became human.

In apocalyptic circles, the natural world is characterized not only as transient, but also by the fact that angels and demons exercise power in it. In general, the view of Jewish eschatology is that the evil of the world comes from demonic powers, and that angelic beings have, with God's permission, established themselves between God and humanity. Among them is the Angel of Death, who despite a sinister office, is thought of as standing in the service of God. In its simplest form, the conception of redemption is that the messianic kingdom puts an end to demonic power.

It is against this background that the New Testament is written. Jesus, as well as Paul and other early Christians, assumed that demons and angels exercise power in the world. The Gospels indicate that Jesus believed the mentally afflicted to be possessed by demons. Not only possession, but also bodily suffering was for Jesus the work of the demons (Matt. 10:1). The fact that Jesus heals the possessed is explained by the Pharisees as his receiving power from Beelzebul, the "ruler of the demons" (Matt. 12:22–24). Jesus, however, explains that the ruler of demons has now lost power, and therefore is obliged to allow Jesus' healing ministry. Jesus compares Satan to a strong man who is overcome and bound by a stronger, and now can only stand by while his house is plundered (Matt. 12:25–29).

Jesus calls the ruler of the powers of evil The Evil One, as we learn from the Lord's Prayer (Matt. 6:13). This Evil One, also called Satan or the devil, is regarded not only as lord of the demons but also as an angelic power opposed to God, as is made clear from the saying about the eternal fire prepared for the devil and his angels (Matt. 25:41). The eschatological perspective also determined the Christian conception of Jesus' death, which is viewed as diminishing the power of evil. Eventually, as heavenly regent, Jesus is expected to return from heaven "with his mighty angels" (2 Thess. 1:7) to terminate the work of Satan, to overthrow all evil, and to end the struggle with the angelic powers (Rom. 8:38). One after another Christ will destroy "every ruler and every authority and power. . . . The last enemy to be destroyed is death" (1 Cor. 15:24, 26). In Revelation 6:8, Death and Hades appear as horsemen, with power to bring harm to one-fourth of the earth. Following the messianic kingdom, Death and Hades are compelled to give up their dead, and are themselves thrown into the "lake of fire" to undergo eternal torment (Rev. 20:13–14). Paul addresses the vanquished

Spirit/Angel of the Lord

Angel of Death in 1 Cor. 15:55 when he declares: "Where, O death, is your victory? Where, O Death, is your sting?"

In ancient Judaism, angels were widely understood to be superhuman messengers of God, standing between God and humans and mediating God's will on earth. In the Hebrew Bible it is striking that various angels sometimes appear on earth in human guise. This includes a figure known as "the Angel of the Lord," who is regarded as the chief angel. In some passages he is identified as God, while in others he appears as a human. An example appears in Genesis 16, where the Lord speaks to Hagar, servant of Sarah, who has been exiled to the wilderness, pregnant with Abraham's child. The Angel of the Lord appears to her and tells her to return to her mistress. The author then surprises us by indicating that the angel is none other than Yahweh, the Lord. Hagar, of course, is astonished that she had "seen God and remained alive after seeing him" (Gen. 16:13).

A similar ambiguity occurs in Genesis 18, this time with Abraham. In 18:1 we are told that "the Lord" appeared to Abraham, but when the episode is narrated, we learn that "three men" come to him. One of these three is later identified explicitly as "the Lord" (Gen. 18:13). Such ambiguity continues in the famous episode of Moses and the burning bush in Exodus 3. In 3:2 we are told that the Angel of the Lord appears to Moses, yet later we are told it is "God" who calls to him out of the bush. There are numerous other texts that describe angels as God and, equally important, as human.

From this evidence New Testament scholar Larry Hurtado formulates a key thesis: "I propose the view that the principal angel speculation and other types of divine agency thinking . . . provided the earliest Christians with a basic scheme for accommodating the resurrected Christ next to God without having to depart from their monotheistic tradition."[1] In other words, if humans could be angels, and angels humans, and if angels could be gods, and if the chief angel could be Yahweh, then to make Jesus divine, one simply needs to think of him as an angel in human form.

While the evidence for Angel Christology in the New Testament is slight, it does exist. Once we take into consideration the widespread evidence that Christian theologians and church leaders worshipped Jesus as angel during the patristic period, even as the preexistent Angel of the Lord that appeared in passages of the Old Testament, and we place such worship against the background of ancient Jewish angelology, certain key passages of the New Testament make perfect sense. For instance, it helps

---

1. Hurtado, *One God, One Lord*, 82.

us to explain Paul's view that the water-providing rock, which follows the Israelites in the wilderness, is actually the preexistent Christ (1 Cor. 10:4). Likewise, it explains Paul's view in 1 Corinthians 15:47 that unlike Adam, who was "from the earth," Christ "is from heaven," meaning that he existed there before he came into this world. It also provides clarification of Revelation 14:14–15, where the reference to "another angel" in verse 15 suggests that the Son of Man of verse 14 (Christ?) is also an angelic being.

As recent christological studies show, a compelling argument can be made that Paul holds to "incarnation" theology, and an examination of neglected passages such as Galatians 4:14 seems to bear this out. Here Paul appears to call Christ an angel, using the construction "but as . . . as" to do so. When he uses that grammatical language elsewhere (see 1 Cor. 3:1; 2 Cor. 2:17), he is not contrasting two things but rather is stating that two things are the same. If Paul understand Jesus to be an angel, as is likely, Jesus is not just any angel but probably God's chief angel, known in the Hebrew Bible as "the Angel of the Lord." If that is so, as New Testament specialist Susan Garrett argues,[2] then "virtually everything Paul says about Christ throughout his letters makes perfect sense. As the Angel of the Lord, Christ is a preexistent being who is divine; he can be called God; and he is God's manifestation on earth in human flesh."[3]

Angel Christology in Paul's "Christ Hymn" (Philippians 2:6–11)

When we apply this information to the "Christ Hymn," an early poem cited by Paul in Philippians 2:6–11, things fit beautifully. When it says in Philippians 2:6 that Jesus was "in the form of God," this need not mean that Jesus was the equal of God the Father, but rather that he was "Godlike" or divine, like the chief angel (the Angel of the Lord) referred to in Genesis 16:7, 13; 18:1—19:1; and Exodus 3:2. As New Testament scholar Charles Gieschen states, this Angel of the Lord is either the "visible manifestation" of God or a distinct figure, separate from God, who is bestowed with God's own authority.[4] If this is what Paul believed about Jesus, that he is the figure who appeared to Hagar, Abraham, and Moses, who is sometimes called "God" in the Hebrew Bible, then that helps to explain the meaning of the final

---

2. Garrett, *No Ordinary Angel*, 11.
3. Ehrman, *How Jesus became God*, 253.
4. Gieschen, *Angelomorphic Christology*, 68; Ehrman, ibid., 57.

two stanzas of the "Christ Hymn" (Phil. 2:10–11). There we find statements that allude to Isaiah 45:22–23, in a context where the prophet Isaiah states explicitly that it is to God alone that "every knee shall bow and every tongue confess." In the Philippians poem, Jesus is granted the status and honor and glory of Almighty God himself. If that is Paul's Christology, it is exceedingly "high." This is not to say Jesus is the Father, since the Father exalts him. And Jesus is definitely not "equal" with God in his preexistent state, for after his death he is exalted even higher than before his act of obedience, though still not the equal of God (see 1 Cor. 15:28).

It is important to note that the preceding interpretation, while intriguing, is not the standard explanation to the "Christ Hymn." It is introduced as a possibility because it supports our theme and because it supplements other interpretations. The ongoing scholarly debate over the interpretation of this passage revolves primarily around two explanations, the first viewing Christ as a preexistent divine being, who gave up his deity (his "equality with God") at the incarnation, when he came to be born as a human and to die for the sin of the world. It is called the "kenotic theory" because Christ's obedience involved "emptying himself" (the Greek word *kenosis* denotes "to empty or divest oneself"). For that reason Christ was exalted to a degree higher than before.

The second explanation views Jesus as a "second Adam." Here Jesus is neither preexistent nor divine but fully human. Unlike the first Adam, who was made in the "image of God" (Gen. 1:26–27) but who succumbed to the temptation to "be like God" (Gen. 3:5), Jesus, the perfect human, reversed the course of human affairs brought about by the first Adam, removing the curse of sin (see Paul's Second Adam Christology found in Romans 5:12–21). Taking this latter interpretation, the second half of the poem can be interpreted in an "adoptionist" way, as Christ's exaltation at his resurrection, or humanistically, as a glory which he enjoys in virtue of his uniquely *human* status.

Of the two explanations, the first seems most likely, as a close reading of the text makes clear. That the poem's opening statement envisions Christ as a preexistent divine being rather than Jesus in his human state is supported by two related arguments, one textual and the other circumstantial. In the first line of verse 6, Jesus is described as having existed "in the form of God" (*morphē theou*), a phrase whose meaning is greatly debated. Is the phrase synonymous with "image of God" (*eikōn theou*), the expression used to characterize Adam (humankind) in the Genesis creation account (Gen. 1:27)? The answer is clearly negative.

The term *morphē* ("form") is never used of Adam or of humankind in the Septuagint (the Greek translation of relevant Genesis passages), nor is it used in any allusion to Adam in the New Testament or in any other Jewish or Christian text that contains an allusion to Adam. So the alleged use of *morphē theou* to link Jesus with Adam in Philippians 2:6 "would be a singular case without any analogy or precedent."[5] Furthermore, in Philippians 2:6–8, there is not a single verbal allusion to the Genesis creation or temptation accounts. Nowhere in Genesis or in references to Adam in any other text is Adam linked with the serpent's statement in Genesis 3:5 that eating the fruit of the forbidden tree will make the humans "like God/gods." In the Genesis passage the serpent's insinuation is made to Eve, but no such references to Adam can be found there or in subsequent passages. In short, if the intention of the Philippians hymn is to allude to Adam or to refer to Jesus as the perfect or ideal Adam, such allusion is particularly inept.

In Philippians 2:6 Jesus' "being in the form of God" is clearly intended to contrast with his "taking the form of a slave" in 2:7. If the latter represents his status and mode as an earthly human figure, then "being in the form of God" surely is best taken to represent a different and prior mode of being much higher than human.

The notion of Jesus' *heavenly* preexistence underlying the opening words of Philippians 2:6 is corroborated by the idea of Jesus' preexistence and "incarnation" in 2 Corinthians 8:9, where Paul tells his audience that though Jesus "was rich, yet for your sakes he became poor, so that by his poverty you might become rich." It is precisely this reflection of God's glory, which is Christ's by nature, that all God's children, as Christ's fellow-heirs, are destined to share by being "glorified with him" (Rom. 8:17).

---

5. Hurtado, *How on Earth*, 99.

Session 9

Judge (Son of Man, Part III)

Question for Individual or Group Reflection: When you think of Jesus as eschatological Judge, do you tend to view this role as essentially accomplished in the past (that is, during his earthly ministry), as ongoing in the present, or as strictly a future activity on his part (that is, at the end of history as we know it)? Explain your answer.

Important Biblical Verses and Passages: Mark 8:38; 13:26–27; 14:62; Matthew 25:31–32; John 3:13; 5:25–29; 6:62; Daniel 7:1–28; 2 Corinthians 5:10; Acts 10:42; 17:31; 2 Timothy 4:1, 8; Luke 12:8

Technical Words and Concepts: eschatological Son of Man; Hasidim; Seleucids; Hellenization

BECAUSE OF ITS PROMINENT use in the Synoptic Gospels, the title Son of Man is one of the most important christological titles in the New Testament. This designation is significant because according to the Gospels it is the only title Jesus applied to himself. The term occurs eighty-one times in the Gospels, sixty-nine of them in the Synoptics. And with two exceptions, Luke 24:7 (where the angel quotes Jesus' words) and John 12:34 (where the people ask Jesus regarding his use of the term)—neither of which are true exceptions since both reflect Jesus' own usage—all of the occurrences are attributed to Jesus himself.

It is important to recognize that the Gospel writers did not use this title to express their own faith in Jesus. They were content to recognize him by the messianic designation "Christ." In addition, there is little evidence that there was any extensive use of Son of Man as a christological title on the part of Christians during the first century. Later on, church theologians of the patristic and medieval period would use the term as a way of referring to Christ's humanity as opposed to his divinity, or to his being the Son of God. However, in the first century, the title does not seem to have been useful in preaching the good news. It does not appear in creedal or liturgical formulas. It is almost completely absent in Acts and is found nowhere in the letters of Paul. Apart from the Gospels, the title appears only in the quotation of Psalm 8:46 in Hebrews 2:6–8, on the lips of the dying Stephen in Acts 7:56, and in the parabolic description of the exalted Jesus in Revelation 1:13 and 14:14. It is only in the latter three cases that it is used as a christological title outside of the Gospels. This title, then, is the designation that Jesus used when he spoke about himself, and he did so because it embraced the totality of his mission as no other.

As we have seen, Jesus referred to the Son of Man in three contexts, each with its own distinct meaning. He used this designation of (1) his earthly work and its humble nature (for example, Mark 2:10, 28 and parallels; Matt. 11:19; Luke 9:58); (2) his suffering role, coming passion, and resurrection (Mark 9:9, 12; 14:21, 41); and (3) his future exaltation or work of judgment (Mark 8:38; 13:26–27 and parallels; Matt. 24:27; 25:31–32; John 5:27). On the lips of Jesus, Son of Man functioned less as a title than of how he viewed his ministry. It was not so much about Jesus' identity but about his activity, what he accomplishes. In this session we focus on the third, eschatological, context.

Two factors put matters in perspective. The first is that the Son of Man sayings as they now stand in the Gospels clearly refer to Jesus as the Son of Man, and not to some second person or being. That does not mean that Jesus necessarily saw his role as cosmic redeemer or vindicating judge, but that this is how the evangelists depicted him. The second factor is that the Son of Man tradition in the Gospels contains clear allusions to the vision of Daniel 7. For the moment, then, we turn to the Old Testament background of the title.

The Son of Man in the Book of Daniel

For our purposes, there are essentially three passages in the Old Testament that employ the term Son of Man in a way that elucidates New Testament usage: Psalms 8, 80, and Daniel 7. In Psalm 8:4–6 Son of Man refers to

Judge (Son of Man, Part III)

human individuals as mortals, weak and insignificant, yet exalted by God to the position of vice-regents over God's earthly affairs. In Psalm 80:17–19 the Son of Man ("the one whom you made strong for yourself") is the nation Israel, viewed as a solitary human, humiliated until made strong by God. For early Christians the titular use of Son of Man as a transcendent and glorified redeemer figure seemed most applicable to Jesus in his saving role or in his eschatological role as coming judge. Hence the centrality of Daniel 7.

The book of Daniel is an apocalyptic writing, set in the sixth century BC but not actually written until the middle of the second century BC, during the tumultuous period following the breakup of Alexander the Great's kingdom. While the author of the book remains unknown, he belonged to a resistance movement known as the Hasidim ("faithful ones"), a group of nonconformists who resisted the Seleucid policy of Hellenization, a coercive policy that forced Jews to compromise or abandon key distinctive beliefs and practices.

The book of Daniel consists of two evenly divided halves. The first six chapters contain six accounts of Jewish heroes exiled to the Babylonian court in the sixth century BC. The function of these chapters is to provide role models for members of the Hasidim. The last six chapters of the book contain four of Daniel's visions, functioning to provide assurance to the Hasidim that the future is in God's hands and that all will end well for God's faithful remnant. Chapter 7 is the book's foremost chapter, the fulcrum on which the rests pivots.

This chapter contains a vision of four beasts, described as four successive empires: the Babylonian (a lion with eagle's wings), the Median (a bear with three ribs in its mouth), the Persian (a leopard with four wings and four heads), and the Hellenistic or Seleucid empire (the ten horns refer to Seleucid kings and the little horn "speaking arrogantly" is the tyrant Antiochus Epiphanes, who ruled over the Jewish homeland). The "Ancient One," presiding over the heavenly council at the last judgment, sentences the fourth kingdom to destruction; the other three, whose rule had not been so evil, are deprived of their dominion and permitted to survive for a time (Dan. 7:9–12). Then, with the clouds of heaven, in contrast to the beasts' origin from the depths of the "great sea" (the mythical source of powers hostile to God's creation; cf. Rev. 13:1; 21:1), comes "one like a human being" (literally, "one like a son of man," Dan. 7:13), that is, a figure that appears human but is clearly more than human.

Part IV: God in Christ

The figure "one like a son of man," often taken to symbolize Israel, is sometimes also identified with the archangel Michael, the "prince of Israel" in Daniel 10–12 (see 10:13, 21, and 12:1; for "son of man" see also 10:16, 18). In this case the expression "the holy ones" of 7:18, 21, 22, and 23 would likely be the angelic host, and the "people of the holy ones" (7:27) the Jewish people, or at least those who are faithful to God's covenant (see 12:3).[1] In ancient Judaism, however, the most common interpretation viewed this heavenly figure to symbolize Israel ("the holy ones of the Most High," 7:25, 27). Instead of a temporal kingdom, Israel would receive an everlasting and universal dominion, to be inaugurated after "a time, two times, and half a time" (7:25; see 12:7; cf. Rev. 12:14) of the little horn, a cryptic reference to the three and a half years when Antiochus Epiphanes persecuted the Jews (167–164 BC).

Eventually in Jewish circles, Daniel's Son of Man figure came to be understood as a future deliver, a cosmic judge of the earth, who would defeat God's enemies and vindicate those who had remained faithful to him. Nowhere is this figure described more fully than in the book of 1 Enoch. This noncanonical work is a collection of various texts spliced together by later editors. One portion of the book, called the Book of the Watchers, comprises chapters 1–36. Typically dated to the third century BC, the book contains an exposition of the episode about the sons of God in Genesis 6:1–4. Unlike the figures in Genesis 6, here they are explicitly called "angels." The Son of Man features prominently in a different portion of 1 Enoch, known as the Similitudes (chapters 37–71). In this section, dated to the first century AD and therefore contemporary with the New Testament, the Son of Man is identified as a divine being. We are told that because he is God's chosen one, the one who reveals God's wisdom to the righteous and holy, who will be "saved in his name" (48:2–7), all the earth will worship him. At the end of time, when the dead are resurrected, it is he who will sit on God's throne and function as cosmic judge of the earth.

Whatever the initial meaning of the Son of Man figure in Daniel 7, whether understood along individual lines or in a corporate sense, is not principally our concern. What is important is that Jesus adopted the term specifically because it was ambiguous. We can be certain that Daniel 7 was the source upon which Jesus based his understanding. This is evident in his reference to Daniel's "desolating sacrilege" (Dan. 9:27; 11:31; 12:11) in his Mount of Olives discourse (Matt. 24:15; Mark 13:14) and in his allusion to

---

1. Collins, *King and Messiah*, 78.

the imagery of Daniel 7:13 in that same discourse (Mark 13:26 and parallels), as well as later in his reply before the Sanhedrin (Mark 14:62 and parallels), all with explicit reference to the Son of Man. Evidently, what Jesus meant to say in using this expression of himself was that he was the one in whom this vision of Daniel was fulfilled.

Jesus as the Eschatological Son of Man

In Jewish texts such as 1 Enoch as well as in the New Testament, the primary eschatological function of the coming Son of Man is that of judgment. This is also the Son of Man's function in the important section about the last judgment of the "sheep and goats" in Matthew 25:31-46. In Mark 8:38 and parallels, the Son of Man is both judge and at the same time witness against those who have been ashamed of him. The transference to Jesus of judgment, which the New Testament often ascribes to God (1 Thess. 3:13; Rom. 3:5; 14:10), is directly connected with the Son of Man concept.

The concept of Jesus as Judge is central to the New Testament. In Paul's letters it is clear that "all must appear before the judgment seat of Christ" (2 Cor. 5:10; cf. 1 Cor. 4:5). Jesus also appears as Judge in the parables of Matthew 25:1-13 and 25:14-30. In Acts 10:42 Jesus bears the title "Judge of the living and the dead." Second Timothy 4:8 calls him the "Righteous Judge," and Acts 17:31 connects the former view that God exercises judgment directly with the view that Christ is Judge of the world. From these and other texts (see 2 Tim. 4:1; Acts 10:42; 1 Pet. 4:5) emerges the formula found in the Apostles' Creed: "he shall come to judge the quick and the dead." The function of Jesus as Judge is important in the Gospel of John (note the eschatological reference to the "last day" in John 12:48, along with other references to the "last day" in John 6:39, 40, 44, 54). The eschatological character of Jesus' judgment follows from John 5:27, particularly because the Judge is the Son of Man.

The way in which Jesus took over the idea of judgment shows how he interpreted the Son of Man's role. He understood about the Son of Man in Daniel 7 something often missed or overlooked, that when the writer of Daniel speaks of the glorification of the Son of Man, he means glorification and vindication *through suffering*. According to Daniel 7:21, the "horn" from the fourth beast "made war with the holy ones [a synonym for the Son of Man] *and prevailed* over them"; also in 7:25, this horn [king] "shall wear out the holy ones . . . and they shall be given into his power" for a time. It is significant that Daniel 7, the one passage in pre-Christian Jewish literature that employs the term Son of Man (lit. "one like a son of man") as a title, affirms humiliation and suffering together with vindication and glory. This double meaning of the Son of Man's role is of immense significance for its usage in the New Testament. No doubt Jesus adopted the term Son of Man because of its ambiguous nature, revealing as well as concealing. The title combined elements of suffering and of glory, both aspects of Jesus' ministry. Reaching back to this enigmatic Son of Man figure, Jesus sought to interpret his identity and ministry in terms of glorification and suffering, as fulfillment of Daniel's vision. What he meant by using the Son of Man title was that he viewed himself as that one in whom this vision was realized.

The way in which Jesus took over and reshaped the idea of judgment shows that, while preserving its eschatological framework, he closely connected judgment with the suffering work of the Servant of God, which atones for sin. In addition, the foundation on which judgment is accomplished by the Son of Man is how humans treat one another, particularly the weak and marginalized (Matt. 25:31-46). We see here how the New Testament deepens the concept of the Son of Man as Judge: Jesus is both the representative Suffering Servant of God and the future Judge of humanity.

The answer to the important question whether Jesus ascribed the judging function of the Son of Man to himself within the framework of his earthly ministry seems thus to be answerable in the affirmative. Yet when we examine the Son of Man references in the Gospels, many appear to have a futuristic, eschatological application. When we deal with the New Testament, however, we must guard against such linear, one-dimensional application. For it is clear that Jesus' conviction that in his person the kingdom of God had been introduced must have had significant consequences for his self-understanding as the Son of Man. Because he regarded his coming as inaugurating the end time, concepts that had an exclusively eschatological (futurist) character in Judaism must be transferred into the present when applied to Jesus. Therefore the Jewish belief that the Son of Man would come only at the end of time should not deter us, particularly since, according to Jesus' teaching, the end was already being introduced. His answer to John the Baptist in Matthew 11:4-6 shows this clearly: "Go and tell John what you hear and see . . ." So also his saying in Matthew 12:28: "if it is by the Spirit of God that I cast out demons, then the kingdom of God has come to you."

Judge (Son of Man, Part III)

In view of this, Jesus can speak of himself as the Son of Man already during his earthly ministry. Such an understanding of the Son of Man, as a human operating in an ordinary human environment, is unique to Jesus, for it is foreign to Judaism as well as to the rest of first-century Christianity. The combination of vicarious suffering and atonement, two concepts decisive for Jesus self-consciousness, appears classically in Mark 10:45: "The Son of Man came not to be served but to serve, and to give his life a ransom for many." This view, basic to Mark, the Gospel closest to the historical Jesus, clearly reflects original "Jesus material." Mark 8:31 also expresses this connection, combining the Son of Man title with the Suffering Servant of God: "the Son of Man must undergo great sufferings, and be rejected by the elders, the chief priest, and the scribes, and be killed."

Despite the debate over the Son of Man sayings in the Gospels, whether they originated with Jesus or not, and whether all three classes of "Son of Man" sayings are applicable to him, a good case can be made that the use of the term goes back to Jesus. Despite editorial reworking, Jesus was responsible for the title, filling it with his own meanings. While some scholars believe that the third, eschatological category, was not used by Jesus as a self designation but rather was attributed to Jesus by early Christians, that does not seem likely. There is little evidence in the sayings of Jesus that he anticipated some other eschatological figure to follow him, or some heavenly advocate whose role would be decisive in the final judgment. The same holds true for the rest of the first-century Christian tradition, which shows no knowledge of a heavenly Son of Man with whom the risen Jesus could be identified, despite the many other figures readily featured in Jewish eschatological hope (an angel, Michael, Enoch, et cetera).

Nevertheless, some sayings in the Synoptics about the coming Son of Man imply a certain differentiation between this figure and Jesus. Thus, Luke reports Jesus as declaring: "Everyone who acknowledges me before others, *the Son of Man* will also acknowledge before the angels of God" (Luke 12:8). While this version indicates a unity of function between Jesus and the Son of Man, at the same time it introduces some differentiation between the two figures. Matthew's version modifies the Q saying to read: "Everyone who acknowledges me before others, *I* also will acknowledge before my Father in heaven" (Matt. 10:32). While scholars argue that Luke has preserved the original form of the saying (note also the unique Matthean material in 19:28, where the connection between Jesus and the eschatological Son of Man is implied), the differentiation makes sense once we recognize the tension present in the eschatological framework.

There is no question that in the Gospels as they now stand the term Son of Man is a title, and for a particular individual: Jesus. Nor is it possible to dispute the influence of Daniel 7 on the Synoptic Son of Man references. One final question remains, however: In light of the fact that in the apocalyptic literature of ancient Judaism the Son of man is thought of as preexistent,[2] did the early Christian identification of Jesus as the Son of Man also imply his preexistence? Once we ask that question, particularly in connection with sayings in the Synoptics that allude to Daniel 7:13, we recognize that all refer to the future state and role of the Son of Man. In not one instance where Jesus is portrayed as the Danielic Son of Man is there any implication that Jesus is thereby understood as a preexistent being hidden in heaven prior to his manifestation on earth.

When we look beyond the Synoptic Gospels we do find reference to the preexistence of the Son of Man in at least two sayings found in the Fourth Gospel: John 3:13: "No one has ascended into heaven except the one who descended from heaven, the Son of Man" ; John 6:62: "What if you were to see the Son of Man ascending to where he was before?"; and perhaps also in John 1:51: "You will see heaven opened and the angels of God ascending and descending upon the Son of Man." While it is clear that preexistence is a peculiarity of the Johannine Christology, scholars have found little if any influence of Daniel 7:13 here. The decisive feature in these passages is the descending/ascending motif, which is distinctive of the Fourth Gospel and which cannot be linked with the Son of Man concept prior to the Fourth Gospel.

We conclude that preexistence in the Johannine Son of Man sayings is uniquely Johannine. While the thought of the Son of Man as a preexistent heavenly figure does appear in the New Testament, though only clearly in John's Gospel, that supposition does not seem to have emerged in Christian (or possibly in Jewish) circles prior to the end of the first century AD.

---

2. The Silmilitudes of Enoch (1 Enoch 37–71) provide the strongest evidence for the existence of a Jewish belief in a preexistent divine individual called the Son of Man.

Session 10

Wisdom of God

Question for Individual or Group Reflection: Building on your understanding of the identity and role of Wisdom in the Jewish wisdom literature, what do you believe the writer of Matthew's Gospel had in mind when he characterized Jesus as "something greater than Solomon" in Matthew 12:42?

Important Biblical Verses and Passages: Proverbs 8:1—9:6; Matthew 11:19; 12:42; 13:52; 23:8–10; 28:18; Philippians 2:6–11; Colossians 1:15–20; 1 Timothy 3:16; Hebrews 1:2–4; John 1:1–18

Technical Words and Concepts: divine wisdom; personified Wisdom; Wisdom Christology; gematria; Emmanuel; Christological Hymns; *logos*

THE IDEA THAT WISDOM could be a divine hypostasis—an aspect of God that is a distinct being yet nonetheless is God—is rooted in a fascinating passage of the Hebrew Bible, Proverbs 8. Here Wisdom speaks, and we learn that she existed before creation, that she was the first thing God created, that she acted as God's agent in creation, and that she dwelt with God and revealed God. Elsewhere we learn that she appeared on earth and lived among human beings (Sir. 24:1–12). As a female figure, Wisdom invites to her feast those who are not yet wise (Prov. 9:1–6). In the Wisdom of Solomon, in a brilliant passage celebrating the divine Wisdom (Wis. 7:22b—8:1), the writer connects Wisdom with God's Spirit, Power, and Glory: Here Wisdom is said to be "a reflection of eternal light, a spotless mirror of the working of God, and an image of his goodness" (Wis. 7:26).

Part IV: God in Christ

These passages could be read metaphorically, as ways of celebrating God and God's creation, but some Jewish readers interpreted them literally and understood Wisdom to be a divine hypostasis, an actual being alongside God that was also an expression of God.

In his attempt to bridge the first-century gulf between Jesus the popular preacher from Galilee and the preexistent Logos (viewed as co-creator with God and mediator of eternal life), biblical scholar Martin Hengel points to Jewish Wisdom—the "mother of high Christology"—as the decisive link.

To interpret Christ, the New Testament uses various strands from the Jewish wisdom tradition. Like Wisdom, Jesus is associated with God's Spirit whom God sends to the prophets and the pious, and who inspires and instructs them; like Wisdom in Sirach 24, God sends Christ to Israel that she might take up her dwelling among God's people; like Wisdom, Christ also preexisted all things and dwelt with God (John 1:1–2, 18). The lyric Jewish language about Wisdom being the breadth of the divine power, reflecting the divine glory, mirroring light, and being an image of God, appears echoed in christological passages such as 1 Corinthians 1:17–18, 24–25, Hebrews 1:3, John 1:9, and Colossians 1:15. Like Wisdom, the New Testament applies to Christ the language about Wisdom's cosmic significance as God's agent in the creation of the world (John 1:3, 10; 1 Cor. 8:6; Col. 1:16; Heb. 1:2). All Wisdom's functions—preexistence, mediation of creation, mission into the world, means of revelation—become consistently applied to Jesus Christ.

At various points in the development of the Jewish wisdom tradition stress was placed on the hiddenness of wisdom, and therefore on the need for it to be revealed. It may be that in early Judaism the personification of wisdom arose, at least in part, to cope with and make clear not only that Wisdom is hidden, but also that God intends to reveal it. During the biblical era, no human, either before or after Jesus, identified himself or herself with personified Wisdom. Early Jewish followers of Jesus, having viewed him as both sage and revealer of God's will for humanity, pondered the possibility of going one step further, identifying him as the embodiment of divine Wisdom on earth. Bearing in mind Jesus as prophetic sage, there were times in the prophetic literature when prophets presented themselves as living symbols of God's message for God's people. In this regard, Jesus may be understood not merely as a teacher of wisdom but as Wisdom in person. With respect to the kingdom of God, the dominant aspect of his teaching, Jesus was not content to merely announce its coming, for in a profound way he believed he embodied it. The portrayal of the role of Jesus in the earliest authentic Gospel material is much like the role of Wisdom as described by one of Jesus' near contemporaries: "Wisdom rescues from troubles those who served her . . . she guided him on straight paths; she showed him the kingdom of God, and gave him knowledge of holy things" (Wis. 10:9-10).

This brings us to Matthew 11:28-30, a text with both a precedent and a close parallel in Sirach 6:23-31. In Sirach it is clearly Wisdom's yoke the disciple is to put on, whereas in Matthew it is Jesus' yoke. The authenticity of the Matthean saying must be seriously considered, in view of the fact that the idea of Jesus as Wisdom can be found in most strata of the Synoptic sources (Matthew 12:42 and Luke 11:31 are taken from "Q"; Luke 21:15 from "L"; and Matthew 11:19 from "M"). If Jesus saw himself as a sage, these passages suggest that he did not see himself as just another sage, or even as the final Jewish sage, but rather that he maintained a transcendent self-understanding.

Matthew's Wisdom Christology

The Gospel of Matthew, more than any other book in the New Testament, represents Jesus as Wisdom incarnate. Matthew's Wisdom Christology is evident throughout, but especially at critical junctures such as the Sermon on the Mount (Matt. 5-7), where Jesus is identified as the true Torah, much as the writer characterizes Wisdom as Torah incarnate in Sirach 24. In terms of the Jewish Christian debate on the nature and location of Wisdom, Matthew's approach epitomized the Christian answer: Wisdom is found in Jesus and his teaching.

Matthew's exalted portrayal of Jesus is substantiated by how people relate to Jesus. In this Gospel, insiders (disciples) regularly address Jesus as Lord (8:21, 25; 14:28; 16:22), a term for Yahweh in the Old Testament, whereas when Jewish leaders or strangers address Jesus, it is generally as rabbi or teacher (8:19; 12:38; 19:16; 22:16, 24, 36). Even more revealing is the fact that only Judas among the disciples calls Jesus rabbi (26:25, 49), and only after he is prepared to betray Jesus. What this indicates is that for Matthew it is inadequate simply to call Jesus a rabbi or teacher. Others may call him teacher, which he is, but Jesus alone is the master teacher, as 23:8-10 makes plain: "for you have one teacher, and you are all students. . . . Nor are you to be called instructors, for you have one instructor, the Messiah." This passage exhibits Matthew's Christology most distinctly, for it is uniquely Matthean; the Markan and Lukan parallels have nothing similar (cf. Mark 12:38–40; Luke 20:45–47).

Matthew's Gospel was written by a Jewish Christian for a predominantly Jewish Christian audience. It was probably written from Antioch, a Syrian port city, where many Jews relocated after the Jewish War with Rome in AD 70 and where the followers of Jesus were first called Christians (Acts 11:26). In early Christianity there was urgency to legitimate itself as offering the true interpretation of Jesus, Judaism, Torah, and related matters. To this end early Jewish Christians set up schools or academic settings where teachings of and about Jesus as well as new interpretations of Torah were introduced and passed on to a generation of Christians who had neither been in contact with the historical Jesus nor involved with his earthly ministry. Schools in early Judaism had been established to conserve religious heritage, and it is likely that this conservation was the primary purpose of early Christian schools as well. Matthew's community is believed to have been organized as such a "school" or academy, and it is quite likely that the author of Matthew was a scribe writing for a particular element within that community, a select group trained as scribes and teachers tasked with the ongoing study, transmission, and interpretation of the Jesus tradition.

Among the various attempts to highlight what is distinctive about Matthew's portrayal of Jesus, one of the most popular is to view Jesus as the new Moses, delivering five discourses, the first from a mount. While the depiction has some merit, Matthew nowhere specifically likens Jesus to Moses, and in the series of comparisons in 12:6, 41, and 42, where the evangelist speaks of one present who is greater than the temple, or Jonah, or Solomon, there is no reference to Moses. It seems clear that the author is more interested in how Jesus is unlike Moses as in ways he is like him. Perhaps Matthew's most distinctive christological contribution is to depict Jesus as "Wisdom of God," the messianic Son of David (1:1) like unto but greater than Solomon (12:42), whose intimacy with the Father is modelled in part on the way Wisdom and God are described in earlier sapiential literature.[1]

The starting point for Matthew's christological understanding is the statement, "something greater than Solomon is here" in 12:42, a Q passage (see Luke 11:31). Whereas Luke ends the pericope with the Jonah analogy,

---

1. Witherington, *Jesus the Sage*, 350.

"something greater than Jonah is here" (11:32), Matthew closes the segment with the Solomon analogy, depicting Jesus as superior to Solomon, the biblical figure most representative of divine Wisdom. In the following chapter (13:1–58), Matthew inserts a collection of narrative *meshalim*, using traditional wisdom genre to underscore that Jesus is God's sage, speaking God's Wisdom. At the climactic point in the chapter, just before the saying about the scribe, Jesus asks his disciples if they have understood all he has said, and like wise learners, their response is an unequivocal "Yes" (13:51; cf. Mark 4:13). In light of the Gospel's conclusion, where the disciples desert Jesus and even after the resurrection some continue to doubt (28:16), it seems clear that Matthew wants to stress that for all disciples, whether of Jesus or of Matthew, the process of growing in faith and understanding continues, even after Easter.

If Jesus is greater than Solomon, a royal person who personifies divine wisdom, then one would expect an extraordinary birth, with signs in the heavens announcing his coming, a visit by royal counselors or seers, and involvement in power struggles with other so-called kings; and that is precisely what one finds in Matthew 2: a great star, visits by magi, royal presents fit for a king, and conflict with Herod.

The genealogy in chapter 1 is equally revealing, for there we learn that Jesus is the "Son of David" (1:1; Joseph is said to be the son of David in 1:20). Matthew also organizes his genealogy according to a pattern of three sets of fourteen generations, as he states in 1:17. In order to create this symmetry, he takes some liberties, relying on Jewish gematria, whereby Hebrew letters equal numbers (the letters for the name "David" add up to the number fourteen). In Judaism the name of David was connected with messianic titles and promises, thus enabling Matthew to construct a genealogy for Jesus that supports his contention that the royal birth of Jesus signified the coming of Emmanuel, which means "God with us" (1:23), thereby fulfilling Isaiah's prophecy (Isa. 7:14).

The sapiential character of the Sermon on the Mount (Matt. 5–7), which might be better called the Teaching on the Mount, is well known. Suffice it to say that this material consists primarily of wisdom material, including beatitudes (5:3–12); metaphors to promote virtuous deeds (5:16); instructions to uphold Torah and its commandments (5:17–20); practical teaching on self-control (5:21–30); prohibition of oaths and revenge (5:33–42); exhortation to love of enemies (5:43–48); exhortation to almsgiving, prayer, and fasting (6:1–18); advice on wealth, health, and loyalties (6:19–23); nature wisdom meant to produce a less anxious lifestyle (6:24–34); prohibitions of judging others and of profanations (7:1–6); and exhortations to seek the will of God, obey the Golden Rule, follow the narrow path, avoid false teachers, and to maintain integrity in word and deed (7:7–23). The discourse ends with the parable of two foundations, which, like the two ways in the book of Proverbs, is typical wisdom imagery. While these topics represent conventional wisdom, Matthew's Jesus is not a conventional teacher, a fact he stresses in the six antithetical sayings in 5:21–48, where the Greek introductory formula adds the emphatic personal pronoun *egō* ("I") to *de legō* ("I say"), meaning, "But I, I say unto you," thereby accentuating the authority of Jesus, and at the conclusion of the discourse, where Jesus' authority is distinguished from that of the early Jewish scribes (7:29). The contrast is between Jesus, who has independent authority (the Teacher), and all other teachers and authorities. For Matthew, Jesus is no mere scribe: he is teacher par excellence, greater and wiser than Solomon.

Matthew 11 is crucial for evaluating the intent of the evangelist. There we are told that "wisdom (i.e. Jesus) is vindicated by her deeds" (11:19). Using parallels and allusions with Israel's wisdom tradition, this passage sums up the first ten chapters of the Gospel. People are offended by Jesus (cf. 11:6), for he associates with tax collectors, sinners, and other undesirable elements of society (11:19), and even John the Baptist wonders about Jesus' identity (11:2–3). Their concerns are answered in 11:19: Jesus is Wisdom, God's agent who reveals God's ways but is often rejected. The book of Proverbs speaks of Wisdom in similar ways: as being refused (1:24–25), as associating with an unlikely audience (1:22–23), and as inviting scandalous guests to her feast (9:4–6). Another wisdom motif appears in Matthew 11:28–30, using words about Jesus found in Sirach 6:23–31 and 51:26. In chapter 12, people again ponder Jesus' identity. Matthew's answer is found in 12:42; there, the ultimate witness is the Queen of Sheba, who heard the wisdom of Solomon and was amazed. The metaphor in 13:52 indicates that Jesus, as the Wisdom of God, embodies the entire Jewish wisdom tradition, uniting conventional and unconventional wisdom, traditional with new.

Chapter 22:41–46 is a pivotal passage in Matthew's Christology. Here one learns that it is not enough to say merely that the Messiah is Son of David, for proclaiming Jesus to be the Son of David falls short of the truth. As the quotation from Psalm 110:1 indicates, Jesus is understood to be David's Lord. If Jesus is by implication claiming to be David's Lord (22:45), then surely he must be seen in more transcendent categories than sage, teacher, or even Son of David. According to Matthew, two ascriptions fit such a claim: Son of God and Wisdom. Like Solomon, Jesus is son of David, only greater. Like Solomon, Jesus is the embodiment of Wisdom; indeed, he is greater than Solomon, for he is God's Wisdom. It is in this light that we can understand Matthew's intention in 28:18: "All authority in heaven and on earth has been given to me." It is hard to imagine a higher Christology than one that begins with a person called Emmanuel (1:23) and ends with a proclamation that to this one has been given all authority in heaven and on earth. Matthew, like the church and its evangelists, was deeply influenced by wisdom literature; he simply would not have been able to develop his Christology apart from the teaching, speculation, and imagery revealed through the Jewish sapiential tradition.

John's Wisdom Christology

Of the canonical Gospels, John is the most persistent in regarding Jesus as incarnate Wisdom descended from on high to offer humans life and truth. Understanding what has been said about Wisdom in the Jewish sapiential literature, particularly Wisdom's origin, mission, benefits, and relation with God, is key to understanding Jesus' identity in John's Gospel: (a) as Wisdom's origin is divine, so is Jesus' (John 1:1–2); (b) as Wisdom existed before creation and was active in creation, so is Jesus (John 1:3); (c) as Wisdom is God's agent on earth, so is Jesus (John 5:36); (d) like Wisdom, Jesus speaks in discourses using the first person pronoun. In the seven "I am" sayings Jesus is described as living bread (6:35, 51), light of the world (8:12), the gate (10:7, 9), the good shepherd (10:11, 14), the life (11:25), the way (14:6), and the vine (15:1, 5). All of these images are found in wisdom literature as proceeding from or characterizing Wisdom.

Thus, for instance, in Proverbs 8:36 Wisdom says: "he who finds me finds life and obtains favor from the Lord." In Wisdom of Solomon 7:26, Wisdom is said to be a reflection of eternal light. In Sirach 24:17, 21, Wisdom is compared to a vine: "Like the vine I bud forth delights, and my blossoms become glorious and abundant fruit.... Those who eat of me will hunger for more and those who drink of me will thirst for more." This passage also seems to inform Jesus' statement in John 4:13–14: "Everyone who drinks of this water will be thirsty again, but those who drink of the water that I will give them will never be thirsty." One may also compare Jesus' saying, "I am the bread of life. Whoever comes to me will never be hungry, and whoever believes in me will never be thirsty" (6:35) with Proverbs 9:5–6, where Wisdom beckons: "Come eat of my bread, and drink of the wine I have mixed. Lay aside immaturity and live and walk in the way of insight"; (e) like Wisdom, one's destiny hangs on whether one accepts or rejects Jesus (3:18; 14:6); (f) finally, like Wisdom, Jesus is said to be the bearer of eternal life (3:16).

Christological Hymns and the Jewish Wisdom Tradition

Three primary sources seemingly were influential in the composition of christological hymns: (1) Jewish discussions about personified Wisdom; (2) early Christian preaching about Jesus, particularly about his death and resurrection; and (3) the christological use of the Psalms, particularly Psalm 110 but also Psalm 8. Early christological hymns, embedded in the New Testament, utilize wisdom motifs to express Christian belief in the incarnation of Jesus (John 1:1–18) and in his cosmic rule (Col. 1:15–20; Heb. 1:1–4). Among the various influences on the New Testament was the identification of Wisdom (Jesus) with divine Spirit (2 Cor. 3:16–18), Word (John 1:1), and Law (Matt. 5:17–20; 7:24–29). Like Wisdom in Sirach and in the book of Wisdom, Jesus is said to have preexisted his historical incarnation; having lived in intimate relation with God, Jesus is now exalted and enthroned in heaven (Phil. 2:6–11).

Once Wisdom became identified with Jesus of Nazareth, and Jesus became an object of worship for early Jewish Christians, some of these same people, steeped in Jewish wisdom traditions, appropriated the hymn-like praise of personified Wisdom in order to express their devotion to Jesus Christ. The christological hymn fragments found in the Pauline corpus (Phil. 2:6–11; Col. 1:15–20; 1 Tim. 3:16), the Gospel of John (1:1–5, 9–14), and Hebrews (1:2–4) are fundamentally expressions of a Wisdom Christology that goes back to early Jewish Christianity. They demonstrate that the earliest thinking about Jesus grew out of worship practices that were modelled after the synagogue service, a pattern that consisted of readings from scripture, singing, and prayer. Such Christology, influenced by Hellenized Jewish traditions, ultimately led to the doctrine of the preexistence of Jesus and in due course to a doctrine of the incarnation.

The earliest use of christological hymn fragments is found in the Pauline corpus, and Paul likely heard such hymns in contexts where Greek was the primary language of worship, since hymns such as the one in

Philippians 2 and particularly in Colossians 1 so clearly draw on the Greek text of the Wisdom of Solomon and were surely first composed in Greek. To judge from the fact that one finds hymn fragments in places as varied as Hebrews, the Fourth Gospel, and the Pauline corpus, such hymns and their composition must have been widespread. These hymns suggest a widely held common form of Wisdom Christology in early Christianity.

Wisdom thinking, to the extent that it is theology, is essentially a form of creation theology, and one should not be surprised to find in Christian wisdom hymns a considerable emphasis on what was true of the Son before and during the event of creation, including the doctrine of his preexistence and in due course a doctrine of the incarnation. In these hymns, Christ's career is envisioned as having both heavenly and earthly scope, and the attempt to express adequately the theological significance of this career led early Jewish Christians to draw on the most exalted language they could find—Jewish wisdom speculation, coupled with messianic interpretation of the Psalms and soteriological reflections on Christ's death.

The Christ (Servant) Hymn: Philippians 2:6-11

The "Christ Hymn," inserted by Paul in his letter to the Philippians, exhorts believers to unity by means of humble service, for which the example of Christ serves as a model. In 2:8 the phrase translated "he humbled himself" is important, for ancient secular writers did not view humility as virtuous. The word had a negative connotation, something like "shabby" or "base-minded," in its adjectival form meaning the mentality of a slave. But this is Paul's meaning, that Jesus, the exemplar of what humility truly means, took the form of a servant (*doulos*, 2:7).

In the Hebrew scriptures one occasionally finds humility and lowliness exalted. Some scholars ask whether the servant language, which is unique to this hymn, draws primarily on material from the Servant Songs of Isaiah or on Jewish wisdom material. If there is correspondence with Isaiah, particularly 52:13—53:12, such correspondence is indirect. It is more likely that the wisdom ideas here predicated of Christ, including the concept of servanthood, are drawn from material in Sirach and the Wisdom of Solomon. For example, after talking about the wisdom that formed humans, "Solomon" in Wisdom 9:4-5 prays: "give me the wisdom that sits by your throne, and do not reject me from among your servants, for I am your servant (*doulos*), the son of your servant girl" (i.e. "wisdom").

Part IV: God in Christ

The Christ Hymn is divided into two parts, namely, what Christ chooses to do (2:6–8) and what God does for him (2:9–11). Both halves are illumined by the material in Wisdom 5–7. For example, in Wisdom 5:16 one hears of the righteous ones (called "servants of [God's] kingdom" in 6:4) who will receive "a glorious crown," or again in 6:3, "for your dominion was given you from the Lord, and your sovereignty from the Most High," for being obedient servants while on earth. These comments culminate in the discussion of hypostasized Wisdom in 7:22–23. Seen in this light, Philippians 2 celebrates a royal figure who, like Solomon, humbles himself by becoming God's servant, obeys God, and is rewarded in royal fashion in the end. Similar is material in Sirach such as "The wisdom of the humble lifts their heads high, and seats them among the great" (11:1) or "The greater you are, the more you must humble yourself. . . . For great is the might of the Lord; and by the humble he is glorified" (3:17–18).

Like these passages, Philippians 2 tells about the exaltation of the obedient servant, who humbled himself willingly. The juxtaposition of preexistence language, servant language, humility and exaltation language, and the bestowal of kingship and kingdom in Philippians 2 are also found in Sirach and Wisdom of Solomon. Indeed, the whole of Philippians 2:6–11, except such Pauline additions as "even death on a cross" (2:8c), probably derived from early Jewish Christian attempts to paint an adequate portrait of Christ reflecting on and utilizing Jewish wisdom material.[2] With regard to this hymn, one can say with confidence that as early as the mid-50s, when Paul adopted and modified it, a new view of monotheism was emerging in Jewish Christian circles, which involved viewing Christ as God's Wisdom in person—as someone who once had and continues to have equal attributes with God, and in the end is given the same throne name ("Lord," 2:9–11). Biblical scholar N. T. Wright views the reference to "the name of Jesus" in Philippians 2:10 as an example of "christological monotheism," which, while affirming the divinity of Christ, at the same time "never intends to assert that Christ is divine in a sense apart from or over against the one true God."[3] Confessing "Jesus is Lord" (likely the earliest Christian confession) does not detract from but in fact enhances God's glory (2:11).

---

2. Ibid., 261–62.
3. Wright, *Climax of the Covenant*, 116.

The Wisdom Hymn: Colossians 1:15–20

Due to numerous verbal parallels between this hymn and the Wisdom of Solomon, we can be fairly certain that barring editorial additions by the author of Colossians (such as "the head of the body" and "the church" in verse 18 and much of verses 18–20), the rest of the hymn is dependent on the book of Wisdom.[4] While the authorship of Colossians is disputed, the majority of scholars are likely right in seeing the Wisdom Hymn as pre-Pauline.

As in Philippians 2, the hymn in Colossians 1 boldly attributes to Jesus divine names as well as ascribing to him deeds only deity can perform. In regard to the meaning of the hymn, two terms used in 1:15 of Jesus need clarification: (a) when Jesus is said to be the "image" of the invisible God, the term used is "icon," meaning Christ makes visible what is invisible. If God could be seen, then this is what God would look like (cf. Col. 2:9); (b) when Jesus is called the "firstborn of all creation," this does not mean that he is himself created, for the hymn declares Jesus to be the agent of all creation. "Firstborn," used legally, declares Christ to be the sole heir of the Father, meaning that he stands on the side of the Creator in the creator-creature distinction. "Firstborn" emphasizes Christ's relationship to the creation, just as "image" emphasizes the relationship to the Creator. "Firstborn" possibly reflects the idea in Psalm 89:27 where God promises to make the king the firstborn, meaning "supreme in rank." In Colossians 1:18, where "firstborn" is used in conjunction with "beginning" and resurrection, the meaning is priority and supremacy; the notion of being created is not present. In the writings of Philo, the first-century Alexandrian Jewish author, "image" and "beginning" are used interchangeably and are predicated of heavenly Wisdom. Similar statements are made about Wisdom in Wisdom 1:7 and Sirach 43:26.

The concept of incarnation, present in every christological hymn, is most likely a development of the idea found in Sirach 24:23, which suggests that Wisdom expressed herself in concrete historical form in the Torah, the law of Moses. While this association is not equivalent to the idea of personal incarnation, such development is not totally unexpected, particularly by early Christians who began transferring what had previously

---

4. Witherington identifies points of correspondence between the following passages: Col. 1:15a and Wis. 7:26; Col. 1:15b and Wis. 6:22; Col. 1:16a and Wis. 1:14; Col. 1:16d and Wis. 5:23d; 6:21; 7:8; Col. 1:16-17, 19 and Wis. 7:24b; Col 1:17b and Wis. 1:7-8; and Col. 1:17a, 18d and Wis. 7:29c; see *Jesus the Sage*, 267.

been said about Wisdom, in particular Wisdom as manifested in Torah, to Jesus. The notion of incarnation, not so much stated as implied, is present in Colossians 1:19–20. While it is unique to talk about the preexistence and incarnation of a personal being who took on flesh and became Jesus Christ, the Jewish wisdom tradition prepare the way for such an idea. It is not accidental that the most clearly incarnational hymn, the Johannine prologue, is also the most clearly sapiential.

The Character Hymn: Hebrews 1:2b-4

The influence of Wisdom on the hymn fragment in Hebrews 1 is clear and may be summed up in the following points: (1) verse 2, with its idea of an agent through whom God created all worlds, is found in the Wisdom of Solomon, where Wisdom is called "the fashioner of all things" (7:22), an "associate in [God's] works," and the "active cause of all things" (8:4–5), but the notion of agency may already be present in Proverbs 8, where Wisdom is seen to be at God's side during the creation, "like a master worker" (8:30); (2) verse 3, which speaks of Christ as the "reflection of God's glory," seems to be a direct use of Wisdom 7:25; (3) Hebrews 1:3b ("and he sustains all things by his powerful word") is related to Wisdom 1:7 (cf. Sir. 24:3), which describes Wisdom as holding all things together; (4) Hebrews 1:3d ("he sat down at the right hand of the Majesty on high") is related to Wisdom 9:4, which speaks of Wisdom sitting beside God's throne (see 9:10), and Psalm 110:1; (5) the reference to angels and superiority over them in Hebrews 1:4 ("having become as much superior to angels as the name he has inherited is more excellent than theirs") may in part reflect 1 Enoch 43, where Wisdom is said to take her place among the angels, yet as being superior to them.[5]

The Logos Hymn: John 1:1–18

This passage has impacted belief in the divinity and preexistence of Christ more than any other New Testament passage. Here the early church derived its Logos Christology (i.e. the Son of God as the "Word") and its basic understanding of the incarnation.

Four beautifully crafted poetic stanzas make up the Logos Hymn in John's prologue: first strophe (1:1–2); second strophe (1:3–5); third strophe

---

5. Ibid., 281–82.

(1:10–12b); and fourth strophe (1:14). Some include 1:16–18, though probably they should not. The following themes appear to be central in this hymn: (1) the preexistent Logos (1:1–2); (2) the Logos and creation (1:3–5); (3) the rejection of those created (1:10–12b); (4) the incarnation and revelation (1:14a); and (5) the response of the faithful community (1:14b).[6]

There is in this hymn an obvious dependence on Genesis 1. Both documents begin with the words, "In the beginning," and in both God creates by means of the spoken word. The use of the Genesis material in the hymnic material about Wisdom both in the Hebrew Bible (see Prov. 3; 8:1—9:6) and in the later Jewish wisdom tradition inspires the ideas in this hymn. In that tradition one learns that personified Wisdom was present at creation, and that she calls God's people back to ethical living and offers them life and divine favor. These are the same things said of the Word in John's prologue. By the time of Ben Sira, this sort of Wisdom speculation includes Torah, seen as the consummate expression of Wisdom (cf. Sir. 24). At the end of the Logos Hymn it is said that the Son eclipses this Torah, for through Torah came the law, but through the Logos come grace and truth (1:17).

One need not reiterate all the parallels between this hymn and the Jewish wisdom literature, although central to that correspondence is that Wisdom provides life and light (see John 1:4 and Wisdom 7:26, where Wisdom is said to be the reflection of eternal light, and Wisdom 7:25a, where she is the very life breath of God). Some question why *logos* ("word," a masculine term) and not *sophia* ("wisdom," a feminine term) is used of Jesus in John 1. Although the answer cannot be known with certainty, it seems doubtful that the reason is because Jesus was male, for other evangelists certainly used *sophia* of Jesus (cf. Matt. 1:19; Luke 11:49). In Wisdom 9:1–2 "word" (*en logo*) and "wisdom" are used in synonymous parallelism, an idea that Philo explores fully. The Wisdom of Solomon personifies *logos* in 18:15, when it declares that God's "all-powerful word leaped from heaven, from the royal throne" (18:15). Since Wisdom 9:10 had already said that Wisdom was present and sent forth from the throne, one can see how interchangeable the terms "wisdom" and "word" are in Wisdom of Solomon. This is also the case in Sirach 24:3, where Wisdom is said to come forth from the mouth of God. As Witherington explains, "It may be that [John] simply used the term *logos* to better prepare for the replacement motif—Jesus

---

6. Ibid., 282–83.

superseding Torah as God's *logos* [1:17]."[7] Another idea unique to John's prologue, the tabernacling of the Logos with God's people (1:14), is also manifest in Sirach 24:8, where the Creator chooses a place for Wisdom to tent, namely in the earthly tabernacle in Zion (24:10).

When the early Jewish Christians composed christological hymns, they searched for exalted language from their heritage that gave adequate expression to their newfound faith in Jesus Christ. No language seemed better suited for their task than the poems about personified or hypostasized Wisdom found in Proverbs 8, Job 28, Sirach 24, and Wisdom 7 and 9. In particular, it was the latest of these sapiential writings, the Wisdom of Solomon, that had the greatest impact. It seems unlikely that one christological wisdom hymn spawned the others, or that some sort of borrowing occurred, whereby the Colossians hymn grew out of the Philippians hymn or the Johannine hymn grew out of earlier hymns. Each hymn is distinctive enough to make such an argument implausible. Rather, it seems that sapiential themes were widely shared and expressed in a variety of ways by early Jewish Christians.

When the sapiential liturgical material was applied to the historical Jesus, the result is a very high Christology, predicating preexistence, incarnation, and even divinity to a historical person. The existence of these hymns in so many different sorts of sources—Pauline, Johannine, and in Hebrews—strongly suggests that Wisdom Christology was both widespread and popular with a variety of Christian writers and their audiences. The fact that one finds such Christology already in Philippians 2 suggests that this Christology had developed within the first two or three decades of early Christianity. That is, this Christology existed *before* the writing of any of the canonical Gospels. To be sure, John 1 represents a further amplification, especially of the ideas of incarnation and divinity, but such ideas are already present, though not as fully expressed, in the earlier hymns.

---

7. Ibid., 285.

Session 11

Word of God (Logos)

Questions for Individual or Group Reflection: John's prologue (John 1:1–18) is central for Logos Christology. Explain the meaning of the term "Logos" for first-century Jewish Christians, and why the term is used so prominently in John's Gospel. Evaluate the merits of the statement: John's prologue "cannot be confined to historical or factual descriptions but rather bursts out of the mundane to tell us something about early Christians and their perception of reality."

Important Biblical Verses and Passages: John 1:1–3, 12–13, 14; 8:23

Technical Words and Concepts: Logos Christology; the Word; Christ; Stoics; Platonists; Philo

IT CAN BE ARGUED that there are three fundamental concepts of Christ in the New Testament: adoptionist, agency, and incarnational. (1) *Adoptionist Christology* suggests that Jesus was a man who, because of his obedience to God, was adopted as God's Messiah. This adoption may have taken place sometime during the ministry of Jesus, such as at his baptism or his transfiguration, but more often it is associated with the resurrection. (2) *Agency Christology* is more common in the New Testament. This view understands Jesus to be God's agent, sent as God's personal representative to perform a revelatory and saving function. This kind of thinking is present in passages which stress that God "sent" Jesus. It is commonly found in John's Gospel (3:34), but is found elsewhere in the New Testament as well. (3) The boldest of the claims for Christ is embodied in *incarnational Christology*, which stresses Christ's preexistence with God as well as his incarnation in human flesh. The prologue to John is the clearest statement of incarnational Christology in the New Testament, though Colossians 1:15–20 and Philippians 2:6–11 express similar views.

When we think of the incarnation, it is important to recognize that in no serious theology, ancient or modern, has the preexistent Christ been identified ontologically with God. In the earliest period, as we have seen, the preexistent being was pictured as the Son of Man or possibly sometimes as an angelic being of the highest rank. Later, Christ was thought of as the Son of God, Wisdom, or Word (Logos) of God, all of these denoting a metaphysical relationship of great intimacy. But never was the preexistent Christ identified with God in any simple or exhaustive sense. It must be so because God (understood in a unitary way) could not become incarnate and still be God.

Logos Christology

When in its doctrine of the Trinity the church speaks of "God the Father, God the Son [or Logos], and God the Holy Spirit," it not only affirms three hypostases or personal modes of the divine being, but it also recognizes that it was specifically the divine Logos, "God the Word," who in Christ was made flesh. This distinction by no means identifies Jesus of Nazareth with that preexisting, and always existing, hypostasis. As the reality of God is not exhausted in the Logos, yet is fully present in it, so the reality of the Logos was fully present in the "Christ event," of which the human life of Jesus was the center, and therefore preeminently in that human life itself, but without being simply identical with Jesus.

In his important work on the incarnation, *The Word Incarnate*, Norman Pittenger affirms that in terms of Trinitarian theology, there can be no preexistence of the human mind, nature, self, or ego of Jesus. The only possible justification of such a theory would be to follow Origen, the patristic theologian, in his view that all souls preexist and that Jesus' soul was "united with the Word" in that preexistent state. But this view was rejected by the church as unnecessary if not absurd. "Hence we must reject outright any idea of a preexistence of *Jesus* and along with this rejection an incredible amount of pious error and confusion. Something *did* preexist: it was the Eternal Word of God who is incarnate in Jesus. Or, in the kind of language which we have been using, the Word, who is universally operative in the natural world, in human history, and in the depths of man's life, is focally expressed in our Lord's full and true humanity."[1]

When speaking of the incarnation, it is helpful to avoid talk of unity in essence or nature and rather to emphasize unity in the function of the preexistent one as revealer of God's *action* in history. For Christology, then, the important question is not "How was God *in* Christ?" or "How did God *become* human?" but rather "What was God *doing* in Christ? To identify God's presence in Christ in this dynamic way is to conceive of the action as inseparable from God's reality. God's "action" is really God acting. Logos language is functional, not ontological. If by Logos is meant the activity of God continually and everywhere acting to create and redeem, then, in the human life of Jesus we can see the focus of this Word in history. However, if we are speaking with precision, we cannot simply identify Jesus, for all his importance, with one of the "persons" of the Trinity. To do so is to distort the doctrine of God and to discredit the incarnation. In John's Gospel we do hear concerning the Logos that "in the beginning was the Word, and the Word was with God, and the Word was God" (John 1:1), but almost as if the writer feared further ontological speculation, he moves immediately from concern with ontology (being) to the *act* of revelation: "All things came into being through him . . . and the Word became flesh and lived among us." Despite the availability of wisdom language and conceptuality, John prefers to speak of Logos, a term that offers a rich complexity of meanings.

Although Logos became the predominant designation for Jesus in the patristic age of the church, and to a great extent came to be considered the essential concept in Christology, we find it as a title only in one group of New Testament writings, the Johannine (those associated with the apostle John). Even there it occurs only in a few passages: the prologue to the Gospel of John ("Word"), the first verse of 1 John ("Word of Life"), and Revelation 19:13 ("Word of God"). While the term is important, indeed indispensable to the writer of the Fourth Gospel, particularly when he wishes to speak of the relationship between the divine revelation in Jesus and his preexistence, it appears infrequently.

John does not, like Mark, identify the beginning of the history of Jesus with the appearance of John the Baptist, because for him the beginning lies in the preexistence of Jesus, which directs our attention to the absolute beginning of all things. Nevertheless, the evangelist is not interested in speculation about this pre-temporal existence of the Logos, but only in

---

1. Pittenger, *Word Incarnate*, 218–19.

the Word's close connection with the work of Christ, whose human life is the center of the history of divine revelation and salvation. Because Christ is the center of history, the Gospel of John emphasizes the participation of the preexistent Christ in creation—even more strongly than the other New Testament writings in which we find the same idea. We must not overlook the fact that John begins with the same words as the book of Genesis: "In the beginning." In his Gospel, the evangelist is presenting us with a new Genesis account, from the perspective of the mediator of revelation.

The Logos in the Hellenistic World

Since Logos as a concept was widespread both before Christianity and contemporaneous with its start, we need to consider the place of the conception in Judaism and among the Greek philosophers. Ancient Greek philosophers known as the Stoics held the concept of Logos in high esteem. For them it meant "word," as in the act of speaking, but it carried much deeper meaning. The word Logos, from which we get the English term "logic," also means "reason," and the Stoics believed that Logos (reason) was a divine element that infused all reality. There is, they believed, a rationality to the way things work, and if one wants to understand the world and how best to live, then one must seek to understand this underlying logic. Such understanding is both possible and practical because Logos was believed to reside in every human being. Each person, it turns out, has a portion of Logos within, and if we apply our minds to the world, we can understand it. And if we understand this underlying logic, we can live peaceful, enriched lives.

Thinkers who stood directly in the line of the great philosopher Plato took the idea of the Logos in a different direction. For them the Logos functions as a mediator or bridge between the two essential constituents of reality, connecting spirit and matter. For Platonists, the eternal Logos is what allows spirit to interact with matter, the nondivine with the divine. Though humans are thoroughly immersed in the material world, the presence of the Logos within our material bodies allows us to escape our material entrapment and attain spiritual wisdom and enlightenment (see John 1:9).

Familiarity with some of these ideas enabled Jewish thinkers to connect these Stoic and Platonic ideas with their own. In the Hebrew Bible, for example, God creates all things by speaking a "word": "And God said, 'Let there be light'; and there was light" (Gen. 1:3). Jewish thinkers, influenced by Greek thought, naturally associated the "Word of God" with the Logos.

Word of God (Logos)

For them the Logos comes from God, and since it is God's Logos, in a sense it is God. However, once this Word is stated, it comes be to be understood as a distinct entity, separate from God. Thus the Logos came to be seen in some Jewish circles as a hypostasis (such a possibility is implied already in the Hebrew Bible; see, for example, 1 Samuel 3:1, 7). The outworking of this conception is evident in the most famous Jewish philosopher of antiquity, Philo of Alexandria (20 BC–AD 50), a contemporary of Jesus.

Philo maintained that the Logos was the highest of all beings, the image of God according to which and by which the universe is ordered. God's Logos was, in particular, the model according to which humans were created. It is easy to see that Philo is taking functions assigned to Wisdom, such as creating and ordering all things, and attributing them to the Logos. The two are so closely associated by Philo that there is a sense in which Wisdom gives birth to Logos. Philo uses a wide array of terms to describe Logos, including: "firstborn son," "archangel," Name of God," and "governor and administrator of all things." Because the Logos is God's Logos, it is divine and can be called by divine names. Philo also describes the full complement of divine attributes, which include "the creative power," "the royal power," "the gracious power," and the legislative powers by which God prescribes and prohibits acts, and over all these he places the "divine Logos" as chief of God's powers. Because the Logos is God, and God is God, Philo sometimes speaks of "two gods," and elsewhere of Logos as "the second God." But there is a difference for Philo between "the God" and "a god," and Logos is the latter.[2]

As a divine being apart from God, Logos sounds a lot like the Angel of the Lord discussed in Session 8. In fact, Philo sometimes equates Logos with this angel. Philo's Platonic influence is clearly at work, for in the more than fourteen hundred occurrences of the term "logos" in Philo's writings, in many the Logos appears as God's means of communication. For Philo, God does not speak directly to humans; rather, God speaks through the Logos. Likewise, when God is manifest to humans, it is the Logos that makes the appearance. In sum, for Philo this complex figure exists outside God but on occasion it becomes the actual figure of God, who appears "like a man" so that humans can know and interact with its presence. In some cases it is a divine being distinct from God, yet also somehow God. While it cannot be proved that the concept of the Logos or Word of God held by

---

2. For further discussion, see Ehrman, *How Jesus Became God*, 72–75; Hurtado, *One God, One Lord*, 44–46.

Philo influenced the New Testament writers, it is only a step from such conception to New Testament Christology.

Logos Christology in the Gospel of John

The christological use of Logos in the Johannine writings is based upon the conviction of Jesus' cosmic lordship adapted to the appreciation of a particular audience for whom the expression was especially meaningful. Both in New Testament times and later, the Johannine Logos offered rich christological possibilities. In addition to expanding our understanding of the possibility of identification and distinction—words can be understood as an extension of the speaker and yet as distinct from the one speaking—the concept offered an effective bridge to contemporary culture, opening the way for Christians to dialogue meaningfully with non-Christian thinkers. By maintaining that the entire world was created by Logos, early Christians universalized their understanding of Jesus as divine agent of all creation and therefore as cosmic Lord.

While the topic of Christology is central to John, the Gospel does not approach the topic abstractly or metaphysically but relationally, in association with the notion of discipleship, with what it means to be a believer. While religious traditions rooted in a historical figure traditionally develop claims for the uniqueness of the founder as well as his or her revelation, for John it is not Jesus' experience that is central but rather it is the believers' experience of Jesus.

The presence of Logos Christology, inserted in the prologue but obviously central to the Fourth Gospel, takes a concept current in Hellenistic philosophies but also central to Jewish thought and plies its imaginative richness to suggest that in one person Jesus fulfills simultaneously the variety of religious and philosophical views of the universe. For John, Jesus Christ is Stoic Logos, Hebraic Word of God, and Jewish Wisdom all in one. Nevertheless, the thrust of the prologue seems to be that for the Christian, Logos is a person and not an abstract philosophical concept.

Of the many affirmations about the Logos in John's Gospel, the first constitutes the highest: the Logos existed from the beginning, before things began. For John, as for the Synoptic Gospels, Christ is so vital that he could not have come into being like any other person or object. The authors of Matthew and Luke implied this when they incorporated the stories of Jesus' virgin birth and his conception by the Holy Spirit. The fourth evangelist

Word of God (Logos)

goes one step further to say the same thing: Christ existed before creation, meaning he is not a created being. Another affirmation about the Logos is that he was the agent of creation: "All things came into being through him" (1:3). As agent of creation, he is the source of a new kind of life, a life attuned to the divine purpose for human existence.

A central concern in John is the relationship of this preexistent, creative Logos to God. If we ask whether the evangelist is suggesting full divinity, along the lines of the later Nicene or Chalcedonian Christology, such formulation presses the imagery too far. In John 1:1, a key text for John's Christology, the author may simply be teasing the reader: "The Logos was with God, and the Logos was God." Insofar as the preposition "with" suggests relationship, this sentence makes two different claims: the Logos is a distinct being, yet identical with God. This means there is both *individuality* and *identification* in the relationship between God and Logos. That is as far as John goes. We should not make the prologue read like a treatise on the Trinity, since it was written long before the church wrestled with this concept.

Yet we find here the paradox at the heart of Christianity, that somehow individuality (distinctiveness, twoness) and identity (equivalence, oneness) coexist in the person of Jesus. The paradox may be addressed by appealing to the analogy of personality, which views persons as having two sides or dimensions, an inward side, known only to themselves and rarely expressed, and an outward side, revealed to others. Understood in this way, the Logos is the expressive outward side of God. This does not mean that God is exhausted in the Logos, but that the Logos is that dimension of God that has come to expression for the comprehension of humans.

This leads to John 1:14, the most complete statement of incarnational Christology in the New Testament: "And the Word became flesh and lived among us." Here the divine nature of the preexistent Logos is most clearly affirmed, and here the humanization or enfleshment of that Logos is openly declared. Such claims and understanding are poetic and imaginative in the most profound sense. John's Logos imagery, expressed in the language of liturgy, articulates a model of meaning and a cosmic perspective that encompasses the experience of a worshipping community. The prologue cannot be confined to historical or factual descriptions but rather bursts out of the mundane to tell us something about early Christians and their perception of reality.

Part IV: God in Christ

Apart from the prologue, John never expressly states that Jesus is the divine Logos. However, he affirms that Jesus utters the *logos* of God (the revelation or Word of God), which, in accordance with Jewish and Christian tradition, is conceived as embodied in scripture. In a profound sense the Word of God is found in the words of Jesus. So in John 17:14 Jesus says, "I have given them your word (*logos*), to which he adds, "your word is truth" (17:17). Thus the *logos* of Jesus is the *logos* of God. In view of the equation of the divine *logos* with "truth," it is significant that Jesus says, "I am the truth" (14:6). Hence Jesus not only gives the word of God, which is truth, he *is* truth; he not only gives life, but *is* life; he not only gives the bread of life, he *is* the bread. As we discover in 6:63, Jesus' words are "spirit and life." It is only a step from that to say: "Jesus is the Logos."

The word of Jesus—the word he proclaimed—plays such an important part in the Gospel of John that one can hardly assume the evangelist did not think also of this "word" when in the prologue he identified Jesus as the Logos. The supposition that he did so is suggested even more strongly by the basic Johannine thought that Jesus not only *brings* revelation, but also in his person *is* revelation. Jesus brings light, and at the same time is Light; he bestows life, and he is Life; he proclaims truth, and he is Truth. More properly expressed, he brings light, life, and truth expressly because he himself is Light, Life, and Truth. So it is also with the Logos; he brings the word because he is the Word.

To many readers, both in antiquity and more recently, the depiction of Jesus in John's Gospel appears docetic, static, and unhistorical. Yet, in John's defense, such judgment is rash and inaccurate, for not one but two figures of Jesus appear in the Fourth Gospel, so intricately interwoven as to be inseparable. There is the Jesus who appears as a god incarnate in flesh, but more like a god who is in the world but not of it, a god who dips into the stream of history but scarcely getting wet. Then there is the Jewish Jesus, the Galilean Jew whose father's name is Joseph, an unlettered man whose origin is known, who is subject to arrest and who suffers and dies on a cross. Yet the author is not naïve, and so we wonder whether it is not we who have introduced such a polarization.

On further reading, with the tools not only of science but of literature, with the comprehension not only of psychology but of theology, and with the eyes not only of fact but of faith, the message of the Gospel, and the source of its distinctive depth and irony, is that there are two levels at which everything about Jesus can and must be judged. It is not that one is true

Word of God (Logos)

but not the other, or that one is real at the expense of the other. If both were not equally valid there would be no misunderstanding, no offence, and therefore no faith. It is possible at one level to know completely where Jesus comes from and yet at another to know nothing. Yet both sources of origin—his earthly father and his heavenly father—are equally real. To suggest that the former is merely a sham is to destroy the tension and texture of the Gospel.

In John's Gospel, which manages to hold the two pictures of Jesus together most paradoxically, there is no contradiction between coming (being sent) from God and being utterly and genuinely human. No other Gospel uses so frequently the word "man" for Jesus as John (John 1:30; 3:27; 9:11; 10:33). "Man" is employed of Jesus exactly as it is of John the Baptist (see John 1:6). It is characteristic of John's Gospel that for all its stress on Jesus' otherness, the language used to designate Christ in his profoundest relationship to the Father is the same applied to humans in general. If Jesus is unique, it is not because he does not share the human origin and condition or the relationship to God open potentially to all other human beings (John 1:12–13; 8:41; 9:31; 10:35; 14:12; 15:7–11, 30; 17:21–23, 26). Thus, to "come into the world," which might suggest a special kind of supernatural entry, is used identically of Jesus and of everyone (for example, compare John 9:39 with 1:9). There is continuity also between the distinctive language John uses to describe Jesus' sonship and that of others (compare John 10:36 with 8:41). Likewise, the apparently exclusive union of Jesus with the Father (John 10:37) is like that to which the disciples are called (John 15:5–10; 17:21–23, 26). While in John only Jesus is designated "son," others are God's "children" (John 1:12–13).

Yet these concepts are contrasted by the most uncompromising statements about Jesus' unique origin and sonship. Jesus is indeed for John the unique revealer and mediator of God. Jesus is and Jesus does what no other human being can be or do. Yet in order to be this and to do this, he is a human in complete continuity with other humans. There is no suggestion in this Gospel, unlike Matthew and Luke, that he enters this world in any other way. Being born, "not of blood or of the will of the flesh or of the will of man, but of God," is for John a description not of Jesus but of believers in general (John 1:13). Of course, it is also true at this level of Jesus; he is par excellence the one who "comes from above" (3:31), yet not in a way to deny the physical links (6:42) or to separate him from others. The real difference in this Gospel is that the "designatory" language found elsewhere in the New Testament, which appears by subsequent standards "adoptionist," John places firmly at the beginning. In this Gospel Jesus is "sealed" (John 6:27) and "sanctified" (John 10:36) by God, in language reminiscent of the Epistle to the Hebrews, where Jesus is "appointed" as Son, only in Hebrews this takes place only after Jesus is "made perfect." In John it happens from the start. In neither case, however, it it implied that because Jesus is Son, he does not stand in the same human relationship to God as every other person. On the contrary, it is because he is the one completely obedient human, who does his Father's will to the end (John 17:4), that he is the perfect reflection or representation of God. Consequently, anyone who has seen this human being, has seen the Father (John 12:45; 14:9).

Yet the impression lingers that this is not truly a human story. And this is intentional. For the evangelist is deliberately telling two stories at once, and superimposing them on each other. The first is the story of the Logos, the story of the wisdom and light and love of God. This story comes to its climax in Jesus and is so totally incarnate in him that he can speak directly in the name of God and utter the divine "I am." The source and ground of this story is not "this world" (John 8:23; 17:14, 26) but the world above (John 8:23). In this story it is God speaking and acting; consequently, its origin is not the moment of Jesus' birth, but is before Abraham (John 8:58), before the world (John 17:5, 24), and indeed at the beginning of all things (John 1:1–2). As the embodiment of this "I am," Jesus does not act or speak of himself (John 5:19, 30; 7:16–18, 28; 12:49).

Yet this does not mean that it is not himself speaking. For John is also telling another story, the history of a human being who comes from Nazareth in Galilee and whose connections are known to all (John 1:45; 7:27, 52; 18:4). There is no mystery about his origin, and it is absurd to say of this historical individual that he is preexistent. To mix up the stories, to confuse the categories, is to make nonsense of everything. Yet the possibility, and indeed the inevitability, of misunderstanding is for John an essential part of the story. We might wish he had made clearer what to take as theology and what as history, for in our age it has become important to distinguish such things. Yet it is integral to John's purpose that certain statements be taken both ways, at two levels. With the eye of faith, "by the true light, which enlightens everyone" (John 1:9), it is possible to view both in focus, and then to see the glory incarnate (John 1:14). There is, John is saying, a way of having the languages both of humanity and of preexistence.

Word of God (Logos)

This is not to say, however, that we must be committed to the language of preexistence. The earliest Christians were not, although there is little doubt that either in New Testament times or soon thereafter the transition from one set of presuppositions to another did take place. That is precisely the function of Son of God language in the New Testament, to serve as a bridge between the functional manner by which Jesus and the earliest Jewish believers denoted Jesus' unique relationship with God and the ontological elaboration and extension of meaning in its use by later Christians, who used Son of God designation to say something about the Son's identity of substance with the Father. Thereafter Christian doctrine became committed to an understanding of incarnation that involved the veiling in flesh of a heavenly being.

Part V

Christ in God

WE PROPOSED EARLIER THAT the first Christians adapted the "chief agent" tradition in ancient Judaism and posited Jesus in such a capacity. They also expanded this category, most notably in the conviction that Jesus was to be worshipped together with God. In the pre-Pauline "Christ Hymn" of Philippians 2:6–11, an early liturgical poem or hymn used in Christian worship no later than the second decade after the crucifixion, Jesus is extolled as Lord of all, to whom all living beings should offer confession and worship (Phil. 2:9–11). In the eyes of at least some Jews at that time, such practice was abhorrent, even blasphemous. The initially vigorous opposition to the Jesus movement by the young Pharisee, Saul of Tarsus, was likely prompted at least in part by this practice.

The origin of this "binitarian shape" of early Christian devotion, reflected in 1 Corinthians 8:6, which involved the veneration of Jesus alongside God and a refusal to venerate all other divine figures, constituted a major problem for the followers of Jesus. Awareness of the distinctive binitarian form of early Christian devotion over against the monotheistic emphasis of early Judaism, coupled with the fact that Christianity began as a Jewish sectarian movement, led scholars in the past to explain the veneration of Jesus as due to the influence of the veneration of a wide variety of divine figures in Greco-Roman paganism. However, given the general antipathy of ancient Judaism toward pagan religion, and after careful consideration of the evidence available concerning the earliest stages of Christian tradition, such a view has become virtually untenable. We now know, however, of traditions in ancient Judaism that practiced binitarian worship, encouraging pious Jews to accommodate a second figure alongside God as an object of religious devotion.

An important biblical text that has played a prominent role in discussions of Jewish monotheism is Deuteronomy 32:8–9. The Hebrew text reads: "When the Most High (Elyon) apportioned the nations, when he divided humankind, he fixed the boundaries of the peoples, according to the number of *the sons of Israel*; the Lord's own portion was his people, Jacob his allotted share." In place of "the sons of Israel," the Septuagint reads "the angels of God," and the Hebrew text of Deuteronomy found at Qumran (among the Dead Sea Scrolls) reads "the sons of God." The traditional Hebrew reading appears to have been modified due to concern over monotheism.

Concerning the relationship of the two divine names in this passage (Most High and Yahweh), there are two ways of reading the text. One way views the Most High and Yahweh (the Lord) as the same. According to this reading, in God's exercise of universal sovereignty over the nations (as the Most High), God allocates rule over the nations to the angels or to the members of the heavenly court ("the sons of God"), but reserves Israel ("Jacob") for his own direct rule (as Yahweh). According to the alternative reading, the Most High apportions the nations to his sons ("the angels/sons of God"), among whom Yahweh is favored.

If this latter reading is the original meaning of the text, thereby implying that Yahweh may have been worshipped in pre-exilic times as the son of the high God, it is possible that this belief survived to influence early Christology, in which Jesus was identified with Yahweh and God his Father with the Most High. As scholars have observed, the book of Deuteronomy does not deny the existence of other gods. The Jewish Shema (Deut. 6:4) and the first commandment of the Decalogue (Deut. 5:7) require monolatry (the exclusive devotion of Israel to Yahweh), but do not deny the existence of other gods. According to this interpretation, passages such as Deuteronomy 4:35, 39 and 32:39 (see also 1 Kgs. 8:60; Isa. 45:5, 6, 14, 18, 22; Joel 2:27) are taken to mean that Yahweh is uniquely faithful to Israel (Deut. 7:9) and therefore is the only God for Israel (see Deut. 10:17).[1]

Another poetic passage, Psalm 82:1, also bears mention, not so much for the interpretation conveyed by the English translator, but for its reading in the Hebrew text: "Elohim (God) will stand up in the assembly of El, in the midst of the Elohim he judges." Two comments are necessary: the first

---

1. MacDonald, *Deuteronomy and the Meaning of Monotheism*, 79–85.

Part V: Christ in God

use of "Elohim" is treated as singular and the second as plural. If the first refers to Yahweh, commonly translated "God" (see Genesis 1:1 and wherever the term "God" appears in translation), then "El" must be a different deity, likely the "Elyon" of Deuteronomy 32:8.

As we discover in the letters of Paul, the earliest Christian writing we possess, within twenty years of the beginning of Christianity Paul regarded the resurrected Jesus as occupying a unique position of heavenly authority and honor. In his letters he wrote of the exalted Christ and reverenced him in ways that seem to suggest that Paul treated him as divine. Additionally, nothing in Paul's letters indicates awareness that his view of Christ was unique or that he had made serious innovation in the way Christians before him had regarded the exalted Jesus. This, coupled with Paul's hostility toward the worship of Jesus prior to his conversion, exhibited in opposition to practice established within a few years of the beginning of the church, demonstrates how deep-rooted was the devotion of Jesus by Jewish-Christian groups at the dawn of Christianity.

Although Paul insisted that the basis for his Christian faith and apostleship lay in the direct call of God, coupled with the divine revelation to him of Jesus as the Son of God (Gal. 1:11–17), he also made clear that his message, including the beliefs and practices he urged upon his converts, came from the faith of other, earlier, Christians (1 Cor. 11:23–26; 15:1–8). Paul's letters also include passages that reflect the devotion of Christians prior to Paul's gentile mission, such as creedal statements (Rom. 1:3–4; 10:9–10); fragments of church prayers (Rom. 8:15; 1 Cor. 16:22; Gal. 4:6); and possibly liturgical poems and hymns (Phil. 2:6–11; cf. also Col. 1:15–20). Some of these fragments of early church tradition take us back to churches of a Palestinian setting and to Christians whose native language was Aramaic (see the untranslated Aramaic prayer fragment in 1 Corinthians 16:22: "*Marana tha*," meaning "Our Lord, come!"; this phrase can also be read "*Maran atha*," meaning "Our Lord has come!").

These glimpses of Christian devotion, therefore, must have emerged from Jewish Christian groups very close in time, culture, and geographical setting to the origin of Christianity. The indications are that already in these groups the exalted Jesus had begun to play a significant role as the object of religious devotion, indeed as an object of cultic veneration. In the gatherings of the Christians with which Paul was familiar, it appears that they sang "hymns" honoring and celebrating Christ, baptized converts "in the name of Jesus," and likely had rituals of "calling upon" Jesus and "confessing" him as "Lord" (Rom. 10:9-10; 1 Cor. 12:3). In this activity they seem to have seen themselves as reflecting the heavenly and eschatological veneration of Jesus anticipated in Philippians 2:9-11 (cf. Rev. 5:1-14).

That early Christian worship of Jesus was understood to include Jesus in the worship due only to God is confirmed by two additional passages that speak of human worship given to Jesus. In Matthew 28:8 and 17 the disciples are said to have worshipped the resurrected Jesus. In 28:17 this act of worship introduces Jesus' declaration, "All authority in heaven and on earth has been given to me" (28:18). This scene forms an antithesis to the temptation of Jesus, in which the devil offers Jesus sovereignty over all the kingdoms of the world (Matt. 4:9), something the devil has no power to give. The second text is John 5:23, the Fourth Gospel's one clear reference to the worship of Jesus: "that all may honor the Son just as they honor the Father." While the verb "to honor" may not seem adequate to describe the worship due to God, the term is so used by Philo and Josephus. But more important are the two activities cited in John 5:19-21 (sovereignty over life and the ability to pronounce final judgment), uniquely divine activities. The context depicts the Son's activity as the exact replication of the Father's.

This unit focuses on the early cultic veneration of Jesus as a divine figure by Jewish Christians, whose religious background placed great emphasis upon the uniqueness of God. It is evident that their devotion had its own distinctive shape, a kind of binitarian reverence that included both God and the exalted Jesus. It is also obvious that these Christians did not have the benefit of the prolonged and intricate developments and discussions that led to the theology reflected in the Nicene Creed. For that reason, we must refrain from reading them back into the earlier period with which we are concerned. The evidence suggests that well before these later developments, within the first two decades of Christianity, Jewish Christians gathered in Jesus' name for worship, prayed to him and sang hymns to him, regarded him as exalted to a position of heavenly rule above all angelic orders, and appropriated to him titles and Old Testament passages originally referring to God. They also sought to bring fellow Jews as well as Gentiles to embrace Jesus as the divinely appointed redeemer, and in general redefined their devotion to the God of their ancestors to include the veneration of Jesus. Moreover, they apparently regarded this redefinition not only as legitimate but also as something demanded of them.

The basic conviction that Jesus had been exalted to a heavenly and divine status, whether through adoption or by virtue of preexistence, and

Part V: Christ in God

that this demanded the cultic veneration of him in early Christian gatherings, does not seem to have been generated by the use or adoption of any particular christological title. Rather, the veneration of Jesus probably generated a new and deeper connotation for such titles as "Lord," which is attested with special frequency in connection with earlier liturgical formulae (1 Cor. 12:3; Rom. 10:9–10). The veneration of Jesus also explains in part why other titles, including "Messiah/Christ" and "Son of God," quickly underwent redefinition in early Christian circles, pointing to a figure holding heavenly and divine status, even if not characteristically conveying such connotation in pre-Christian usage.

Session 12

Lord

Question for Individual or Group Reflection: In your estimation, what did the first Christians mean when they confessed Jesus as Lord? If possible, identify one statement or idea from this lesson that best exemplifies for you the meaning of the Lordship of Christ.

Important Biblical Verses and Passages: 1 Corinthians 1:2; 8:5–6; 15:28; 16:22; John 20:28; Revelation 1:12–16; 3:21; 5:13; 7:9–17; 11:15; 19:16; 22:13, 20; Isaiah 42:8; Psalm 110:1; 2 Corinthians 4:6; Romans 9:5; 11:36; 2 Peter 3:18; Mark 2:7; Colossians 1:18; Philippians 1:21; Ephesians 1:23; 4:4–5

Technical Words and Concepts: Kyrios; Kyrios Christology; *marêh*; Adonai; two powers in heaven (binitarian worship); doxology; the Lamb; Maranatha; new creation; anthropology; I-Thou; panentheism; pantheism

Kyrios Christology

Christians applied the title "Lord" (*Kyrios* in Greek) to the crucified and risen Jesus very early in Christianity. Our oldest Christian document, 1 Thessalonians, calls him by that title twenty-four times. In the New Testament, the "word of the Lord," to which Old Testament prophets so often appealed, becomes "the word of the Lord Jesus" (1 Thess. 1:8; see 2 Thess. 3:1; Acts 8:25; 12:24). In the Old Testament deliverance is promised to those who "call upon the name of the Lord," whereas in the New Testament Christians "call upon the name of our Lord Jesus Christ" (1 Cor. 1:2). Passages in the

Old Testament that call God "Lord," the New Testament refer to Christ (Rom. 10:13 cites Joel 2:32; Heb. 1:10–12 cites Ps. 102:25–27). Philippians 2:10–11 echoes Isaiah 45:23–24, a classic Old Testament passage celebrating Yahweh as the one and only God of the whole world. What is implied by reapplying to Jesus the Old Testament name for Yahweh is made quite explicit when Thomas calls Jesus "my Lord and my God" (John 20:28). Not surprisingly, it is not always clear whether the New Testament means God or Christ when it speaks of *Kyrios*.

Christ is understood to share God's lordship over all created beings "in heaven and on earth and under the earth" (Phil. 2:10). In particular, Christ's lordship makes him sovereign over all angelic beings (Col. 1:16–17; 2:8–10; 1 Pet. 3:22). Likewise, the two opening chapters of Hebrews claim repeatedly that Christ is superior to the angels. Unlike them, he bears "the exact imprint of God's very being" (Heb. 1:3). No wonder then that the angels also bow down before Christ in worship (Rev. 5:11–14). As "King of kings and Lord of lords" (Rev. 19:16), Christ merits the adoration of all.

The Jewish Background of Kyrios Christology

The cultic veneration of Jesus in early Christian circles is the most important context for the use of christological titles and concepts. This context indicates what they signified and gives us insight into how they functioned. For example, "lord," either in Greek (*kyrios*) or in Aramaic (*marêh*), had a wide spectrum of meanings in the ancient world, extending from a polite "sir" to a title for God. Various people who met the historical Jesus and saw in him a teacher, healer, eschatological prophet, or a mysterious person transcending these categories could have all addressed him as *marêh*; yet each person could have intended a different degree of reverence. The title therefore provided a living link between the circle of disciples around its rabbi Jesus and the post-Easter church worshiping its risen Lord.

However, once we see this title in the context of the early Christian cultic actions of prayer and hymn, it acquires a much more specific connotation. The term "lord" in either language does not automatically connote divine status. Nevertheless, the use of the title in cultic contexts implies much more than simple social superiority of or respect for the figure to whom it is attributed. When early Christians attributed the title Lord to Jesus, particularly in the context of worship, how would they have understood such attribution? Surely they were aware of passages in the Hebrew scriptures such as Isaiah 42:8: "I am the Lord (Yahweh), that is my name; my glory I give to no other, nor my praise to idols." Were they attributing deity to Christ, calling him God?

As noted in our study of angelology in Session 8, passages in the Hebrew scriptures about divine beings who beget semidivine beings (Genesis 6:2–4), and fascination with mysterious individuals such as Enoch, Abraham, Moses, Jacob, Elijah, and the quasi-human/quasi-divine "son of man" figure in Daniel 7, led to a vast literature that told of humans who became angels, angels who became human, and humans who became gods.

Psalm 82 portrays God as having a divine council, angelic beings with whom God consults; they are called "children of the Most High" but also "Elohim" (Ps. 82:6), the Hebrew word for "God." These angelic beings are called "gods." As we have seen, the Hebrew Bible grants the kings of Israel a uniquely close relationship to God, so much so as to consider them sons of God (see Ps. 2:7). However, what is truly astonishing is the reference in Psalm 110:1: "The Lord says to my Lord, 'Sit at my right hand until I make your enemies your footstool,'" a statement widely applied to Jesus by the New Testament writers.[1] The first use of the term "Lord" in this passage is the Hebrew name of God, often spelled Yahweh. The second use of the term "Lord" is a different term in Hebrew, Adonai, a common term for God but also used by pupils or slaves of their teacher or master. What is striking here is that Yahweh is speaking to "my Lord" (the king, in this case) and telling him to "sit at my right hand." The king is not God Almighty, but in being exalted to the level of God's throne, the king "is being portrayed as a divine being who lives in the presence of God, above all other creatures."[2]

Possibly more surprising is Psalm 45:6–7, where the king is addressed as a god: "Your throne, O God, endures forever." It is clear that the person addressed as "Elohim" (O God) is not God Almighty but the king, because of what follows: God Almighty, the king's God, anoints him with oil. One final example comes from Isaiah 9:6, which celebrates the coronation of a new king by ascribing to that king epithets seemingly attributable only to God Almighty: "Mighty God, Everlasting Father." At his coronation, a "child" has been given to the people, meaning that a king has been made

---

1. The widespread use of this text in the New Testament writings (twenty-one quotations or allusions scattered across the twenty-seven books of the New Testament) is contrasted by its infrequent use in Jewish writings of late (Second Temple) Judaism (only one probable allusion in a five-hundred-year period); Bauckham, *Jesus and the God of Israel*, 21–22.

2. Ehrman, *How Jesus Became God*, 78.

the "son of God." As the Son of God, the king is exalted to the level of God and has such divine status as to be called God.

Philo of Alexandria, the learned Jew living in the first Christian century, wrote a biography of Moses that praises the great lawgiver. For Philo, Moses was "the greatest and most perfect man that ever lived."[3] Even though Philo never equates Moses with God Almighty, he plays with levels of divinity, arguing that Moses was gradually becoming divine. Since Moses was a prophet and friend of God, it follows that he would "partake of God himself and of all his possessions as far as he had need."[4] As a result, Moses was to be God's heir. Philo indicates that Moses appeared to others as a god, to the extent that he "was called the god and king of the whole nation."[5] Here we find Moses called what the king of Israel was called, and what, in a different context, the Roman emperor was called: god. At times Philo goes even further and imagines Moses as a kind of preexistent divine being sent to earth for a time.

Kyrios Christology in the New Testament

In 1 Corinthians 8:5–6, a key christological passage written slightly more than two decades after the crucifixion of Jesus, Paul summarizes the distinctive nature of early Christian devotion. At the same time, he identifies the problem he will investigate: "Even though there may be so-called gods in heaven or on earth—as in fact there are many gods and many lords—yet for us there is one God, the Father, from whom are all things and for whom we exist, and one Lord, Jesus Christ, through whom are all things and through whom we exist."

Here, Paul distinguishes Christian devotion from other varieties in the Greco-Roman world of his day. He does so by rejecting the plurality of deities almost universally accepted in varying ways among his pagan contemporaries as legitimate manifestations of "the divine," insisting that for Christians there can be only "one God." In maintaining this strict monotheistic stand, Paul and the early Christians were affirming the common position taken by Judaism. However, by referring to Jesus in the same breath, linking Jesus with God and conferring on him what is here a title of divine honor, Paul also distinguishes early Christian faith from the Jewish

3. *Life of Moses* 1.1.
4. Ibid., 1.27.
5. Ibid., 1.158.

background. Although we do not have first-century Jewish documents that tell us directly what Jewish religious leaders thought of Christian devotion, they most likely would have agreed with the attitude reflected in slightly later Jewish sources, which apparently reject cultic devotion to Jesus as constituting an example of the worship of "two powers in heaven," that is, the worship of two gods.[6]

We may have indirect evidence of this suggestion in the letters of Paul. It is likely that Paul's persecution of Jewish Christians (Gal. 1:13-14; 1 Cor. 15:9) prior to his conversion experience was occasioned at least in part by the reverence they gave to Jesus. Paul describes his change of heart as brought about because God "was pleased to reveal his Son to [or "in"] me" (Gal. 1:15-16), which suggests that his conversion experience forced him to embrace a view of Jesus' relationship to God that he, as one zealous for the traditions of his ancestors, had previously been unable to accept. Our premise, then, is that though their devotion to Jesus may have caused other Jews to regard early Jewish Christians as having violated the uniqueness of God, such Jewish Christians, like Paul after his conversion, apparently felt justified in giving Jesus reverence in terms of divinity, yet at the same time thought of themselves as worshiping one God.

One of the most debated verses in Paul's letters is Romans 9:5 (translations such as the NRSV or NIV note the variant readings in the footnotes). Here, in a passage enumerating the advantages given to the Israelites, Paul concludes by saying that "from them comes the Messiah, according to the flesh, who is over all, God blessed for ever, Amen." This translation (NRSV) ascribes divinity to Jesus; here Christ is "God over all." While this view comes close to "incarnation" theology, as Jesus is portrayed in John's Gospel (see John 1:18, which speaks of Jesus as "God the only Son"), many scholars believe such a Christology is "higher" (more advanced and therefore later) than anything found elsewhere in Paul and even in the Synoptic Gospels. Thus they translate Romans 9:15 differently, such as "From them comes the Messiah according to the flesh. God who is over all be blessed for ever, Amen," thereby calling Christ Messiah and then concluding with a blessing to God. However, if it is true that Paul here explicitly calls Jesus "God," it would the only place in his letters where he does so, though as we now understand, calling Christ "God" is something a Jewish Christian could do

---

6. For an investigation of the ancient Jewish criticism of "two powers," see Segal, *Two Powers in Heaven*.

without implying that Christ is actually God Almighty, or in this case, God the Father.

Three doxologies (ascriptions of praise) to Christ alone appear in the New Testament (2 Tim. 4:18; 2 Peter 3:18; Rev. 1:5), evidence that within a generation or two of his crucifixion, orthodox churches were worshipping Jesus as Lord. The author of 2 Peter, exhorting Christians to "grow in the grace and knowledge of our Lord and Savior Jesus Christ," ascribes to Jesus everlasting glory. Likewise John of Patmos, confessing Jesus Christ as "ruler of the kings of the earth," ascribes to him "glory and dominion forever and ever." Doxologies were a Jewish form of praise to the one God. In John's case, their use cannot simply be attributed to Gentile Christian carelessness but "must be regarded as a development internal to the tradition of Jewish monotheism, by which Jewish Christians implicitly included Jesus in the reality of the one God."[7]

The book of Revelation regularly depicts Jesus jointly with God in scenes of heavenly power, praise, and glory. At times, as in the initial throne room scene in 4:3, the figure seated on the throne is not identified. Other passages in Revelation depict Jesus as exalted ruler of the universe who is worshipped in heaven and who shares the throne of God (3:21; 5:7–14; 7:9–17). In traditional Jewish imagery the final judge is of course God, though in some later apocalyptic traditions the heavenly "Son of Man" was authorized by God to judge on his behalf, as his representative. By failing to specify the figure on the heavenly throne as well as on the great white throne on the day of judgment (20:11), John is able to avoid the necessity of distinguishing between God and Christ. Like other New Testament authors, John believes that the glory of God is seen in the face of Jesus Christ (cf. 2 Cor. 4:6).

The picture of Jesus that results from reading Revelation assumes a preexistent, heavenly being who enters the human world as Jesus, who dies as a faithful martyr, and who is exalted to share God's throne and to act forever as God's vice-regent. How would this portrait of Christ have been heard by John's contemporaries? The Christology of Revelation is not unlike reflections about the divine throne in ancient Jewish literature from the second century BC to the third century AD. While numerous references to the divine throne in ancient Jewish sources view only one figure present,

---

7. Bauckham, *Theology of Revelation*, 61.

in some references a second figure, said to be in human or angelic form, is implicitly or explicitly present.[8]

In Revelation John initially portrays Christ with all the attributes of deity (1:12–16). Furthermore, in the seventh trumpet scene the kingdoms of the world become the "kingdom of our Lord and of his Messiah" (11:15). Such a blurring between Christ and God appears elsewhere in John's imagery and theology. For example, the "Lamb" is never an independent figure, but always Lamb-as-representative-of-God; likewise, God is never a figure defined apart from Christ, but always God-who-defines-himself-by-Christ.

In Revelation 1:8 God declares himself to be the Alpha and the Omega, and again in 21:6, where he adds, "the beginning and the end." This expression appears also in 22:13, with the insertion "the first and the last." All three expressions mean much the same. If they apply to Christ, as surely they must in 22:13, then they set Christ apart from all created beings, since none other than God could share in these titles.

Here we see the developing Christology of early Christianity taking shape. Christian prophets such as John played an important role in this process. As a way of stating unambiguously that Jesus Christ belongs to the fullness of the eternal being of God, John's Christology surpasses anything in the New Testament.

The Lordship of Christ

The expression "Jesus is Lord" belongs to the very earliest stratum of Christianity. In his writings Paul often used the phrase "the Lord Jesus Christ" in conjunction with the mention of God the Father (1 Thess. 1:1; 2 Cor. 13:14). Paul, like the author of Acts, says that no one can say "Jesus is Lord" except by the Holy Spirit (1 Cor. 12:3). Paul also uses the term "Lord" (*Kyrios*) in connection with the hope of Christ's return (Phil. 3:20; 4:5; 1 Thess. 3:13), and, as noted earlier, at the conclusion of 1 Corinthians he utters the Aramaic prayer: *Maranatha*, "Our Lord, come!" (16:22), a hope central to the author of Revelation (see 22:20: "Amen. Come, Lord Jesus").

The confessional statement "Jesus is Lord," uttered by the first Christians concerning a penniless first-century preacher from Galilee, ranks among the most astounding claims professed by mortals of another mortal.

---

8. Textual references to the divine throne may be found in Charles H. Talbert's essay on "The Christology of the Apocalypse" in Powell and Bauer, *Who Do You Say That I Am?*, 172–79.

The statement can be understood on two levels, politically and religiously. As *a political claim*, Christians were affirming that their primary allegiance belonged to Jesus and not to the Roman emperor, government officials, tax collectors, bankers, businessmen, traders, the religious elite, or the military establishment. Historians traditionally attribute to Domitian, who ruled Rome from AD 81 to 96, the start of compulsive emperor worship. One of his decrees began: "Our Lord and God commands that this be done."[9] To the early Christians, such lords and gods were false and their worship blasphemous. The author of the book of Revelation implies that Christ, as "King of kings and Lord of lords," is the only emperor whom Christians can recognize. To say "Jesus is Lord" conveyed the notion of loyalty, directly challenging allegiance to Rome and to all temporal authorities. Such a claim had social, political, and economic implications, for it signified disloyalty to the state and to the Roman gods who guaranteed the state's wellbeing.[10]

As *a religious claim*, Christians were affirming that Jesus Christ was the personification of God, the one in whom heaven and earth met. Looking at him, and contemplating his death and resurrection in particular, they believed they could see directly into God's world, understanding God's purpose in ways previously unimagined.

To ascribe to Jesus the term "Kyrios" as a title involves an almost incredible paradox, both for the Jew trained in the Old Testament and for a Gentile from the Hellenistic world. Why incredible? Because the title "Lord" would bear a precise meaning for a Jew steeped in scripture. In the Septuagint (the Greek) version of the Hebrew Bible, *Kyrios* is used for Yahweh, the name of God; indeed, it translates several divine names. And in Jewish liturgies, both in Palestine and in the Jewish communities across the Mediterranean world, *kyrios* was a common word referring to God. Any Jew, therefore, examining the Christian claims for Jesus, would interpret the affirmation "Jesus is Lord" to mean that Jesus is for the Christian what God is for the Jew.

In the Hellenistic Gentile world, which did not necessarily know the Septuagint, the word *kyrios* had a different meaning. In the Oriental and Hellenistic religions prevalent in the Roman empire at the beginning of the

---

9. Suetonius, *Domitian*, 13.

10. The author of 1 Peter, who is much more friendly to the Roman Empire, exhorts his readers to honor the emperor but to fear God (2:17) and to sanctify Christ as Lord in their hearts (3:15).

Christian movement, lordship—whether ascribed to a deity or to a ruler—meant absolute power and authority.

If confessing Jesus as Lord meant either of these two things—deity and authority—then one questions whether Christians were not contradicting Jesus' self-awareness as Servant of the Lord and his mission as the rejected suffering Son of Man (see Mark 8:31; 10:45). As the temptation stories make clear, Jesus decisively rejected political ambitions. When Peter declared Jesus to be the Christ/Messiah, Jesus responded by speaking of suffering.

Jesus' self-understanding as Messiah may well have reflected Old Testament hope that the community he forms consummates the older idea of a messianic community to be gathered at the time of the new age. However, a better description of Jesus' relationship to the Old Testament might be this, that in his ministry he embodied what the Old Testament means by "Israel," which must suffer as a means for the redemption of all. But Jesus cannot be confined to this understanding, for in some ways he embodies what the Old Testament means by "God." Jesus is said to forgive sins, something God alone can do, and this is one of the decisive grounds for the scribes' suspicion of Jesus as a blasphemous claimant to the status of God (Mark 2:7). Jesus was and is what Israel longed for, but he did not come in the form expected.

Against this background of meaning, the essence of the confession "Jesus is Lord" become clear. Jesus is the lowly one who suffered and died, and this is what divine lordship means. We find this understanding of lordship already in the hymn Paul quotes in Philippians 2:6–11. Here we find the church wrestling with the fact of Jesus' earthly humiliation ("he humbled himself and became obedient to the point of death—even death on a cross"), yet daring to say that in this very lowliness he is Lord.

In the form of a humble servant God is present, and therefore the one decisive name by which this Jesus is to be known is Lord, which is to say, either to a Greek or to a Jew, the one through whom God meets you. In this way the church wrestled with the tension between power and weakness, between sovereign divinity and suffering humanity. "For you know," Paul writes, "the generous act of our Lord Jesus Christ, that though he was rich, yet for your sakes he became poor, so that by his poverty you might become rich" (2 Cor. 8:9). The purpose of Christ's grace is not that we might become divine, but that we might come to know and meet God.

The church, thus, gives the name of Lord to the humiliated one who was killed on a cross. In so doing, it proposed the most radical revision of conventional ideas of divinity that can be imagined. Christianity's greatest contribution may well be this, that lordship is servanthood, that lordship is love.

A distinction remains, however, between the Lordship of Christ and the Lordship of God. For in his resurrection, the humanity of Jesus was not left behind; rather it was retained, yet exalted and transfigured. When, at Chalcedon, the church insisted on the unity of two distinct natures, the divine and the human, in the one person of Christ, it did so to safeguard the recognition of the humanity of Christ. Many today criticize this formula as making an unnatural dualism in the Christ portrayed in the Gospel accounts, and the criticism is not unjust. We would not naturally express the belief in those terms today. However, many Christians today perpetuate the error of thinking that Jesus, in his exalted state, is solely divine and no longer human. The church's belief in the incarnation prevents such thinking, for if Jesus was truly human on earth, he did not cease to be human when he departed from this world. Jesus remains human, and this continuing humanity is essential to his "lordship." He is Lord in the distinctive sense that this term has in the church's devotion only because we can think of him, not only as having once been with us and of us, but also as being with us and of us still. According to the church's confession, Jesus was "raised to the right hand of God." Such declaration is not in the least incompatible with the acceptance of the reality and normality of his earthly human nature. At his exaltation, Jesus was not divested of his humanity, but rather his humanity became divine and divinely redeeming.

Much as the church cannot deny the humanity of Jesus, since it "remembers" Jesus thus, so it cannot deny the divinity, since it knows him as the divine Lord. Actually, however, Christians do not experience the humanity and divinity of Christ in ways as separate as this language suggests, but as together. This is explained, in large part, by the realization that the divine Lord is none other than the human Jesus exalted—his humanity thus being a transformed (and therefore a redemptive) humanity. But it is also true that the church senses the presence of divinity within his earthly life.

It is this divinity—or rather divinity in this sense—that makes Jesus' life different from all others. The uniqueness of the earthly Jesus does not consist in some peculiarity of his nature that would make him more, and therefore less, than human. Nor does it consist in extraordinary moral

Part V: Christ in God

excellence or extraordinary genius, or even in extraordinary spiritual sensitivity or depth. These qualities can be affirmed, but such characteristics would distinguish him only relatively from others, whereas the distinction of Jesus is absolute. The uniqueness of this person, this human being, lies in the affirmation that in him and through him, the God of heaven and earth, of all nature and history, brought into being a redeemed humanity.

It is in this new humanity, which we know in Christ, that incarnation continues. For although the "new creation" is essentially eschatological, the church's existence in history, however broken and partial, represents "the grace of our Lord Jesus Christ" and "the fellowship of the Holy Spirit" on earth, here and now. It is the actual experienced reality of this communal existence to which every christological statement ultimately refers and by which its truth or adequacy must be tested. For so central is Jesus, remembered and still known, within the church's existence, and so fully identified is he with it, that to speak of Jesus in any significant way is to speak also of it. Jesus is more that the historical cause or occasion of the church; he is, and always has been, the decisive center of its life. As he is our Lord, by the same token he is the Lord, whether recognized or not, of heaven and earth. As such, he is one with us: we are his "body," and he is "head" (Col. 1:18). Our own true life is so intimately with him that we can speak of it as being in him: "For me," writes Paul, "living is Christ" (Phil 1:21).

The affirmation of the church is this: "There is one body and one Spirit, just as you were called to the one hope of your calling, one Lord, one faith, one baptism, one God and Father of all, who is above all and through all and in all" (Eph. 4:4–5). If it is true that Christians cannot think of themselves as reconciled without thinking of Jesus, it is equally true that they cannot think of him without thinking also of God. For early believers, the very word "God" meant "the God and Father of our Lord Jesus Christ." No wonder Christians found themselves speaking of Jesus as the Mediator or the Great High Priest. Christ one with us, Christ one with God—can these inseparables in the existence of the church and in the experience of the Christian provide context for our understanding of the two natures of Christ?

The story of the only-begotten Son of God, who divested himself of divinity and became one with us in our humanity in order to set humans free to experience fully the goodness God created us to be—this story became the way in which the earliest church tried to explain its own existence. This story of incredible love and self-giving brings to humanity, like a sacrament, the concrete reality of God in Christ, of Christ in us, and of us in God.

We may differ about the story, its interpretation, and its true form, but we must not differ about the reality that story expresses. Him whom we remember and love as brother, we also love and adore as Lord. Him whom we have known in the flesh and whom our hands have handled, we now know also as the reality of God's presence in our midst and in our hearts—judging, cleansing, healing, restoring. This we know, and this the church proclaims through its life and witness. This is the meaning the story of Jesus Christ expresses. Less than this we cannot say.

Who, then, is Jesus? Is he human, fully human, God's human, preexistent being, divine hypostasis, a god, Second Person of the Trinity, God in human flesh, God for us, God for all? Our struggle to understand what Jesus was and the meaning of his mission was shared by the writers of the New Testament. One of the first facts that strikes us in the New Testament record is the reticence Jesus had in accepting traditional messianic titles. Why was he so evasive?

Jesus' reticence is explained, surely, by his desire to remove any possible barriers between ourselves and God. If some traditional title had been clearly affirmed about his work and words, wouldn't his admirers confidently pigeonhole him, and, having understood him, left him alone. Because God was claiming humankind through Christ, Jesus carefully removed all possibility of a simple definition of his work that might lead us to make peace with him too readily.

Such understanding of Jesus and his mission cannot be forced, or externally imposed. It must be arrived at through experience, by the process of searching and pondering, and ultimately in affirmation.

The Beyond in the Midst

As we have discovered, Christology is not simply about Jesus and who he was. It is also about anthropology—about sin and salvation and what it means to be human—and it is necessarily about God, the ineffable mystery of reality. Contemporary theologians are in agreement that a dualistic model of the universe is no longer viable. Whether examined from the outside or the inside, reality is now viewed as a whole. The traditional divisions with which theology has worked—body and soul, earth and heaven, this world and the next, the secular and the sacred, the natural and the supernatural, the two natures human and divine, I and Thou—are decreasingly useful. In our pluralistic world, however, this need not mean a repudiation of uniqueness or individualism.

For theology, the implication is not the reduction of the transcendent to pure naturalism. Rather it is an apprehension of the "beyond in the midst," of the transcendent in, with, and under the imminent. It is the refusal to see any final discontinuity between the human spirit and the Spirit of God.

The best theological model—perhaps the only appropriate model today—for a satisfactory conception of God and of the incarnation, is named "panentheism." This perspective finds the Being of God including and penetrating the entire universe, but (as against pantheism) God's Being is more than the universe. According to this view, God is in everything and everything is in God. Yet God is greater still. Unlike pantheism, which depersonalizes and dehistoricizes, panentheism personalizes reality, seeking God as the inner truth, depth, and center of all being.

When speaking of God, words are bound to fail. Paucity of words has always been a mark of the mystics, as acknowledged by the ancient Daoist poet Lao Tzu: "He who knows does not speak. He who speaks does not know."[11] One of the insights of our time is that the transpersonal character of God is better expressed not by envisaging God as a bigger and better Individual, nor as a collective Personality incorporating all other persons, but in terms of the interpersonal. In this sense the Jewish philosopher Martin Buber taught that in the beginning—and in the end—is not the individual, the "I" or even the "Thou," but the joint "I-Thou." This image of God goes beyond pantheism, deism, and traditional theism, in that it views the whole of reality ultimately not in terms of a monarchical Being supreme among individual entities, but of a divine "field" in which finite Thous are constituted in the freedom of personalizing love. This is the vision to which the New Testament points, of God as "all in all" (1 Cor. 15:28; cf. Rom. 11:36; Eph. 1:23).

Ultimately, of course, there are things we cannot think up or express, but when we hear them or see them we say, "Yes." There is the sense that what is most real is before us; we are simply catching up to it, entering into it. Pascal's remark is haunting: "You would not be seeking me if you had not found me." Life is response—and hence responsibility—to "the beyond in the midst." The Christian gospel is that human beings are

---

11. *Tao Te Ching*, 56.

responsible—terrifyingly so—in freedom to a God whose strength is made perfect in weakness (2 Cor. 12:9).

One of the central and distinctive features of this gospel is the utterly intimate relationship that it sums up in Jesus' word for God: *Abba* (Father or Daddy). It is a word we too can use with regard to God (Rom. 8:15–17). It is this relationship at the heart of the universe, at the core of reality, that biblical Christology addresses.

Epilogue

God in All: The Scandals of Divine Love

Important Biblical Verses and Passages: 1 Corinthians 1:21–31; John 13:3–8; 14:6; Genesis 12:3; Galatians 3:14; Romans 5:8; 10:4; 11:32; Colossians 3:11; Hebrews 6:20

Technical Terms and Concepts: scandal of the cross; scandal of the incarnation; scandal of particularity; scandal of imparticularity; legalism; the Atonement; the Fall; transcendence; immanence; Pantocrator

FROM ITS INCEPTION, CHRISTIANITY was perceived as scandalous, on at least three fronts (to which we add a fourth), all interrelated. The first front is *the scandal of the cross*. Paul, writing to the Corinthians a mere twenty-five years after the death of Jesus, to a cosmopolitan city proud of its pluralism, multiculturalism, and inclusivism, identifies the scandal thus: "Has not God made foolish the wisdom of the world? . . . For Jews demand signs and Greeks desire wisdom but we proclaim Christ crucified, a stumblingblock to Jews and foolishness to Gentiles. . . . But God chose what is foolish in the world to shame the strong; God chose what is low and despised in the world, things that are not, to reduce to nothing things that are" (1 Cor. 1:21, 23, 27–28).

Ancient Jews rejected the idea that God should be a victim. Ancient Greeks, likewise, rejected the idea that a god would elect to die. Can omnipotence suffer? Can eternity die? So we can understand the shock experienced by first-century Jews and Greeks when they confronted the Christian claims of a suffering God. The scandal is resolved in divine love, which unites two natures—human and divine—in one Person. Because these two distinct natures are said to be united in Jesus Christ, Christians affirm that God truly suffered and died on the cross.

If antagonists overcome the first element of shock to allow for the reality of Christ as God, they might ask, "Why did God suffer and die?" At that moment, they open themselves to the profound truth that God is love, and that brings us to the second front, *the scandal of the incarnation*. Ancient Jews rejected the incarnation as scandalous: a monotheistic God does not become man. The Greeks, likewise, rejected the idea of a human person being at the same time a god. Yet for Christians God is not the Absolute that remains outside the world, indifferent to pain, suffering, and death. God is Emmanuel—with humanity, sharing our nature and participating in our destiny. The crucified Christ is proof, early Christians affirmed, of God's solidarity with humanity, of God being "for us and not against us" (Rom. 8:31). God gave his Son to reveal himself as Love.

The concept of "God in Christ" exemplifies the third front, made famous in Gerhard Kittel's phrase as *the scandal of particularity*. This phrase refers to the resistance many people have to the idea that God, the Creator of the universe, would enter human history in a localized way—incarnating in one person, revealing divine love in one religion and one culture; that Jesus of Nazareth represents the only divine way, truth, and life.

Divine love is not primarily a "teaching," a communication of knowledge, but rather an action that God undertakes, a mystery seen in nature, in the incarnation, and on the cross. Here is everything that appeals to the mind, the heart, the senses, and the imagination. Here is vision that transforms life from a problem to be solved to an adventure to be enjoyed.

Contemporary Christians and non-Christians who have trouble with the finality of Christ may not simply be stumbling over the "scandal of particularity," but with a particular understanding of that finality that today many believe to be false, namely, that only devout Christians—particularly those who believe certain things about Jesus or join the right church or participate in the right ritual—or only devout Muslims or Jews or members of some enlightened sect, preordained race, appropriate social class, or orthodox ideology are loved and accepted by God. According to the New Testament Jesus is the person of God, the Son of God, precisely as he is not the person for himself or even for an elite clique. Rather Jesus Christ is the man for others. He is the representative person, who dies—and lives—for all. He is the universal person, the person for all space and all time.

God in All: The Scandals of Divine Love

The first Christians—at least some of them—may have believed that Jesus Christ did literally represent finality for all time. That is what many people today think is what the Fourth Gospel means when it quotes Jesus saying he is "the way, and the truth, and the life" (John 14:6). However, as we know now, if Paul's language about "the first Adam" need not require a literal historical individual at the beginning of the world, then Jesus Christ as "the last Adam" can have different implications for our thinking today about uniqueness and finality. In an evolutionary cosmos it is unthinkable to believe that there is no further development or truth after the historical character Jesus of Nazareth. In fact New Testament writers affirm this when they attach finality not to the historical Jesus but to the coming Christ (see 1 Peter 1:7, 13). Furthermore, as Paul makes clear, the purpose of Jesus is not to make all people Christian, but to extend the blessing of Abraham to all people (Gal. 3:14; Rom. 4:16–18; see Gen. 12:3).

The concept that Jesus is the person "for others," and this includes the marginalized and all those viewed as outsiders (see Matt. 25:31–46), brings us to the fourth front, *the scandal of imparticularity*.[1] For some insiders today the greatest scandal is God's unconditional love for the world, including love for his despisers. Yet that is Paul's teaching in Romans, that God's grace extends to all (Rom. 11:32), for "while we were yet sinners, Christ died for us" (Rom. 5:8).

Christians and non-Christians will inevitably view Christ differently. He can be final for one in a way that he cannot be for the other. In the words of Bishop Lesslie Newbigin, "To claim finality for Jesus Christ is not to assert that the majority of humans will one day be Christian or that all others will be damned. It is to claim that commitment to him is the way by which human beings can become truly aligned to the ultimate end for which all things were made."[2]

Read literally, a passage like Acts 4:12 seems unequivocal: "There is salvation in no one else, for there is no other name under heaven given among mortals by which we must be saved." Yet the situation before us today has parallels with that which Paul faced with regard to Judaism and Mosaic law (Torah). Because ancient Jews viewed Torah as the supreme embodiment of God's will, they believed it could never be superseded.

---

1. I borrow this phrase from Bishop John A. T. Robinson. The ensuing segment is adapted from his discussion of this topic in *The Human Face of God*. See his closing chapter, "Man for All," particularly the argument in pages 230–36.

2. Newbigin, *Finality of Christ*, 115.

God in All: The Scandals of Divine Love

Christians must become Jews first, they argued, an assessment held as well by some of the first Jewish converts to Christianity (see Acts 15:1). Paul disagrees. While agreeing that God's law "is holy and just and good" (Rom. 7:12), he adds that through Christ the requirement of the law is fulfilled (Rom. 8:4). Though Paul refuses to say that faith annuls the law (Rom. 3:31), yet he categorically states that Christ is the end of the law (Rom. 10:4). In saying this Paul is not thinking of the law as the content of the will of God but as an exclusive system of salvation. In that respect, the law is powerless to bring the newness of life it intends and demands. Legalism, as a system of salvation, fails to accomplish the divine reconciling intention. Just the opposite, it leads to death (Rom. 7:10). Christ is the end of the law as its goal, namely, trust in God (see Rom. 3:1), but also its end as the means to a relationship with God.

There is a positive sense in which Jesus Christ represents for Christians the goal of faith, the fulfillment of God's revelation, and the ultimate end for which all things were made (Col. 1:15–20). There is no other of whom it can be said that to have seen him is to have seen the Father. Not only morally, but in terms of wholeness or salvation, to be found in Christ is to be found in God. That conviction the Christian cannot abandon without ceasing to be Christian. But that is very different from saying that Christianity as a religion is the only true path to salvation. The finality or universality of Christ is not to be identified with the finality or universality of the Christian religion. It might be nearer the truth to say that Christ is the "end" of Christianity as he is of Judaism. Just as Gentile Christianity forced Paul to differentiate the two aspects of Jewish Torah, so in our day we are being compelled to distinguish the truth of Christ from the form of religion in which Christians (like ancient Jewish views of Torah) have equated dogma and truth.

In his discussion of particularity and imparticularity, Bishop Robinson questions the practice in Christian theology of referring to dogmatic beliefs by using the definite article combined with a capital letter, in phrases such as "the Atonement," "the Resurrection," "the Incarnation," and "the Parousia" (the Second Coming of Christ). When this is done intentionally, it is a way of asserting finality and universality for Christ and Christianity, yet such assertions have the effect of removing Christ from universal common experience. If we are asked whether we believe in *the* Atonement or in *the* Parousia, the expected response is to something Jesus supposedly accomplished on the cross or to what may happen at the end of the world.

However, when one leaves out the definite article, the effect is quite different. To say one believes in atonement or in resurrection or in parousia personalizes the discussion, making it more present, accessible, and experiential. Such an approach creates openness and space and more effectively universalizes the affirmation or conviction.

While it is difficult to speak this way without appearing to threaten the link of Christian truth with history, that is not the intent. Rather, to historicize the Christ event "by giving it definition in certain once-and-for-all moments of 'sacred history' is to isolate it from continuous relevance to ordinary history."[3] Take the Atonement, for example, a doctrine that affirms Christ's full, perfect, and sufficient sacrifice on the cross for the sins of the world. Such language, foreign to modern experience, serves more as an obstacle today than as a facilitator of the truth it seeks to communicate. This is the case not merely because the metaphors used in the past to relate atonement to experience—justification, sanctification, sacrifice, ransom, satisfaction, et cetera—are obsolete, but because the whole notion of an objective transaction of this nature, accomplished once and for all, no longer has the effect of changing our lives. In like manner, people today cannot be expected to see the fall of Adam as describing an objective event that has forever altered the human condition. While "the Fall" is a profound mythological representation and interpretation of certain realities of human experience, it does not function as an event that in itself changes human experience. What, then, is the place of atonement, resurrection, and parousia for us today? While the traditional Christian answer has been to point backward to historical events, people rightly ask how one man's death and resurrection can alter their lives *today*. Thus understood, the place of atonement, resurrection, and parousia is wherever (and whenever) we *experience* reconciliation, release, and renewal with life.

For many people in the past, "the Creation" was synonymous with a single divine act at the beginning of the world, just as "the Fall" was synonymous with a single human act. Now we are coming to appreciate that creation, like incarnation and resurrection, is "co-extensive with the duration of the world."[4] Incarnation and resurrection, though they broke through with Jesus as new possibilities for life and freedom in the Spirit, are not confined to the birth of Jesus or to "the third day" after his crucifixion. Parousia, too, is not a single "second coming" at the last day, but a

---

3. Robinson, *Human Face of God*, 231.
4. Teilhard de Chardin, *Science and Christ*, 64.

continuing dimension of incarnation. Thus understood, incarnation speaks of the openness of all history to the pervasive presence, the constant coming, of Christ into every aspect of life, now and forever.

The Christian church, likewise, has failed to grasp the totality of incarnation by limiting incarnation to itself as the "body of Christ." The ancient formula, "Where Christ is, there is the church," is often reversed to declare, "Where the church is, there is Christ." A better distinction is to say that the body of Christ "subsists in" the church, not that it consists of it. Otherwise we lose sight of an equally vital New Testament emphasis: "as all die in Adam, so all will be made alive in Christ" (1 Cor. 15:22). "In that renewal," the new humanity envisioned by the New Testament authors, "there is no longer Greek and Jew, circumcised and uncircumcised [that is, religious and irreligious] . . . but Christ is all in all!" (Col. 3:11).

The question has been posed: Is Jesus "Lord" because we cannot question his power and authority, or is he "Lord" because we have found and affirmed his unique ability to shape our lives? Whatever its truth of old, there is little doubt that for us today Jesus becomes Lord in our experience. We start there, rather than with authority. The question is more likely to ring true in the form, "Can you see your humanity as defined and authenticated in Jesus Christ?" rather than, "Can you believe in this individual as the Son of God?" What most of us seek today is not a messiah, or even a Christ-figure, but the deeper truth that Christianity claims, that where and when the Word becomes flesh, we no longer find ourselves alone, fragmented from one another and alien before God.

Transcendence within Immanence

The images of Jesus that resonate with compelling power for most of us today are those that begin "from below" and move from immanence to transcendence, from relationships to revelation, rather than the other way around. Whether we view Jesus as servant, healer, martyr, victim, prophet, sage, or saint, even in these we recognize the embodiment of the divine. When Bonhoeffer coined his now famous phrase, "the man for others," it was in answer to the question "Who is God?" The implication is clear: unless the dimension of the transcendent, the unconditional, is visible, however broken or imperfect, there is no Christ at all. Whether God-talk is a help or hindrance, "transcendence within immanence" is experiential and therefore relatable and meaningful. As Adam prefigured the one who was to come (Rom. 5:14), so Jesus is the prototype of the new humanity (Heb. 6:20). The problem is that the preliminary sketch has been taken as the finished portrait, and in the past this portrait was made the closed subject of Christology. But the open subject of Christology is the "humanity of God" and "the glory of man." When such incarnation is denied, whether the divine in the human or the human in the divine, the consequences are disastrous: political and social fragmentation and psychological and spiritual alienation.

Who Christ is for us today remains a matter of discernment. Whatever our answer, we must retain the unity in Christ of the human and the divine. This means affirming Christ not simply as Jesus according to the flesh or simply as a being alive in some divine superworld, but as incarnate reality, around us and within. Participation in Christ, to use the realistic language of the New Testament (see 1 Cor. 1:9)—partaking of his body and blood, to use Eucharistic language (see 1 Cor. 10:16–17)—is less likely to occur in communities that are self-sufficient and self-assured, but rather where humanity is injured and impaired, as the body of Christ is broken and shed for all.

Our image of Christ today is unlikely to be that of the *Pantocrator*, the Sovereign Christ of the Byzantine dome, sitting serene above the fray. His lordship is known more in the taking of the towel (John 13:3–8) and by those who take the towel. In Schweitzer's haunting words, which close his classic book, *The Quest of the Historical Jesus*:

> He comes to us as One unknown, without a name, as of old, by the lake-side, he came to those men who knew Him not. He speaks to us the same word: "Follow thou me!" and sets us to the tasks which He has to fulfil in our time. He commands. And to those who obey Him, whether they be wise or simple, He will reveal Himself in the toils, the conflicts, the sufferings which they shall pass through in His fellowship, and, as an ineffable mystery, they shall learn in their own experience Who He is.[5]

For Schweitzer, as for us, the importance of Jesus is not that we get our theology or Christology straight, but that we follow him in cruciform ways. As we follow him into the fray, we will discover Who He Is, and in that discovery, experience God's scandalous love.

---

5. Schweitzer, *Quest*, 403.

Appendix A

A Chronology of Biblical Events

Patriarchal Period	1850–1700 BC
The Exodus from Egypt	c. 1250
Period of the Judges	1200–1025
United Kingdom (David and Solomon)	1025–926
Northern Kingdom (Israel)	926–722
Southern Kingdom (Judah)	926–586
Babylonian Exile	686–538
Maccabean Revolt	167–142
Second Temple Constructed	520–515
Alexander the Great's Conquests	336–323
The Hebrew Torah Translated into Greek (Septuagint)	c. 250
Book of Sirach (Ecclesiasticus) Written	c. 180
Rule of Antiochus IV Epiphanes	175–163
Maccabean Revolt	167–142
Publication of Book of Daniel	c. 165–164
Roman Conquest of Jerusalem (Pompey)	63
Assassination of Julius Caesar	44
Rule by Herod the Great	37–4
Emperor Augustus (Octavian)	30 BC–AD 14

Appendix A

Philo of Alexandria	20 BC–AD 50
Book of Wisdom (Wisdom of Solomon) Written	c. 20
Birth of Jesus	c. 6–4 BC
Rule by Herod Antipas	4 BC–AD 39
Judea Becomes a Roman Province	AD 6
Birth of Paul	c. AD 8
Emperor Tiberius	14–37
Paul Studies in Jerusalem; Becomes a Pharisee	c. 20–30
Pontius Pilate (Roman governor of Judea)	26–36
Crucifixion of Jesus	c. 30
Paul Persecutes Followers of Jesus	c. 30–33
Conversion of Paul	c. 33
Paul in Arabia, Damascus, and Jerusalem	33–36
Paul Preaches in Tarsus and Surrounding Region	c. 36–44
Emperor Caligula	37–41
Emperor Claudius	41–54
Paul Teaches in Antioch	44–46
Paul Visits Jerusalem with Barnabas and Titus	46
Paul's First Missionary Journey	47–48
Jerusalem Council	49
Paul's Second Missionary Journey	49–53
Paul Writes 1 Thessalonians	
Paul's Third Missionary Journey (3-year stay at Ephesus)	53–58
Paul Writes Galatians, Philippians, Philemon, 1 and 2 Corinthians	
Paul Writes Romans	57 or 58
Emperor Nero	54–68
Paul Arrested in Jerusalem	58
Paul Imprisoned at Caesarea	58–60
Paul's Voyage to Rome	60–61
Paul Under House Arrest in Rome	61–64

A Chronology of Biblical Events

Paul's Martyrdom under Nero	64
Revolt of Jews Against Rome	66–70
Gospel of Mark Written	c. 69–70
Fall of Jerusalem	70
Deutero-Pauline Epistles Written [Colossians, Ephesians, and 2 Thessalonians]	c. 80–100
Pastoral and General Epistles Written [1 and 2 Timothy, Titus; Hebrews, James, 1 Peter, 1, 2, and 3 John]	c. 80–100
Gospel of Matthew Written	c. 80
Gospel of Luke Written	c. 85
Book of Acts Written	c. 85–90
Gospel of John Written	c. 95
Book of Revelation Written	c. 96
Books of Jude and Second Peter Written	c. 98–120

Appendix B

Guidelines for Leading a Group Study or Workshop on Biblical Topics

Note about Participants

PEOPLE WHO CHOOSE TO attend a group study or workshop on biblical topics do so for a wide variety of motives and bring with them varied levels of readiness and ability. When individuals are invited to attend a group Bible study, they should be made aware from the beginning that this is not a study where the leader does all the work of preparation and presentation. Every participant is expected to have read the assigned chapter and to have completed the assigned study questions prior to each session.

Given the busy schedules most people have, there may be times when persons come to a session with minimum preparation. You should not compromise the expectation of adequate preparation, because the experience for the whole group will suffer if the reading is not taken seriously. In such situations, encourage persons who have not read the material or done the homework assignments not to participate in the discussion until others have had a chance. Also, when working in small groups, try to ensure that those who are not prepared are distributed among the groups rather than grouped together.

Some participants will have had a lot of experience with studying the Bible, while for others this may be their first experience with Bible study. It is important for each person to feel that he or she belongs to the group.

Encourage both experienced and inexperienced participants to be mindful and appreciative of each other.

One way to ensure full participation is to ask participants to keep a journal, to write in it regularly, and to bring it to each session. The journal will be used to record the weekly homework assignment as well as to take notes on their reading and on class interaction. In addition to a journal, participants should bring to class a Bible as well as a copy of the secondary text (in this case *The Scandal of Divine Love*).

Planning a Session

This study is designed to be completed in twelve sessions, each *60 to 75 minutes in length*. Each session follows a fourfold pattern:

1. *Opening*, 5 minutes (a time of prayer and scripture reading, run by the leader or by someone appointed in advance; the leader may ask if there are any prayer requests).
2. *Overview*, 15 to 30 minutes (this can be in the form of a presentation by the leader and may include group discussion on the topic of the homework assignment).
3. *General or small-group discussion*, 20 to 30 minutes (depending on the size of the class, the leader may divide the class into groups of threes or fours to discuss one or more topics from the passage).
4. *Closing*, 5 to 15 minutes (run by the leader or by someone appointed in advance). This may include a report and general discussion on the small-group activity, a time of reflection or a comment by the leader and a closing prayer.

If sessions last *45 to 60 minutes*, the recommended time allotments and activities should be adjusted accordingly.

Types of Discussion Leaders

Many factors contribute to the effective, productive working of a group. What follows is an attempt to summarize several important considerations about effective group leadership.

There are numerous types of leaders. Which kind do you wish to be?

1. An *autocratic leader* is one who assumes all the responsibility for the group, and who is primarily concerned about accomplishing a task. There are times when such an approach is necessary, but this study of the Bible will be most successful when the leader does not do all the work for the group.

2. The *laissez-faire leader* is one who sits back, enjoys what is happening, and lets the group go its own way. It is important at times not to be too agenda-conscious, but this study of the Bible assumes that the leader is actively engaged in guiding the group's process.

3. The *democratic leader* functions in a partnership style. This approach to the study of the Bible will be most effective when led by persons who seek to involve others in sharing their questions, insights, and affirmations.

Leaders of this study are encouraged to keep the following guidelines in mind:

- Adults are responsible for their own learning;
- Adults learn best when they can participate directly in the process of their own learning;
- Learning is reinforced best when adults have opportunities to practice skills and to express ideas in their own words.
- Learning occurs within an environment of trusting relationships.

Therefore, the activities should represent a cooperative, collaborative, non-threatening style of learning.

Leadership and Group Dynamics

Because participants will have questions, opinions, and insights about many aspects of the study of the Bible, *leaders need to keep the group focused on the topic or task*, knowing when to let the discussion proceed with its own momentum and when to direct the discussion back to the topic. It is common in a group to have one person who is both well informed and quite verbal do most of the talking. Others in the group may be intimidated or discouraged or have little desire to talk. Such a circumstance is not healthy for the long-term life of the group. *When one person dominates the discussion*, the leader may need to be direct, speaking privately with that

Guidelines for Leading a Group Study

participant or inviting others to speak by saying, "What do others think about . . . ?" or "Let's share as many ideas as we can about . . ." If leaders encourage members to be participants, to think and speak for themselves and to interact regularly with one another, there will be times *when people offer a contradictory point of view* to that of the author or of the group. When disagreements occur, you can accept what persons say without agreeing with them. You can encourage them to clarify what they mean or to provide evidence for their position. It is not necessary to defend the author or even an accepted view from scripture. However, it is important that you and the others in the class have read carefully and worked hard to understand the text.

A basic premise of this study is that the leader is a learner among other learners. It is not necessary for leaders to be fully knowledgeable in all subjects of the study. It is much more important to know where to turn for the needed information (such as a Study Bible, a Bible handbook, a Bible dictionary, a theological text, or an appropriate Bible commentary). In such cases, I recommend the following resources:

- Study Bibles: *The Harper Collins Study Bible, The New Oxford Annotated Study Bible,* and *The New Interpreters Study Bible;* The *Eerdmans Dictionary of the Bible.*

- One Volume Bible Commentaries: *HarperCollins Bible Commentary, The New Jerome Biblical Commentary, The New Interpreter's Bible Commentary.*

- Bible Dictionaries: *HarperCollins Bible Dictionary;* the *Anchor Bible Dictionary,* or the *New Interpreter's Dictionary of the Bible.*

How will you respond when you do not know the answer to a question? Nothing is more frustrating to a group than a leader who tries to bluff his or her way through a topic or a question. At such times it is helpful to encourage the group to work toward its own understanding and to be willing to admit that you do not know something.

If leaders desire to involve persons in serious interaction with one another and with the subject of the session, they need to ask effective questions. Questions may be one of the most valuable resources available to the leader as well as to the participants. Generally speaking, there seem to be three different types or levels of questions: (a) *information questions,* which presume right answers; (b) *interpretation questions,* which require participants to think about, analyze, explore, and evaluate a subject, and

Appendix B

(c) *personalized questions*, whereby leaders encourage participants to apply the subject to themselves in a personal way that helps them to express their own identity.

When you lead, try to use all three types, but be intentional about making room for the latter. Questions at this level are essential if persons are to grow in their faith and life commitments. In using questions of a personal nature, we must be careful to avoid embarrassing participants by getting too personal or putting them "on the spot."

When preparing to lead a discussion that utilizes a variety of questions, the following guidelines will be helpful to keep in mind.

1. Ask questions that are open-ended, analytical, or probing, rather that questions with only one right answer or implying a "yes" or "no" response.
2. Ask only one question at a time; more than one question is confusing and lacks focus.
3. Present questions to the whole group, rather than putting one person "on the spot."
4. Provide feedback after a person responds, so participants know they have been heard;
5. After asking a question, give participants time to think.
6. Use an inquiry style rather than an interrogative style; some examples are "what are your thoughts about . . . ?"; "why do you suppose . . . ?"; "who do you think will . . . ?"; "what is the possibility of . . . ?"; or "what are some reasons . . . ?" Inquiry conveys to the group that you are interested in what they think and say, whereas interrogation puts persons on the defensive and inhibits creativity.
7. Encourage people to ask their own questions, and let them know you value them and their perspective, whether you agree with it or not.

In order for effective group process to develop, there are simple yet significant things you can do as leader:

- Know the participants' names and speak inclusively so that everyone feels free to participate and share of themselves with one another.
- Arrange the room so that persons are in a circle or square, preferably seated at tables so they do not have to juggle Bibles, books, and cups on their laps.

Guidelines for Leading a Group Study

- Make sure that the group adheres to the class time, and try not to make a habit of going past the allotted time.
- Be sure the meeting space is comfortable with regard to heat, lighting, and seating.
- Always make room for mystery and uncertainty. Nothing destroys Bible studies more than threatening attitudes, condescending language, or a competitive environment where there are winners and losers. The losers may not return and eventually only one or two people will show up, blaming others for failure.
- In order to build a community of trust and a place for participants to share their experiences with God, leaders should remind the group that information shared in class should be kept confidential.
- Acknowledge the presence and influence of the Holy Spirit at all times, and in all relations and situations, allow the gifts of the Spirit full sway (see Galatians 5:22–23: love, joy, peace, patience, kindness, goodness, faithfulness, gentleness, and self-control); without God's Spirit, our efforts are vain.

Bibliography

Allison, Jr., Dale C. *Constructing Jesus: Memory, Imagination, and History*. Grand Rapids, MI: Baker Academic, 2010.
———. *The Historical Christ and the Theological Jesus*. Grand Rapids, MI: Eerdmans, 2009.
———. *Jesus of Nazareth: Millenarian Prophet*. Minneapolis: Fortress, 1998.
Baillie, Donald M. *God Was in Christ*. New York: Charles Scribner's Sons, 1948.
Barclay, William. *The Mind of Jesus*. London: SCM, 1960.
Bauckham, Richard. *Jesus and the God of Israel*. Grand Rapids, MI: Eerdmans, 2008.
———. *The Theology of the Book of Revelation*. Cambridge: Cambridge University Press, 1993.
Borg, Marcus J. *The God We Never Knew*. New York: HarperSanFrancisco, 1998.
———. *Jesus in Contemporary Scholarship*. Valley Forge, PA: Trinity, 1994.
———. *Meeting Jesus Again for the First Time*. New York: HarperSanFrancisco, 1994.
Borg, Marcus J., and N. T. Wright. *The Meaning of Jesus: Two Visions*. New York: HarperSanFrancisco, 2000.
Brunner, Emil. *The Christian Doctrine of Creation and Redemption*. Dogmatics. Vol. 2. Philadelphia: Westminster, 1952.
Buber, Martin. *I and Thou*. 2nd ed. New York: Charles Scribner's Sons, 1958.
Caird, G. B. *The Language and Imagery of the Bible*. Philadelphia: Westminster, 1980.
Collins, Adela Yarbro, and John J. Collins. *King and Messiah as Son of God*. Grand Rapids, MI: Eerdmans, 2008.
Creed, John M. *The Divinity of Jesus Christ*. Fontana ed. London: Collins, 1964 [1938].
Crossan, John Dominic. *Jesus: A Revolutionary Biography*. New York: HarperSanFrancisco, 1995.
Crossan, John Dominic, and Richard G. Watts. *Who is Jesus?* Louisville: Westminster John Knox, 1996.
Cullmann, Oscar. *The Christology of the New Testament*. Philadelphia: Westminster, 1959.
Dunn, James D. G. *Christology in the Making*. Philadelphia: Westminster, 1980.
Ehrman, Bart. *How Jesus Became God*. New York: HarperOne, 2014.
———. *Jesus: Apocalyptic Prophet of the New Millennium*. New York: Oxford University Press, 1999.
———. *Jesus Before the Gospels*. New York: HarperOne, New York: HarperOne, 2016.
Forsyth, P. T. *The Person and Place of Jesus Christ*. London: Independent, 1948 (1909).
Fuchs, Ernst. *Studies of the Historical Jesus*. London: SCM, 1964.

Bibliography

Fuller, Reginald H. *The Foundations of New Testament Christology*. New York: Charles Scribner's Sons, 1965.
Garrett, Susan R. *No Ordinary Angel: Celestial Spirits and Christian Claims About Jesus*. New Haven, CT: Yale University Press, 2008.
Gieschen, Charles A. *Angelomorphic Christology: Antecedents and Early Evidence*. Leiden: E. J. Brill, 1998.
Grillmeier, Alays. *Christ in Christian Tradition*. 2nd. ed. London: Moubrays, 1976.
Grindheim, Sigurd. *Christology in the Synoptic Gospels*. London: T & T Clark, 2012.
Haberer, Jack. *Godviews: The Convictions that Drive Us and Divide Us*. Louisville: Westminster John Knox, 2001.
Hahn, Ferdinand. *The Titles of Jesus in Christology: Their History in Early Christianity*. London: Lutterworth, 1969.
Hamilton, William. *The New Essence of Christianity*. New York: Association, 1966.
Hengel, Martin. *The Son of God*. Philadelphia: Fortress, 1976.
———. *Studies in Early Christology*. Edinburgh: T. & T. Clark, 1995.
Holmes, Urban T. *The History of Christian Spirituality*. New York: Seabury, 1980.
Hurtado, Larry W. *How on Earth Did Jesus Become a God?* Grand Rapids, MI: Eerdmans, 2005.
———. *Lord Jesus Christ: Devotion to Jesus in Earliest Christianity*. Grand Rapids, MI: Eerdmans, 2003.
———. *One God, One Lord: Early Christian Devotion and Ancient Jewish Monotheism*. Philadelphia: Fortress, 1988.
Jeremias, Joachim. *The Central Message of the New Testament*. London: SCM, 1965.
Kelly, J. N. D. *Early Christian Doctrines*. 2nd ed. New York: Harper & Row, 1960.
Knox, John. *The Humanity and Divinity of Christ*. Cambridge: Cambridge University Press. 1967.
———. *Jesus, Lord and Christ*. New York: Harper Brothers, 1958.
Longenecker, Richard N. *The Christology of Early Jewish Christianity*. London: SCM, 1970.
MacDonald, Nathan. *Deuteronomy and the Meaning of Monotheism*. Tübingen: Mohr Siebeck, 2003.
Mackintosh, H. R. *The Doctrine of the Person of Jesus Christ*. Edinburgh: T. & T. Clark, 1913.
Macquarrie, John. *Jesus Christ in Modern Thought*. London: SCM, 1990.
Marshall, I. Howard. *The Origins of New Testament Christology*. Downers Grove, IL: InterVarsity, 1976.
Martin, Ralph P., and Brian J. Dodd. *Where Christology Began: Essays on Philippians 2*. Louisville, KY: Westminster, 1998.
Marxen, Willi. *The Beginning of Christology*. Philadelphia: Fortress, 1969.
McGrath, Alister E. *Christian Theology: An Introduction*. 5th ed. Malden: MA: Wiley-Blackwell, 2011.
Meier, John P. *Jesus the Jew: Rethinking the Historical Jesus*. 5 vols. Anchor Bible Reference Library. New York: Yale University Press, 1991–2016.
Moule, C. F. D. *The Origin of Christology*. Cambridge: Cambridge University Press, 1977.
Newbigin, Lesslie. *The Finality of Christ*. London: SCM, 1969.
Newman, Carey C. *Jesus & the Restoration of Israel*. Downers Grove, IL: InterVarsity, 1999.
O'Collins, Gerald, S.J. *Christology: A Biblical, Historical, and Systematic Study of Jesus*. 2nd ed. Oxford: Oxford University Press, 2009.
Pannenberg, Wolfhart. *Jesus: God and Man*. Philadelphia: Westminster, 1968.

Bibliography

Pittenger, W. Norman. *The Word Incarnate: A Study of the Doctrine of the Person of Christ.* New York: Harper Brothers, 1959.

Powell, Mark Allan, and David R. Bauer. *Who Do You Say That I Am? Essays on Christology.* Louisville: Westminster John Knox, 1999.

Rahner, Karl. "Current Problems in Christology." In *Theological Investigations* 1:215–29. Baltimore: Helicon: 1961.

———. "The Two Basic Types of Christology." In *Theological Investigations* 13:213–23. New York: Seabury, 1975.

Richardson, Peter Tufts. *Four Spiritualities.* Palo Alto, CA: Davies-Black, 1996.

Robinson, John A. T. *Honest to God.* Philadelphia: Westminster, 1963.

———. *The Human Face of God.* Philadelphia: Westminster, 1973.

———. *Jesus and His Coming.* 2nd ed. Philadelphia: Westminster, 1979.

———. *Twelve More New Testament Studies.* London: SCM, 1984.

———. *Twelve New Testament Studies.* London, SCM, 1962.

Sanders, E. P. *The Historical Figure of Jesus.* London: Penguin, 1993.

———. *Jesus and Judaism.* Philadelphia: Fortress, 1985.

———. "Jesus: His Religious Type," *Reflections* 87 (1992) 4–12.

Schillebeeckx, Edward. *Christ: The Experience of Jesus as Lord.* New York: Seabury, 1980.

———. *Jesus: An Experiment in Christology.* New York: Seabury, 1979.

Schweitzer, Albert. *The Quest of the Historical Jesus.* New York: Macmillan, 1968 [1906].

Segal, A. F. *Two Powers in Heaven.* Leiden: E. J. Brill, 1978.

Spong, John Shelby. *This Hebrew Lord.* New York: HarperOne, 1993.

Teilhard de Chardin, Pierre. *Science and Christ.* London: Collins, 1968.

van Peursen, Cornelis. "Man and Reality – The History of Human Thought." In *A Reader in Contemporary Theology*, edited by John Bowden and James Richmond, 115–26. Philadelphia: Westminster, 1967.

Vermes, Geza. *The Changing Faces of Jesus.* New York: Penguin, 2002.

———. *Jesus the Jew: A Historian's Reading of the Gospels.* London, Collins, 1973.

Witherington, III, Ben. *The Christology of Jesus.* Minneapolis, Fortress, 1990.

———. *Jesus the Sage: The Pilgrimage of Wisdom.* Minneapolis: Fortress, 1994.

Wright, N. T. *Jesus and the Victory of God.* Minneapolis: Fortress, 1996.

Zetterholm, Magnus, ed. *The Messiah in Early Judaism and Christianity.* Minneapolis: Fortress, 2007.

Zimmerli, Walter, and Joachim Jeremias. *The Servant of God.* London: SCM, 1957.

Subject and Name Index

abba, 78, 173
Abraham (patriarch), 24, 82, 84, 98,
    100, 103, 115, 117, 162, 176
Adam, x, 24, 29, 72, 98, 102, 118, 119,
    120, 176, 178, 179
    second, 119, 176
adoptionism (exaltationism), 10, 12, 13,
    20, 101, 102, 119, 143, 152
Allison, Dale, xv, 64
Angel Christology, 110, 114–20
    in Paul, 118–20
Angel of Death, 116, 117
Angel of the Lord, xi, 111, 117, 118
angelomorphic language, 114
angels, xi, 117, 162
anhypostasia, 24, 70
aphorism, 49, 50, 51, 52
Apostles' Creed, 19
Assumption of Moses, 96
atonement, 4, 104, 177, 178

Baillie, Donald, xv, 27
Bauckham, Richard, xv, 162n1
Beelzebul, 116
Bible study
    guidelines for leaders, 184–89
binitarian worship, 155–56
Bonhoeffer, Dietrich, 4, 179
Borg, Marcus, 65
Brunner, Emil, xv, 34
Buber, Martin, 29, 172

Chalcedon, Council of, 3, 5, 7, 69, 169
Character Hymn, 140

charisma(ta), 113
Christ. *See* Jesus Christ
Christ Hymn, 3, 118–20, 155
Christianity
    finality of, 177
christological hymns, 118–20, 136–42
christological titles, x, 2–3, 10, 34, 72
    in Paul, 2–3
Christology, ix, x, xi, xii, xiv, 1, 2, 3, 4, 7,
    15–16, 19, 27, 156, 180
    adoptionist, 10, 102, 143, 152
    agency, 143
    classic, 3, 18, 69
    definition of, 1
    development of, 9–14
    from above, 5, 6
    from below, 5, 6, 179
    incarnational, 12, 143–44
    of Revelation, book of, 165–66
Christos, 1, 16, 83
creation, doctrine of, 71, 178
Creed, J. M., 4
creeds, xii, 69
    Chalcedonian, 3, 5, 69
    Nicene, 3, 5, 158
Crossan, John, Dominic, 64
Cullmann, Oscar, xv

Daniel, book of, 123–25
    See also Son of Man, in Daniel
Darwin, Charles, 23, 72
David (king), 24, 84, 86, 87, 133, 134–35
Day of Atonement, 100
Dead Sea Scrolls. *See* Essenes

Subject and Name Index

devil. *See* Satan
divine agency, xi
docetic, docetism, 12, 13, 18, 27
Dodd, C. H., 64
doxa (glory), 81, 120
doxologies, 165
Dunn, James, xv

Ehrman, Bart, xv, 3, 93
eikōn (image), 81, 102, 119, 139
election, 60
Elijah, xi, 59, 66, 86, 107, 115, 162
Elohim, 156–57, 162
Elyon, 156, 157
Emmanuel, 85, 133
Enoch, xi, 108, 115, 127, 162
Enoch, book of, 6, 87, 124
eschatology
   and resurrection, 63
   Christian, 61–66
   Jewish, 60, 62
   realized, 64
Essenes, 39, 76, 87, 97, 98, 156
Exodus, 71

Fall, the, 71, 72, 178
Forsyth, P. T., 33
Fuchs, Ernst, 72
functional way of thinking, 8, 9, 145, 153

Garrett, Susan, 118
gnostic, gnosticism, 6, 18
God
   as Elohim, 156–57, 162
   as Father, 46, 57
   as Yahweh, 156, 167
   immanence of, 179
   kingdom of, 2, 23, 43, 54, 61, 62, 64, 65, 67, 71, 88, 91, 92, 126
   knowledge of, 19
   Most High. *See.* Elyon
   nature of, 18–19
   transcendence of, 19, 109, 179
Golden Rule, 57, 134

Haberer, Jack, xiii
Hagar, 117, 118
Hasidim, 123
Hasmonean, 96, 99
Hebrews, letter to, 9, 11, 19, 26
   Jesus as high priest in, 33, 100–104
   Jesus' humanity and divinity in, 32–33, 106–7
Hengel, Martin, xv, 3
High Priest Christology, 103–4
   in Hebrews, 100–104
   See also Jesus Christ, as high priest
Holmes, Urban, xiii
Holy Spirit. *See* Spirit
hypostasis, 5, 7, 24, 69, 82, 105, 108, 110
Hurtado, Larry, xv, 117

I Am sayings, 20, 135, 152
Ichthys, 96
image. *See eikōn*
incarnation, incarnationism, 4, 8, 12, 13, 17, 71, 72, 102, 105, 107, 108, 118, 119, 120, 139, 140, 142, 144, 145, 164, 169, 170, 172, 175, 177, 178–79, 180
   church as, 170, 179
Intertestamental Period, 109
Israel
   as son of God, 75

Jesus Christ, 2, 169–71, 175
   and Adam, x, 176
   as Alpha and Omega, 18, 166
   as angel, 7, 110–11, 114–20, 161
   as divine agent, 8, 72, 82, 102, 105, 108, 143, 155, 165–66
   as end of the law, xii, 177
   as eschatological prophet, 58–67
   as exorcist, 41–44
   as firstborn, 104, 139
   as forerunner, 104
   as good shepherd, 91–92, 135
   as healer, 41–44
   as high priest, 2, 96–104
   as human face of God, xv, 72
   as King of the Jews, 92, 93
   as Lamb, 166
   as Logos, x, 7, 12, 82, 102, 140–42
   as Lord, x, xii, 2, 8, 9, 34, 155, 159, 160–61, 166–71, 179

Subject and Name Index

as mediator, 103, 170
as Messiah, x, 2, 34, 65–66, 83–85, 88–93, 121, 159, 168
as new Moses, 132
as Pantocrator, 180
as prophetic sage, 51–57
as rabbi, 2, 46
as Savior, x, 94–96
as second Adam, 29, 113, 119, 176
as Son of God, x, xii, 2, 7, 8, 10, 16, 18, 25, 34, 43, 76–81, 102, 135, 159, 179
as Son of Man, x, 10, 18, 20–23, 29, 35, 74, 99–100, 118, 121–22
  as eschatological judge, 21, 23, 125–28
  as human being, 23–27, 29
  as suffering servant, 21, 35–41, 125–26, 127, 168
as Spirit of God, 2, 7, 109–14
  in John, 113
  in Paul, 113
as teacher, 19, 45–57, 131–32, 134
as Wisdom, xi, 7, 50, 82, 130–31
  in John, 135–36
  in Matthew, 55–57, 131–35
biblical information about, xii
crucifixion of, 40, 70
divinity of, 7, 8, 101, 122, 163–66, 169–70, 171
finality of, 18, 177
genealogies of, 24–25
humanity of, 5, 12, 13, 16, 19, 20, 21, 23–27, 29–34, 69–73, 101, 102–3, 106, 107, 108, 119, 122, 169, 171
perfection of, 30–34, 103
preexistence of, 3, 6, 11, 12, 13, 20, 82, 101, 102, 105, 107, 108, 117–18, 120, 128, 144, 145, 152–53, 165
  and virgin birth, 105, 106
self-awareness of, ix, 20–21, 35, 40, 59–60, 61, 66, 72, 76, 78, 80–81, 86, 88–93, 99, 112, 121, 122, 125, 126, 127, 168
significance of, 2, 9
sinlessness of, 32–34

triple office of, 97
two natures of, 5, 7, 18, 69, 70, 71, 169, 170, 171
worship of, 155–59, 163–66
Job, book of, 37
John the Baptist, 23, 59, 61, 64, 65, 67, 95, 107, 126, 134
Jonah (prophet), 67, 132–33
Josephus (ancient author), 34, 158
Judaism
  ancient (late), 6, 8, 108, 115, 117, 155, 163n1, 174, 175
  Hellenistic, 110
  Palestinian, 110
Jung, Carl, 15

kenotic, kenoticism, 11, 13, 119
king
  as son of God, 75
kingdom of God. *See* God, kingdom of
Kittel, Gerhard, 175
Knox, John, xv, 7, 12, 20, 32, 105, 106
Kyrios Christology, 160–61, 163–71
  in Paul, 163–65
  Jewish background of, 161–63
  Old Testament background of, 167–68

Lao Tzu, 172
legalism, 177
Lessing, G. E., xi
Levi, Levites, 97, 100, 103, 104
logos, 1
Logos. *See* Jesus Christ, as Logos
Logos Christology, x, 112, 144–53
  background of, 146–48
  in John, 148–53
  in Philo, 147–48
Logos Hymn, 140–42
Luther, Martin, 5, 32

maranatha, 157, 166
mashal, meshalim. *See* parable
Matthew, gospel of, 38, 39, 55–57, 84–85, 131–35
Melchizedek, xi, 96, 97–99, 104, 108
  in Dead Sea Scrolls, 98–99
  in Hebrews, 100–104

Subject and Name Index

Messiah, 1, 7, 15, 40, 59
   and Son of God, 75–76
   in Old Testament, 85–88
   king as, 85
   suffering of, 40, 168
Messiah Christology, 2, 83–93
   in Luke, 85
   in Mark, 84
   in Matthew, 84–85
   in Paul, 84
   See also Jesus Christ as Messiah
metaphor, metaphorical, xii, 10
metaphysics, metaphysical, 6, 7, 10, 17, 18, 19, 33, 70, 148
Michael (archangel), xi, 98, 99, 115, 124, 127
monolotry, 156
monotheism, monotheistic, 60, 115, 156, 163, 165
morphē (form), 119, 120
Moses, xi, 56, 59, 66, 108, 115, 118, 132, 162, 163
   as prophet, 58–59, 66
munus triplex (triple office), 97
Myers Briggs Type Indicator, xiii
myth, mythical, xi, 18, 71
mythological way of thinking, 6, 8, 9, 10

Nephilim, 76, 115
new, newness, 25
Newbigin, Lesslie, 176
Newman, John Henry, 32, 97
Nicea, Council of, 3, 5, 7, 69, 82

ontological way of thinking, 7, 9, 108, 145
Origen (theologian), 144

panentheism, 172
pantheism, 172
parable, 49, 50, 51, 52–55, 73, 133
   of the Good Samaritan, 53–55
Parousia, x, 23, 71, 177, 178, 179
Pascal, Blaise, 172
Passover (festival), 95
Paul (apostle), 26
   and the historical Jesus, 106
   and incarnation theology, 118

   and the preexistence of Christ, 11
perfection, 103
Peter (apostle), 36, 39, 56, 89
Pharisees, 15, 54, 87, 97, 116
Philo of Alexandria, 147–48, 158, 163
Pilate, Pontius, 18, 73, 93
Pittenger, Norman, xv, 144–45
Prophet Christology, 58–67, 112
   in Luke, 66–67
proverb, 49

rabbi, 56, 131
reincarnation, 107
Resurrection, the, 18, 71, 177, 178
Richardson, Peter Tufts, xiii
Robinson, John A. T., xv, 61, 107, 176, 177

Sadducees, 96, 97
salvation, 33–34, 40, 171
Sanders, E. P., 60
Satan, 116
Savior Christology, 2, 94–96
   See also Jesus Christ, as Savior
scandal
   of the cross, 174
   of imparticularity, 176, 177
   of the incarnation, 175
   of particularity, 175, 177
Schweitzer, Albert, 180
scripture
   reading and interpretation of, xi–xii, 4
second coming of Christ. *See* Parousia
Septuagint, 21, 120, 156, 167
Sermon on the Mount, 55, 56–57, 131, 133–34
Servant Christology, 2, 35–41, 125–26
   in Isaiah, 36–37, 40
   in Mark, 36, 38
   in Matthew, 38, 39
   origin and development of, 39–41
   See also Jesus Christ, as suffering servant
Shema, 156
sin, 33–34, 171
skeptic, skepticism, xii, 18, 19
Solomon (king), 132–33, 135

Subject and Name Index

Son of God
  angels as, 76
  in John, 81–82
  in Mark, 78
  in New Testament, 76–81
  in Old Testament, 75–76
  origin of, 74–75
  See also Jesus Christ, as Son of God
Son of God Christology, x, 2, 74–82
Son of Man, x, 20–23
  as Israel, 124
  definition of, 21, 22, 35
  in Daniel, 21, 23, 115, 122–25, 125–26, 128, 162
  See also Jesus Christ, as Son of Man
sophia, 141
Spirit
  as divine attribute/hypostasis, xi, 108, 110, 111
  as Paraclete, 111, 114
  in Old Testament, 111
Spirit Christology, 111–14
spirituality, xiii
  and personality, xiii
Suffering Servant, 21, 36, 37, 38, 39–41, 168
  as Israel, 37

Teilhard de Chardin, Pierre, 4
Ten Commandments, 115
Torah, 54, 56, 110, 111, 131, 132, 176–77
Trinity, 2, 4, 5, 7, 24, 69, 108, 144, 145

Vatican Two, 97
virgin birth, 25, 26, 27, 105, 106, 108

Wisdom
  and christological hymns, 136–42
  as divine attribute/hypostasis, xi, 129–30
  as Jewish literature, 48–49, 51, 52, 53
Wisdom Christology, 129–42
  in John, 135–36
  in Matthew, 131–35
  See also Jesus Christ, as Wisdom
Wisdom Hymn, 139–40
Witherington, Ben, 49, 139n4, 141–42
Word, xi, 7
  See also Jesus Christ, as Logos
Wright, N. T. 64

Yahweh, 60, 110, 131, 156, 167
Yom Kippur (festival), 110

Zionism, 15

www.ingramcontent.com/pod-product-compliance
Lightning Source LLC
Chambersburg PA
CBHW060607230426
43670CB00011B/2015